Śūnya Puruṣa

— Bauddha Vaiṣṇavism of Orissa —

Utkal Studies in Philosophy

General Editor
Tandra Patnaik

Editors
S.C. Panigrahi, A.K. Mohanty

Volume One	:	Action, Freedom and Responsibility
Volume Two	:	God, Time and Evil
Volume Three	:	Studies on the Purusarthas
Volume Four	:	Reality and Mysticism
Volume Five	:	Social Justice
Volume Six	:	Facets of Humanism
Volume Seven	:	Varnadharma, Niskama Karma and Practical Morality
Volume Eight	:	Persons, Mind and Value
Volume Nine	:	Darwanism and Philosophical Analysis
Volume Ten	:	Kant's Concept of the Sublime
Volume Eleven	:	Karma
Volume Twelve	:	Śūnya Puruṣa : Bauddha Vaiṣṇavism of Orissa

Utkal Studies in Philosophy – XII

General Editor : Tandra Patnaik

Śūnya Puruṣa

Bauddha Vaiṣṇavism of Orissa

Tandra Patnaik

D.K. Printworld (P) Ltd.
New Delhi

In Association with

Department of Special Assistance in Philosophy
Utkal University, Bhubaneswar

Cataloging in Publication Data — DK
[Courtesy: D.K. Agencies (P) Ltd. <docinfo@dkagencies.com>]

Patnaik, Tandra, 1947-
Śūnya puruṣa : Bauddha Vaiṣṇavism of
Orissa / Tandra Patnaik.
xx, 268 p., 23 cm. — (Utkal studies in philosophy ; 12)
Includes bibliographical references (p.)
Includes index.
ISBN 8124603456

1. Sunyata. 2. Vaishnavism — India — Orissa — History. 3. Buddhism — India — Orissa — History. 4. Philosophy, Hindu. I. Title. II. Series: Utkal studies in philosophy ; 12.

DDC 181.043 095 413 21

ISBN 81-246-0345-6
First published in India in 2005

Published by:
D.K. Printworld (P) Ltd.
Regd. Office: 'Sri Kunj', F-52, Bali Nagar
New Delhi-110 015
Phones: (011) 2545-3975; 2546-6019; *Fax*: (011) 2546-5926
E-mail: dkprintworld@vsnl.net
Website: www.dkprintworld.com

in association with

Department of Special Assistance in Philosophy
Utkal University, Bhubaneswar (Orissa)

Printed by: D.K. Printworld (P) Ltd., New Delhi

for
Pihu

Dārubrahma svarupāya tasmai buddhātmane Namaḥ
— *Nilādri Mahodayam*, 6.22b

My salutation to Buddha
who is manifested in the form of
the wooden Brahman — Jagannātha

Prologue

WORKING on this project for me was like setting out on a voyage from the mid-sea to the *terra firma*. How and why I reached the uncertainties and tumults of the mid-sea, I do not myself know. It must have been a sort of frenzy that forced me to leave the shore as quickly as possible. The culture of the post-Independence period oriented me to act as a rootless mirror to reflect all that was happening philosophically in the Western world. I basked in the glory of the acquired knowledge without ever realizing that I have to find out my own roots so that I do not have to float aimlessly. My work on Orissan philosophy and culture is thus a reverse journey.

My initial attempts to delve into the Santha (*bhakti*) literature of Orissa that spanned almost 400 years (fifteenth to nineteenth century CE) really amazed me. I came across a philosophical tradition that is religious in letter but secular in spirit. Here is a philosophical tradition that accommodated the concept of God. But it is no ordinary personal God but a symbol of *Śūnya Puruṣa* — the formless, non-qualitative, inconceivable principle. Here is a tradition that argues that being śūdra is an advantage, and one must approach the Almighty with a sense of humility that characterizes the śūdra class. It is also a tradition that rejects all the trappings of religion and believes that there can be no God outside one's own body and mind. I realized that unravelling such a tradition was no less adventurous than understanding the intricacies and technicalities of philosophy of language that have pre-occupied me so far. So with a sense of admiration and awe I undertook this study never bothering about what others have to say about the philosophical proprieties involved in undertaking such a study.

India has an extremely rich and varied cultural heritage. Innumerable and diverse cultures grew and flourished here during its long history. In fact, it is the variations that add to its richness and strength. Almost in every generation and in every part of the country, unique and original thoughts have come forth that have made Indian culture so very fascinating. But when it comes to recording the history of this great tradition for the modern generation our scholars have faltered. There seems to be a lot of bias and lack of objectivity in their projections. As a result the culture and history of those parts of India that are considered to be backward are totally forgotten. Orissa is one of such backward regions. Hence, it is natural that the contribution of Orissa to the enrichment of Indian cultural history has never been given its due. There was no dearth of scholars in Orissa who wrote in English, but they were never taken as erudite enough to be consulted. The result is painful and humiliating for any sensitive person eager to know about the culture of this region. A look at any encyclopaedia or any compendium on cultural and philosophical heritage of India reveals that the culture, philosophy and literature of Orissa have been pushed to the oblivion.

This land, like other parts of India, has witnessed the rise and fall of varied religious and spiritual forms. But it has absorbed and amalgamated these streams of ideas to produce a very unique kind of religio-philosophical tradition. This land has a great literary history of its own. It has produced a great history of ideas that can add to the pride of Indian tradition. However, all these dimensions of this culture have been simply overlooked. I take here as examples two of the most consulted works on concepts and ideas related to India to prove my point. *The Cultural Heritage of India*, one of the most authentic encyclopaedic book on Indian culture, makes no mention of the Vaiṣṇavism of Orissa that stands apart from all other forms of Vaiṣṇavism. One is likely to be equally frustrated if one tries to gather some objective information from the *Encyclopaedia Britannica*. Though it admits the existence of Oriyā as an independent language, nothing is mentioned about the philosophical and *bhakti* literature it produced in this vernacular language. With much difficulty one may find the name of Jagannātha Dāsa, the composer of *Śrīmad Bhāgavata* in Oriyā. But this great Santha-philosopher is mentioned merely as a disciple of Caitanya, which is again a misrepresentation of facts. "Pañcasakhā," the famous group of five *santhas* (including Jagannātha Dāsa), who brought about a cultural renaissance in the areas of Oriyā *bhakti* tradition, are just glossed over in most of the compendiums on the cultural history of India.

When one comes to the religious history of India, it is all the more frustrating. The theories about the genesis and development of the diverse sects of Tāntric Buddhism, like Vajrayāna and Sahajayāna, can be taken here as a case in point. All the available modern literatures on Tāntric Buddhism keep repeating that such Buddhist schools were nurtured in Bengal during the Pāla dynasty. But scholars seem to be unaware of the Bhaumakara rulers of Orissa who used the epithet *Parama Saugata* to indicate their Buddhistic affiliations. In fact, Orissa has innumerable *vihāras* and temples dedicated to the gods and goddesses of Vajrayānic order, mostly constructed during the Bhaumakara rule. Buddhism received royal support in Orissa as late as seventh century as is evident from the travel accounts of the Chinese and Tibetan pilgrims.[1] It is all the more surprising that the contributions of Orissa in nurturing this new form of Buddhism is never acknowledged despite the fact that Uḍra or Uḍḍiyāna (which is the name of the ancient Orissa) has been identified as one of the *pīṭhas*[2] (centres)

---

1. (i) Mkhan Po Sumpa, *Pāg Sām Jon Zāng*, ed. S.C. Das, Calcutta, 1908.
   (ii) D.P. Chattopadhyaya (ed.), *Tāranātha's History of Buddhism in India*, Simla: Indian Institute of Advanced Study, 1970.
2. *pīṭhaṁ jālandhraṁkhyātaṁ oḍḍiyānaṁ tathaivaca*
   — *Hevajra Tantra*, VII.12.

of Tāntric sects of Buddhism. It is unfortunate that such misinformation is still dished out even after such pioneering works like *Modern Buddhism and its Followers in Orissa* by N.N. Vasu[3] published as early as 1919; even after the archaeological excavations carried out in Lalitagiri, Udayagiri and Ratnagiri of Orissa had conclusively established by 1869 the existence of the Buddhist *vihāra*s of the Vajrayānic order. Perhaps there is no corner in Orissa where images of Buddha and Buddhist gods and goddesses are not found. On the other hand, scholars are happily oblivious of the fact that very few archaeological evidences are there in Bengal in support of the claim that the Pāla dynasty was the only dynasty to nurture Tāntric Buddhism in that belt. Though such pioneering works like *Antiquities of Orissa* by R.L. Mitra[4] (1913), *Historical Geography of India* by Cunningham[5] (1924), *Buddhism* by Monier-Williams[6]

3. N.N. Vasu, *Modern Buddhism and its Followers in Orissa*, Delhi: Gyan Publishing House, 1986 edn. (first published in 1919).

   In this work the author very meticulously argues that the Oriyā Vaiṣṇava Santhas were crypto Buddhists. He also elaborates how Tāntric Buddhism is still followed by certain tribes of Orissa.

4. R.L. Mitra, *Antiquities of Orissa*, vol. I & II. (1980). Reprinted as *Indian Studies, Past and Present*, Calcutta, 1961-63.

   He writes, "During four centuries preceding Christian era, Orissa generally and the district of Purī in particular were under the dominance of the Buddhists," vol. II, p. 175.

5. Cunningham, *Historical Geography of India*, Calcutta, 1924.

   He notes, "The Buddhist origin of Jagannātha figures is proved beyond all doubts by their adoption as the representation of the Brāhmiṇical '*avatāra*' of Buddha in the annual almanacs of Mathurā and Benares." p. 63.

6. Monier-Williams, *Buddhism*, New Delhi: Munshiram Manoharlal Publishers Pvt. Ltd. 1995, latest edn. (first published in 1889).

   He observes, ". . . in Orissa, where a temple once dedicated to Gautama Buddha, and supposed to contain a relic of his burnt body, was afterwards dedicated to the Jagannātha form of Kṛṣṇa and supposed to enshrine one of its bones, and where low caste and high caste both eat together the food cooked in the house of that popular God." pp. 165-66.

(1889), *History of Orissa* by R.D. Bannerjee[7] (1930) and *A History of Orissa* by W.W. Hunter[8] were published long back, nobody wants to check the intimate relation between Buddhism and the cult of Jagannātha of Orissa. The existence and impact of a cult can be judged by posterity on the basis of archaeological and literary evidences. In case of Orissa, besides abundant archaeological evidences, the vast literature produced during thirteenth to nineteenth century proves the impact of the *śūnya*-centric metaphysics of Buddhism on Oriyā literary and philosophical tradition. But this aspect of its history is kept under the wrap due to inexplicable reasons. Similar is the case with the history and the influence of Nātha cult. There is no mention about the presence of this cult in Orissa. Yet two of its important theories — *piṇḍa-brahmāṇḍa tattva* and *kāyā sādhanā* — are very important components of the philosophy of the Oriyā *santha*s of the medieval age. The same attitude is noted when it comes to the contribution of Orissa in the development of the Tāntric philosophy, even if *Kālikā Purāṇa*, one of the important works of this school, mentions Uḍra or Orissa as its primary *pīṭha*.[9] My study of different authentic works on these areas made me wonder why such a treatment has been meted out to such a rich culture. Is it because Orissa is economically a backward state? Or is it because of the fact that Orissa came under British rule very late? Or is it simply because of the apathy of the people of Orissa? The answer is difficult to pinpoint. Despite such remarkable publications as *History of Orissa* by H.K. Mahatab[10] and *Buddhism in Orissa* by

7. R.D. Bannerjee, *History of Orissa*, vol. I & II, Calcutta: R. Chatterjee, 1930-31.
8. W.W. Hunter *et al.* (ed.) N.K. Sahu, *A History of Orissa*, vol. I & II, Calcutta: Sushil Gupta (India) Ltd., 1956.
9. *uḍrākṣyaṁ prathamaṁ pīṭhaṁdvītīyam jalaśailakaṁ* ।
   tr̥tīyaṁ pūrṇapīṭhaṁtu kāmarūpaṁ caturthakaṁ ॥

   Kālikā Purāṇa, Vangavasi edn., 410, qtd. in N.K. Sahu, *Buddhism in Orissa*, Bhubaneswar: Utkal University, 1958, p. 144.
10. H.K. Mahatab, *History of Orissa*, vol. I & II, Cuttack: Prajatantra Prachar Samiti, 1959-60.

N.K. Sahu[11] and in recent times such books as *The Cult of Jagannātha and Regional Traditions of Orissa* by Eschmann, Kulke and Tripathi,[12] the contributions of Orissa in the field of culture are yet to receive significant notice. My desire to take up the project on the Orissan *santha* tradition is partly driven by this sense of hurt and neglect.

Once I started working on the project I realized enormities of hazards associated with any study in this area. The bulk of the works of these Oriyā *santha*s are voluminous. Some of them are not available in print. But the most important problem I faced was in finding properly edited versions of these works. Most of the works of these *santha*s are published by Dharma Grantha Store, a publishing house that caters to the needs of the rural people with very cheap editions. These people are no scholars. These books are in demand as these simple people still draw solace from works of the *santha*s that are mostly composed in lyrical forms. So most of the scripts are not properly edited or documented. There may be variations in the readings of the texts. Only a miniscule portion of such voluminous literature is properly edited. So a scholar working on the area is likely to be confused about the authenticity of the use of certain crucial words. Moreover, a lot of terms with heavy religious and Tāntric symbolisms were in vogue during the period. With the lapse of time and lack of interest of the scholars of the subsequent period, these symbols have become all but decipherable. *Santha Sāhitya Śabda Koṣa*, a pioneering work by Ratnakara Chainy, is the only available work dealing with the lexicon of the Oriyā *santha*s. This work is of immense help to scholars working in this area. But that is not enough. Besides, most of the writers who have done serious work on this area have approached the subject from a literary rather than philosophical angle. However, such invaluable books like

11. N.K. Sahu, *Buddhism in Orissa*, Bhubaneswar, Utkal University, 1958.

12. A. Eschmann *et al.* (ed.), *The Cult of Jagannātha and Regional Traditions of Orissa*, New Delhi: Manohar, 1978.

Santha (Bhakti) Sāhitya by C.R. Das and *Oṛisāre Nirguṇa Sāhityara Dhārā* by N. Pradhan and *Oṛisī Vaiṣṇava Dharma* by K.C. Mishra are of enormous help to the scholars uninitiated in this line of thought. Delineating the philosophical positions from this vast and comparatively obscure philosophical literature of the period was a real challenge for me. But I have tried to offer a consistent account of a very powerful philosophical tradition for posterity, as I fear the tradition may die a natural death with the spread of technical education and the all-engulfing culture of consumerism.

However, it was not very easy on my part to make up my mind to tread on this unfrequented path. I have no hesitation in admitting that I imbibed interest in the theme from my son Priyadarshi Patnaik, Associate Professor of English at I.I.T. Kharagpur. While helping him translate some of the poems and lyrical pieces of the literature of this genre I was exposed to this wonderful philosophy. He always felt that I as a scholar of philosophy must do justice to this unknown facet of the medieval *bhakti* tradition of Orissa. However, my typical training in technical philosophy always stood in my way. My last shreds of hesitation vanished with the necessary nod from Professor Daya Krishna, the renowned philosopher and my role model. His dynamism helped me to get rid of my initial vacillation about working on a topic that might not be considered academically suitable for a scholar of philosophy. It was Professor Daya Krishna who asked me to write a paper on this topic for his journal. Since then I have set out on a journey on this arduous path. The passion was so demanding that I had never got time to think even about my personal problems of very serious dimensions. I hope that the work will be able to generate interest of the readers in a culture that had remained in oblivion so far.

Tandra Patnaik

Contents

Acknowledgements

THIS is the seventeenth book published by the Department of Philosophy, Utkal University and the twelfth one to be published under "Utkal Philosophy Series." I record my gratitude to the University Grants Commission for providing funds for publication of this volume under UGC Special Assistance Programme. I am also greatly obliged to Professor K. Bagchi, Retired Professor of Philosophy, Visva Bharati University, for consenting to act as a Referee and recommending the work for publication. I am equally indebted to other members of the Editorial Board, especially to Professor S.C. Panigrahi, for scanning the manuscript and coming out with some constructive suggestions.

My special thanks to Dr. Biraj Mohan Das and Satya Narayan Mishra for providing me some of the rare materials without which I could not have proceeded with the work.

Finally, I express my gratitude to M/s. D.K. Printworld, New Delhi for collaborating with us in the publication of the book.

Tandra Patnaik

Key to Transliteration

VOWELS

अ *a*	आ *ā*	इ *i*	ई *ī*	उ *u*	ऊ *ū*
(but)	(palm)	(it)	(beet)	(put)	(pool)
ऋ *ṛ*	ए *e*	ऐ *ai*	ओ *o*	औ *au*	
(rhythm)	(play)	(air)	(toe)	(loud)	

CONSONANTS

Guttural	क *ka*	ख* *kha*	ग *ga*	घ *gha*	ङ *ṅa*
	(skate)	(blockhead)	(gate)	(ghost)	(sing)
Palatal	च *ca*	छ* *cha*	ज *ja*	झ *jha*	ञ *ña*
	(chunk)	(catch him)	(john)	(hedgehog)	(bunch)
Cerebral	ट *ṭa*	ठ* *ṭha*	ड *ḍa*	ढ* *ḍha*	ण* *ṇa*
	(start)	(anthill)	(dart)	(godhead)	(under)
Dental	त *ta*	थ *tha*	द *da*	ध* *dha*	न *na*
	(path)	(thunder)	(that)	(breathe)	(numb)
Labial	प *pa*	फ* *pha*	ब *ba*	भ *bha*	म *ma*
	(spin)	(philosophy)	(bin)	(abhor)	(much)
Semi-vowel	य *ya*	र *ra*	ल *la*	व *va*	
	(young)	(drama)	(luck)	(vile)	
Sibilants	श *śa*	ष *ṣa*	स *sa*	ह *ha*	
	(shove)	(bushel)	(so)	(hum)	
Others	क्ष *kṣa*	त्र *tra*	ज्ञ *jña*	ळ* ḷ	ॠ* *ṝ*
	(*kṣatriya*)	(*triśūla*)	(*jñānī*)	(*play*)	

अं (ं) *ṁ anusvāra* (nasalisation of preceding vowel) like *saṁskṛti*

अः *ḥ* (*prātaḥ*) *ḥ visarga* (aspiration of preceding vowel)

ऽ 'Avagraha' consonant #'consonant (like:- *ime 'vasthitā*)

Anusvāra at the end of line is presented by म् = m (not ṁ)

HINDI LETTERS (Extras)

ँ *ñ*	ं ṅ	ड़ *ṛa*	ढ़ *ṛha*
(*candrabindu*)	(*anusvāra*)		

* No exact English equivalents for these letters.

Introduction

MANY of my fellow scholars may recoil at the idea of undertaking research in a subject dealing with a school of thought which can at best be described as a religio-philosophical doctrine. They have at their disposal every possible justification for a strong aversion towards anything that does not adhere to the conception of philosophy proper, handed down to us by a Western orientation. They may argue that philosophy being a pure rational activity cannot accommodate a *bhakti*-based system dealing with a specific cult-syncretism. Therefore, it is advisable that the job be better left to anthropologists or historians. This is what I propose to counter in this chapter. So the first thing I owe to my readers is justifying my position that the task I have undertaken is not entirely non-philosophical in nature. Fortunately for me I do not have to strain myself to prove my point. All the great names like Radhakrishnan, T.R.V. Murthy, B.K. Matilal, J.N. Mohanty, Daya Krishna, to name a few, must have faced this predicament convincing the Western world that Indian philosophy is neither pure soteriology nor religion, but a distinct brand of philosophy bearing its own stamp. They have stood by their own conviction that whatever is taken for philosophy in India need not be reduced to what the Western world labels as philosophy. I shall follow the path trodden by them while arguing that what we mean by philosophy in India need not be restricted to accredited systems like Nyāya, Sāṁkhya or Vedānta. If this is the case then we willy-nilly admit that Indian philosophy comes to an abrupt end sometime by the end of the eleventh century. But philosophy in India never came to an end. It continued and will continue though the method of doing philosophy might fluctuate with the changes of clime and time. So I find nothing wrong about exploring this very rich religio-metaphysical tradition of India. In the first section of my introductory note I would like to focus on the typical nuances of what in general is known as Indian philosophy. In the second section I shall throw some light on a much-neglected philosophical tradition spearheaded by the *santhas* during thirteenth to eighteenth century.

The first question that I must address is about the validity of discussing a metaphysics centering on soteriology and religion. We know pretty well that most Western academic philosophers love to nurture the belief that there cannot be anything called philosophy in India. Right from W.T. Stace[1] to Anthony Flew[2] have very blatantly declared that what passes for philosophy in India is nothing more than religion or else a bundle of mystical proclamations. I take these disparaging remarks as the starting point to assess how far we have been fair to our own philosophical tradition in the colonial and post-colonial phases. Most often we have reacted to these observations of the Western philosophers in two extreme ways. Some scholars have capitalized on this libelous attitude and tried to allure the Western mind by presenting the Indian philosophical tradition as esoteric, spiritual and mystical in nature; and thereby giving credence to the allegation that India never had a philosophy in the proper sense of the term. This has done immense harm to a rich and diverse intellectual tradition. But the other reaction coming from the philosophers trained in Western way of thought is no less damaging. Those of us trained in Western analytic tradition have always felt uncomfortable about the application of the term philosophy, to what is known as *darśana* in Indian

1. W.T. Stace, *A Critical History of Greek Philosophy*, Delhi: Macmillan, 1982.
2. Anthony Flew, *An Introduction to Western Philosophy*, London: Thames and Hudson, 1971.

tradition. Matilal rightly points out that for such academic philosophers *darśana* has a "practical end in view, namely, ultimate freedom from *duḥkha* and to that extent the discipline called *darśana* is saturated with soteriology and religious fervour, while academic discipline is devoted to pure pursuit of knowledge, thought, analysis of concepts and meanings, etc."[3] So this group of scholars has been mostly obsessed with convincing the Western world that our brand of Realism, Idealism or Phenomenalism is very much in line with the Western counterparts. Sometimes their distrust for the tradition is so deep that they prefer to bend backwards to prove that our classical systems of philosophy had nothing to do with intuitive experience, soteriology and spirituality. In the process they have produced some excellent works in which the analytic and dialectic acumen of Śaṅkarācārya or Nāgārjuna or Gaṅgeśa are brought to the notice of the Western world. It should be admitted that such salutary efforts have largely been responsible for creating a positive attitude about the Indian philosophy. But most often the other side of the fact is suppressed. These works seldom mention that these great ancient thinkers also talk of soteriology and in some cases about the existence of God. It is really a matter of regret that we have seldom displayed courage to claim that our philosophical tradition always had a place for other elements along with systematic rational analysis. A peep into our philosophical tradition reveals that our ancestors were concerned about all that is claimed to come under the so-called academic discipline, yet they did not mind going beyond this limit. In our philosophical tradition we do not come across a sharp dichotomy between facts and values, theory and practice. That is why a purely metaphysical school of thought like Sāṁkhya could be aligned to a practice-oriented system like Yoga; an epistemology-based critical system like Nyāya could be aligned to the Vaiśeṣika system, primarily concentrating

3. B.K. Matilal, *Perception*, Delhi: Oxford University Press, 1986, p. 70.

on metaphysics. I strongly believe that one need not feel helpless about the way our philosophical tradition has been shaped. Rather the close link between life and philosophy should be seen as a point of strength of our philosophical tradition, never a weakness. There are very few philosophical thoughts in the world that have the potentiality to be translated into a way of life, as it is the case with philosophy or *darśana* in India. At the same time I do not intend to claim that Indian philosophy is purely non-rational and non-academic in nature. There are the elements of high-level speculation as well as rigorous logical and conceptual analysis. But what makes this philosophical tradition distinct from its Western counterparts is the absence of a clear-cut line of demarcation amongst these elements. Unlike Western philosophy "reason" alone does not occupy the central position in the philosophical systems of India. The elements of intuition, experience as well as rational analysis are balanced in a constructive way. The tradition, in general, aims at one goal, i.e., the elevation of life from the material levels of existence to the level of spiritual fulfilment.

Unfortunately, Western philosophers have often failed to appreciate this attitude in the Indian philosophical tradition. So it is seen as a form of mystical rhapsody. I quote W.T. Stace to help us understand their way of misinterpreting a philosophical heritage. He remarks that as "the roots of Indian thought lie in anxiety of the individuals to escape from the calamities of existence"[4] it can at best be called a religion. Such a type of thinking, in his esteemed opinion, is not a rational enterprise. It is nothing more than "passing out of a realm of thought, reason, and philosophy into the dream and shadow land of . . . mysticism, where the heavy scent of beautiful poison-flower drugs the intellect and obliterates thought in a blissful languorous repose."[5] Ironically, Stace makes such quotable remarks in a book that also includes

4. Stace, p. 14.
5. Stace, p. 371.

Plato's mystical interpretation of the highest Reality. To answer Stace and their ilk we have to first of all understand what the term "mysticism" connotes. Mysticism, in the West, is often taken to mean something overwhelmingly God-oriented or else something dealing with the occult. But the metaphysical foundation of Indian mysticism, if we call it mysticism at all, is centred upon the belief expressed as "All is One; and One is all"; and ultimately this One transcends all categorial as well as conceptual discriminations. This theory is eminently portrayed in the Upaniṣadic, Advaitic and Buddhistic philosophies. Yet all these systems are also based on rigorous rational analysis. The conception of an ineffable absolute reality is so powerful that it continued to be a dominant metaphysical trend of philosophy from thirteenth to eighteenth century. If this is mysticism, then we need not be ashamed of it. We should rather be proud of the type of mysticism our culture encourages. It is a mysticism that allows a thinker to transcend all categorial limitations in the quest of the ultimate truth. The basic purpose of Indian thought is not to arouse dogmatic thought in God but to awaken and inspire a man towards the quest of the ultimate reality and truth. If it is a form of religion, then it does not surely mean theology but spiritualism. Contrary to the widespread but mistaken view that in order to lead a profoundly religious life one has to believe in God, the Upaniṣads as well as the systems like Advaita and Mahāyāna Buddhism teach with unrelenting rationality that profound religious life can only arise out of transcending dualism including that of theism versus atheism and of immanence versus transcendence. If such concern is labelled as religion there is nothing more to say.

This trend of being aware of the limitations of the empirical level of existence and focusing on the transcendental and self-abiding truth has helped philosophical musings in India to be closer to life and reality. Despite being known as *guhyaśāstra*, meant exclusively for the intellectual elites, the philosophical speculations in India could never be totally kept away from the common mass. It has always permeated down to the commonest level of the society. Śaṅkara's attempt at resurrecting Hinduism can be taken as a case in point. It is commonly believed that Śaṅkara's philosophy is highly speculative in nature. Hence, it is meant for the intellectuals only. But, history proves it otherwise. Śaṅkara's teachings had such a pervasive impact on our culture that, even today, the illiterate people from the remotest corner of our land can understand concepts like *māyā* or *Brahman* with remarkable ease. Similarly, one may wonder at the amount of influence Buddha and his teachings had on the common people of India. Despite Buddhism being labelled as pessimistic and nihilistic, the people of his time found a new message of hope in its philosophy. They accepted the basic principles of Buddhism and translated them into a way of life. Perhaps in no country in the West could philosophy influence life to such an extent. This shows that in India philosophy is not confined to the four walls of logical and intellectual rigour. Mere intellectual satisfaction is not the aim of Indian philosophers. Philosophy, here, has a typical bearing on the day-to-day life of the people. As life is associated with philosophy, thinkers have felt the necessity to consider all aspects of life including poetry and religion on the ground that they have also some positive contributions in shaping the individual life as well as providing a pattern of social framework based on a moral fabric. In this context S.K. Maitra's remark is worth noting:

> Philosophy is no doubt love of knowledge (from *philos* — love and *sophia* — knowledge), but the knowledge that philosophy craves for is not the knowledge of facts but the knowledge of values, especially the supreme value, namely salvation.[6]

Therefore, philosophy in India implies *darśana* and *tattva*, which mean "vision of truth and reality" and "the nature of the

6. S.K. Maitra, *The Spirit of Indian Philosophy*, Calcutta: N.P., 1947, p. 10.

reality"[7] respectively. It is *darśana* or a vision of the highest values and of truth. Therefore, it is neither merely a chew of the intellectual pieces of the Śāstras, nor only the grasping of the raw materials of philosophy and logic.[8] Philosophy goes beyond these and studies the different aspects of human life in its relationship with the society and charts out a definite programme of life. Hence, it is living and practical, rather than only academic in nature. According to Max Müller, philosophy was recommended in India not for the sake of the knowledge but for the highest purpose that man can strive after in this life.[9] There is no doubt about the fact that philosophy or *darśana* is soteriologically-oriented. Most of the strands of Indian philosophical tradition (both Hindu and non-Hindu) admit release or liberation as the highest value. They might have used different words to mean this ultimate value, might have suggested various methods or modes, yet it is unanimously regarded as the culmination of philosophic culture. This singular emphasis on pursuing the highest goal can be ascribed to the fact that philosophy in India did not emerge merely from wonder or curiosity as it seems to have done in the West; rather it originated under the pressure of a practical need arising from the presence of moral and physical evil in life.[10]

Another important reason why philosophy in India is mistaken with religion is because of the identification of the phrases "Indian Philosophy" with "Hindu Philosophy." Unfortunately the term "Hindu" is primarily understood as a

7. R.K. Puligandla, *Fundamental of Indian Philosophy,* New York: Abington Press, 1975, p. 18.

8. Swami Prajñānanda, *Schools of Indian Philosophical Thought,* Calcutta: Ananda Press, 1973, p. 7.

9. F. Max Müller, *Six Systems of Indian Philosophy,* vol. XIX, London: Longmans Green & Co., 1928, p. 370.

10. M. Hiriyana, *Outlines of Indian Philosophy,* Bombay: Blackie & Son, 1973, p. 18.

form of religious belief. Indian philosophy, though not adverse to religion, is not also religio-centric. The term "Hindu" refers to a group of people having different socio-religious background, such as aborigines, Draviḍians and Āryans, etc. It is a common term encompassing everybody of Indian origin professing the spirit of the Indian culture.[11] The concept had originally a territorial significance. When Persians invaded the land they referred to the people of the Indian side of the river "Sindhu" as "Hindu." In the process, the religion and philosophy of Indians have come to be known as Hinduism for all practical purposes. The word "Hindu" when combined with the word *dharma* creates some confusion for people not associated with the culture of the land. The word *dharma* is often misconstrued as "religion" (as it is understood in English), though it stands for "a way of life." It is seldom realized that even if Hinduism stands for a set of religious beliefs they do not always recommend faith in a personal God, and in some cases even if the notion of God is mentioned. He is viewed as the symbol of an ineffable and non-categorizable reality. Thus, though the conceptions of *dharma* and *darśana* sometimes are mixed up this presents no unsurpassable problem for us. Unlike the Western epistemological tradition there is no place for bi-polarity between faith and reason, knowledge and scriptural authority, religion (not theology) and philosophy in Indian intellectual tradition. The spirit of Indian philosophical heritage can be best summed up in the following words of Swami Abhedananda:

> Of the tree of knowledge, philosophy is the flower and the religion is the fruit. Philosophy is the theoretical side of the religion and the religion is philosophy in practice.[12]

---

11. S. Radhakrishnan, *The Hindu View of Life,* Bombay: Blackie and Son (India) Ltd., 1979, p. 2.

12. Swami Abhedananda, *Philosophy and Religion,* Calcutta: R.K. Vedānta Math, 1951, p. 63.

The philosophy of a land is the product of its environment and its specific modes of cognitive, intellectual, aesthetic, moral and religious experience. Therefore, to evaluate the philosophies of "others" by standards and criteria of one's own culture is not a healthy practice. It is equally unhealthy to assess one's own culture by the norm that is not one's own.

Classical Tradition *vis-à-vis* Medieval Tradition

Now it is time for me to discuss about the question of philosophical propriety involved in exploring a tradition I call Bauddha Vaiṣṇavism. This theory is a part of a great spiritual wave that swept the land during the eleventh to the eighteenth century. It is broadly known as the *santha* tradition. I have already argued that philosophy in India was not always confined to rational and conceptual analysis. It also is a record of the vision of life. With the change of vision depending on change of life in the society, philosophy changes too. We notice that our society has never hesitated to accept any new vision. So there is always a scope for other kinds of interpretations; and an interpretation depends on a specific intellectual and social climate. Naturally, we find varieties of visions or interpretations of the ways of life within the broader ambit of philosophy in India. There has never been a break in the stream of this philosophical culture. It is continuous and living, projecting world-views of different kinds, reflecting the culture of different phases of history.

Unfortunately, the students and teachers of philosophy have gathered a strange belief that the philosophical tradition of India comes to an abrupt end sometime in the eleventh century, may be after Rāmānuja (Navya-Nyāya, being an exception). The reason for such an attitude is not difficult to trace. In the previous section I have mentioned that those trained in Western trend of analytic philosophy find it difficult to accommodate aspects of classical Indian philosophies that deal with soteriology and intuitive experience. The discomfort becomes all the more acute when it comes to the medieval philosophy that mostly highlights the ineffability of the highest Reality and emphasizes *bhakti* as a path of self-realization. The amount of such misgivings can be deciphered from the fact that very few philosophers have come forward to record the metaphysical trends of the medieval period. The task is always left to the scholars of religious history. The twists and turns in the development of philosophical culture during that phase of Indian history may be one of the important reasons for such a disparaging attitude. This was a period marked by great socio-cultural upheaval. The baton of spiritual leadership passed from the *ācārya*s to the *santha*s who emphasized more on social renaissance than hair-splitting intellectual analysis. Their aim was to make philosophy and spiritualism accessible to the common people and the down-trodden. Naturally, the dialectical and logical way of engaging in philosophical activities yielded place to simple and appealing ways of making philosophical statements through poetical creations. Philosophy no longer remained the preserve of the select few but the door was flung open for the commonest of the common. As a result Sanskrit, the language of gods, lost its appeal and yielded place to the vernacular languages. And finally, the term *bhakti,* due to some unknown reason, came to be associated with the philosophical movements of the period.

Today, unfortunately, the term *bhakti* is seen as a theologically loaded concept, with all the trappings mistakenly associated with religion, i.e., blind acceptance of scriptural revelations, dogmatism and narrow-mindedness bordering on fanaticism. It is seldom realized that the philosophers of the medieval period were engaged in the same activity as were undertaken by their predecessors of the classical age. Like the *ācārya*s of the classical age these *santha* philosophers deliberated on the nature of the highest Reality, about the nature of life and the way out of the physical and moral evils. In most cases they talked of *bhakti,* yet they were opposed to the theological interpretation of the term. Therefore, they advanced a metaphysical scheme in which the Reality was presented as a unique principle, transcending all qualifications (*nirguṇa*) and all categorial discriminations (*nirvikalpa*). Making this stand explicit Kabīr, the great *santha* declared: "This unique *tattva* is beyond Vedic injunction, beyond discriminations, beyond *pāpa* and *puṇya*, beyond knowledge and meditation."[13] It is, in general, a metaphysical tradition that beautifully assimilates the basic ideas of Upaniṣads, Advaitism, Buddhism and Yoga and re-assimilates them all in a new form. In no way is the *santha* tradition a religious tradition in the ordinary sense of the term. It is a continuation of the philosophical heritage of the classical period. Even a cursory look at the literature of the period reveals that the philosophical tradition of the past continued with new vigour by absorbing within itself new characters and new forms. Ironically, such a cluster of rich philosophy has never been considered to be a part of the mainstream tradition and has always been treated as the children of lesser gods by the scholars. Nevertheless, it cannot be denied that the philosophical trend of the period from the eleventh to the eighteenth century forms a significant part of our cultural tradition. Therefore, it is all the more relevant to examine some of the basic dimensions of their thought.

The Fundamentals of the Santha Tradition

Before I discuss the basic tenets of the philosophy of the medieval India I would like to point out the exact implication of the word, *santha*. In the present context *santha* is a much-maligned term. Bearded and half-naked persons having large *akhāṛā*s (religious establishments); and gathering at various religious *melā*s are often presented as the *santha*s in the electronic media. They, in their turn, are equally media savvy and try to hog the limelight by proving that they are no less glamorous than any industrialist or film star with a fleet of imported cars and modern electronic gadgets. But the term

13. Qtd. in C.R. Das, *Santha (bhakti) Sāhitya* (Oṛiyā), vol. II, Bhubaneswar: Orissa Sahitya Academy, 1982, p. 146.

santha has a profound implication. According to *Amarakośa* the term *santha* derived from the root *sat*, which signifies "a person endowed with right knowledge." Śaṅkarācārya, on the other hand, defines *santha* as, "persons with a calm and compassionate disposition; always engaged in the welfare of mankind like the spring season."[14] In the opinion of Acyutānanda, the great Oriyā *santha*, truth, love, forgiveness and compassion are the inherent qualities of *santha*-hood. So the word *santha* stands for a person who dedicates his knowledge and moral power for the uplift of the society. Again many people confuse the term *santha* with a person passionately devoted to God (*bhakta*) as the *santha* tradition is closely associated with *bhakti*. But every *bhakta* is not a *santha*, though every *santha* is a *bhakta*. As a path of spiritual realization *bhakti* has a long history of its own. The most popular definition of this term is *parānuraktirīśvare*, i.e., the highest attachment for God. A *bhakta*, thus, indulges in his own self-realization through intense love for God and surrendering of his ego. But *santha*s are more interested in the freedom of mankind from the vortex of ignorance and suffering. In this sense, they are also different from *puṇḍit*s and *ācārya*s. Subtle processes of logic and dialectics do not hold any meaning for them. They are interested in realizing the truths of life, redemption of mankind, and this inner realization serves as the primary inspiration for spreading the message of love and compassion. As far as the urge for inner realization is concerned they are *bhakta*s. So the *santha*s are neither intellectual elites nor social recluses. The society, itself, is the field of their activity. At this point it should also be made clear that *santha*s never aim to create a religion, to divide people, to set one religion against the other. They intend to show the path of spiritual joy. They have only one mission, i.e., mercy. The *santha*s tell us that to realize God one need not undertake religious formalities nor do they expect us to run away from our social responsibilities.

---

14. *śāntā mahānto nivasanti vāsanthavat lokahitacarantaḥ.* Qtd. in Das, p. 33.

Santha tradition is not the name of a unified system of beliefs. This, rather, refers to a cluster of views coming from different directions of India, across several centuries. *Santha* philosophy is vast and varied, and most often, has a regional ambience. To name a few masters of this kind — we have Kabīr, Nānak, Dādū and Razzab from the northern part of India; Tukārām, Jñāneśvar, Narsī Mehtā from Maharashtra and Gujarat, Vīra Śaivas from Karnataka, Tamil *siddhas*, Palikiri Somnath from Andhra, Bauls, Yugīs from Bengal, Śaṁkara Deva from Assam, Swamikal and Ezhuthachan from Kerala, Pañcasakhā (a group of five *santhas*) and Bhima Bhoi from Orissa. They belonged to different parts of India, spoke and wrote in different regional languages, accepted different personal gods as the ultimate object of their *bhakti*, yet their views reflected a uniform pattern of thoughts. The best of the elements of different philosophical traditions were amalgamated by these *santhas* to reconstruct a metaphysics that could respond to the human needs of that period. Therefore, their metaphysics was not a neo-metaphysics from the perspective of the content, but their method and approach were distinctly novel. Vinoba Bhave[15] very rightly observes that the *santha* philosophy is an amalgam of three distinct traits — Upaniṣadic (Vedic), Buddhistic and Tamil *bhakti* philosophy. From Upaniṣads, it absorbed the elements of absolutism, and its emphasis on self-realization through direct intuitive experience; from Buddhism it adopted the principles of *karuṇā* (compassion), *samatā* (equality) and *maitrī* (fraternity); finally the lofty metaphysics was turned by the *santhas* into an accessible philosophy of life by incorporating the elements of *bhakti* from the Tamil *Āḷvārs*. This amalgam resulted in a unique theory about life that reassured human beings of their place under the sun.

---

15. Biyogi Hari, ed., *Santha Sudhāsār*, Foreword, by Vinoba Bhave, New Delhi: Sasta Sahitya Mandal, 1953.

It is not possible for me within the limits of this chapter to go into the details of the *santha* metaphysics. So I shall offer a brief sketch of some of their fundamental principles:

(i) The *santha* metaphysics is mostly Advaitic in spirit. For them the ultimate Reality is one and ineffable. It is beyond all predications, attributes and names. According to Hazari Prasad Dwivedi,[16] *nirguṇa bhakti* is the most fundamental aspect of *santha* metaphysics. But in most cases, we note that the *santhas* conceived the highest Reality as transcending the *nirguṇa/saguṇa* distinction. Of course, there were some *santhas* who were dualists. But that does not come in the way of delineation of their distinct metaphysics of life, because for them the world along with all the created beings is the real manifestation of the highest reality.

(ii) The most important aspect of their metaphysics is their conception of man. Man is the expression of divinity and perfection. Therefore, they put all the emphasis on looking within, not outside for appeasing God by rituals, fasting and pilgrimages. A Sahajīyā *santha* of Bengal puts this idea in the following way: "He is very much inside home, why seek Him outside? You see your husband within, why ask your neighbours where he is?"[17] Another Oriyā *santha* goes one step further to proclaim, Can there be a God outside your mind?"[18] So the *santha* philosophers do not hesitate to be openly critical about idol-worship and the rituals associated with it. The Tamil *siddha* Śivavākkiyar says, "You plant

---

16. Pt. Hazari Prasad Dwivedi, *Madhyakālīn Dharmasādhanā*, Allahabad: Sahitya Bhawan, 1956, p. 94.

17. Qtd. in Jyotibhusan Chaki, "Love-intoxicated Wanderers of Bengal." (Unpublished) presented in the National Seminar on "Sant Literature in India" sponsored by Kendriya Sahitya Akademi and I.I.A.S., 1992.

18. Śiśu Ananta, *Hetu Udaya Bhāgavata* I, Cuttack: Dharma Grantha Store, 1971.

a stone, throw some flowers over it and around it, and utter some *mantras*. Can the planted stone speak, when the Lord is inside you?"[19] Ezhuthachan, the *santha* from Kerala asks us to discard the outer trappings of religion. He says, "Never with studies, penance, charity and rituals is it possible to get the ultimate liberation."[20] Guru Nānak also pointed out several times about the futility of all ritualistic practices.

(iii) The *santha* philosophers claim that man is not essentially different from the universe as well as the creator of the universe. On the basis of this idea some of them offered a theory that is known as *piṇḍa-brahmāṇḍa* identity theory. According to this theory, human being is an extension of the universe and the universe is nothing but manifestation of the ultimate Reality. Thus, they do not hesitate to compare the body with a temple.

(iv) From this sort of view about human nature they could smoothly pass over to the conclusion that there should be no distinction between man and man — be he rich or poor, upper caste or lower, Hindu or Muslim. Thus, they heralded a new confidence in men suffering from low self-esteem, due to the discriminative social structure perpetuated by the Brāhmaṇical order. Many Oriyā *santha* poets preferred to call themselves śūdras because in Indian caste hierarchy śūdra class is allotted the function of "serving others with humility." These *santhas* claimed that this alone is the essential qualification of a man who wants to realize spirituality. Similarly, Dādū, the north Indian *santha*, says, "When

---

19. Qtd. in "Philosophy of the Tamil Siddha" by S. Panneerselvam, *Journal of Indian Council of Philosophical Research*, Special Issue on Philosophical Traditions in the Indian Languages 2002, p. 201.

20. Ezhuthachan, *Adhyātma Rāmāyaṇa*, qtd. in "The Tradition of Dissent," N. Sreekumar, *Journal of Indian Council of Philosophical Research*, Special Volume 2002, p. 301.

the *ātmā* is same everywhere, where is the question of being a Hindu or Muslim?"[21] Madan Baul from Bengal sings, "Varied locks of orthodoxy hang on the doors of love. Madan weeps over the wrangles arising out of differences between *Korān* and *Purāṇa*, rosary and garland."[22] The entire emphasis obviously rests on equality and the bond of love.

(v) The message of human equality and fraternity was already reflected in some Vedic and Upaniṣadic *mantras*, but the *santha* philosophers tried to give these ideals a concrete shape by introducing the element of love through their emphasis on *bhakti*. *Bhakti* has also been defined as *parānuraktirīśvare*, i.e., the ultimate attachment for God, in the presence of which all other worldly attachments pale into insignificance. This attachment leads one to realize that there is no distinction between love and God. According to the Tamil *siddha* Thirumoolar :

> They are fools who say,
> Lord and love are twain.[23]

Man, being a part and parcel of this divine principle of love, cannot afford to be selfish, cannot afford to bother only about his own redemption. Thus, *bhakti* implies compassion for one and all, so that a man can gladly say in unison with the Oriyā *santha* Bhima Bhoi — "let me suffer in hell, but let the suffering humanity be redeemed."[24]

---

21. Qtd. in C.R. Das, p. 121.
22. Jyotibhusan Chaki, "Love-intoxicated Wanderers of Bengal."
23. Qtd. in S. Panneerselvam, "Philosophy of the Tamil Siddhas," *Journal of Indian Council of Philosophical Research*, Special Issue on Philosophical Traditions in the Indian Languages, 2002, p. 199.
24. Bhima Bhoi, *Stuti Cintāmaṇi*, Bhubaneswar: Utkal University, 1972, Poem No. 24.

From this brief outline of the fundamental concepts of the Santhic tradition, it becomes clear that the continuation of the classical tradition of Indian philosophy is not exactly a replication of the past. It seems to assemble many novel elements from the development of philosophical ideas of pre-Śaṅkara and post-Śaṅkara phases. There is little doubt that the tradition is more socially-oriented and therefore closer to human life. It shifts the centre of gravity from the glories of upper ether to this earth of things. In every respect, *santha* metaphysics embodies a series of coherent systems of thought that reflect man's ideals, aspirations, goals and his desire for elevation from the common level to the extraordinary. Its aim is to equate knowledge with life, intellect with experiences, logic with infinite flux of life. It is an amalgamation of unity and plurality, existence and essence. In short, Santhic philosophy stands for those ideas and ideals, which a man can translate into a living experience.

The Santha Tradition of Orissa

Philosophy in a certain sense is culture-specific. This is amply proved by the development of the history of ideas in India. Philosophy, like literature, language, music and social theories, is determined by the limitations of space and time. The history, culture and religion of a land play a vital role in giving shape to the philosophical ambience of the land. Thereby I do not want to claim that each culture has a specific philosophy. There is always scope for variety and novelty. One may notice that this element of "culture-specificness" is more pronounced when the philosophical ideas are expressed in vernacular languages, for such use has a potentiality to be a part of the life-view of the common people and the non-elite. So, even though *santha*s of different parts of India share certain common ideas and ideals, their approaches vary with the cultural ambience of the region. This element of regionalism has made *santha* tradition more culture-specific. The influence of Kabīr's philosophy is more acutely felt in the northern part of India than the southern or eastern parts. Similar is the case with Maharastrian *santha*s like Tukāram and Jñāneśvar. Hence, Orissan *santha* philosophy is largely determined by the religio-cultural factors that flourished in the land.

Here I shall mention some of the important features of the cultural history of Orissa that helped in the making of this unique form of Vaiṣṇavism, which has perhaps no parallel in India. Like other parts of India this eastern region of the country came under the sway of various religio-philosophical streams that evolved during the post-Upaniṣadic period. There were multiple sects of Buddhism, Tantra and Vedānta, along with such Brāhmaṇical sects like Vaiṣṇavism, Śaivism and Śāktism. Besides, the culture of varied aboriginal religions also made its presence felt. But all these cults could not maintain their individual identity for long. The spirit of assimilation seemed to be stronger in this region than in other parts of India. This was further heightened by the cult of Jagannātha that encompassed all forms of religious affiliations that came in its way. Nobody is sure how and when this cult emerged. It is shrouded in mystery. But gradually the evolution of cultural life of Orissa almost became co-terminus with the culture of Jagannāthism. Lord Jagannātha, who is mostly perceived as the sovereign deity of Orissa, is not a deity like any other presiding deities found in other parts of India or even in Orissa. He does not originally belong to any particular class or creed. He too does not have the form and figure of any other god, Hindu or non-Hindu. The iconography of the wooden images of the Jagannātha trinity (actually three deities in the *sanctum sanctorum* of the Jagannātha temple, viz., Jagannātha, Balabhadra and Subhadrā), are peculiar. The deities neither look like Viṣṇu nor like Bodhisattva or Śiva found in the different temples of India. Historians still debate over the origin of this cult. Some look to its aborigine past, while others are of the opinion that the deities represent Buddhists; still others argue that the Jagannātha tradition is the continuation of Vaiṣṇavism mostly conforming to its presentation in the *Bhagavad-Gītā*. However, Jagannātha belongs to all these cults but does not belong to any of them exclusively. Most probably the very idea of Jagannātha is the product of a gradual process of evolution assimilating different elements from different cults that flourished here till it was fully Vaiṣṇavized sometime in the eleventh century CE. The iconographic features as well as the rituals and practices of the Jagannātha temple provide ample indications about its being a fusion of Āryan and non-Āryan, Brāhmaṇical and non-Brāhmaṇical religio-philosophical trends. Naturally, the *santha* tradition that mostly grew around Jagannātha displays certain patterns of fusion of life-views and philosophies. In this case, one comes across the traces of Buddhism (especially its Tāntric versions), Upaniṣadic Advaitism, Nāthism, Vaiṣṇavism and Yoga.

Very much like the cult of Jagannātha it is very difficult to trace the exact philosophical affiliations of the *santha*s tradition of Orissa. The Orissan *santha* tradition appears to be Vaiṣṇavite in form, yet the tradition has virtually nothing in common with the varied versions of Vaiṣṇavism existent elsewhere. These *santha*s are self-proclaimed Vaiṣṇavas and envisage Lord Jagannātha as the Viṣṇu incarnate, yet the same Jagannātha is portrayed as nameless and formless *śūnya puruṣa*, eluding any attempt to catch Him within our conceptual network. He is the object of *bhakti*, yet not realizable by any forms of worship like offerings, pilgrimage, fasting or chanting. These *santha*s strictly adhere to *bhakti* as a means of God-realization, yet their interpretation of *bhakti* has nothing to do with the usual and Vaiṣṇavite interpretation of the term. For them *bhakti* is not a matter of emotional attachment for the Lord supreme but a matter of yogic realization. One may be tempted to categorize these *santha*s as Buddhists, since they stand by the philosophy of *śūnya puruṣa*, yet soon it may be realized that they are not Buddhists. At certain points of time their views seem closest to Śaṅkara's Advaitavāda, yet these philosophers did not accept the conceptual gap between the *Brahman* and *Īśvara*. These *santha*s staunchly believed in the divinity of the body and in *kāyā sādhanā* like the Buddhist Sahajayānīs and the Nātha *panthī*s, yet they did not subscribe to sexo-yogic dimensions of these schools of thought. They seem to be influenced by the Yogācārī theory of mind, yet they were no Yogacārīs. It appears that they encompassed every ideology, every bit of idea that came their way and put them together to formulate a new philosophy. All theoretical positions lost their identity to assume a totally different identity in the form of a new philosophy.

So by what name are we going to identify this distinct type of Vaiṣṇavism of Orissa? Frankly speaking, scholars are not unanimous about the exact nature of its philosophical position. As this philosophy has not received the attention it deserved, no specific name has been assigned to it *a la* Gauḍīya Vaiṣṇavism or Śrī Vaiṣṇavism. If one attempts to find the contents of this philosophical system and accordingly assign a name to it then he is likely to be frustrated. He may be simply at a loss to determine where the predominance of Tāntric Buddhism begins and at what point the entire philosophical speculation is turned towards Upaniṣadic Brahmavāda and Yoga. But this is a predicament not very peculiar to Orissan Vaiṣṇavism alone. We must remember that even the great exponent of non-dualism like Śaṅkarācārya had to earn the sobriquet "crypto Buddhist." Rather the source of our bewilderment may lie elsewhere. This is about the Vaiṣṇavite contents in the so-called Vaiṣṇavism of the *santha*s of Orissa. Unlike other forms of Vaiṣṇavism it swears by pure non-dualism. Not only this, it espouses a theory of *bhakti* that is more yoga-oriented than emotion-oriented. Again, *Śūnya Puruṣa*, not Viṣṇu, is the highest Reality for them. Yet these *santha*s were self-proclaimed Vaiṣṇavas. They formally belonged to different Vaiṣṇava sects. Their *mantra*s for meditation were Vaiṣṇavite; they often sang the glory of Jagannātha, the Viṣṇu, incarnate. So who are these *santha*s? Viaṣṇavas, Buddhists or *yogī*s? Under such peculiar circumstances I feel it is safe to have a closer look at the sources of their philosophical theories. Any such attempt forces us to trace them to Buddhism, both classical and Tāntric. At the same time we cannot avoid using the epithet "Vaiṣṇava" following their proclaimed status. Thus, one may say that they are the Vaiṣṇavas with a Buddhistic leaning. So it will be appropriate to designate this form of Vaiṣṇavism as Bauddha Vaiṣṇavism.

Many scholars on Orissan religious and literary history may find my use of the epithet Bauddha Vaiṣṇavism objectionable. Yet none of them would refute the fact that there are definite stamps of Buddhism in this form of Vaiṣṇavism. So controversy only arises regarding the extent of influence and also to a large extent on the perspectives of the investigators. The famous Bengali scholar N.N. Vasu was so much amazed by the predominance of Buddhism in the literature of the Oriyā *santha*s that he went to the extent of claiming that these thinkers were followers of Buddhism; and they concealed their Buddhistic affiliations apprehending royal persecution.[25] On the other hand, critics like A.B. Mohanty[26] would not find anything wrong with the use of the epithet "Bauddha Vaiṣṇavism." Again there are writers like C.R. Das, who feels unhappy about such unwarranted comparisons though he does not totally discard the role of Buddhism in the development of *santha* metaphysics.[27] A sort of non-committal attitude is discernible in all other literatures on *santha* philosophy of Orissa. Their hesitation to admit the role of Buddhism in the evolution of Orissan Vaiṣṇavism is evident from the fact that the critics and scholars pay virtually no attention to the theory of *Śūnya Puruṣa* that forms the basis of this philosophical tradition. As a result, I am left with a feeling that the conjunction of words Bauddha and Vaiṣṇavism

25. N.N. Vasu, *The Modern Buddhism and Its Followers in Orissa,* Delhi: Gyan Publishing House, 1986, pp. 39 & 59.

26. A.B. Mohanty, "Editorial Introduction" to *Brahma Śaṅkuḷi*, Bhubaneswar: Utkal University, 1970.

27. C.R. Das, *Acyutānanda o Pañcasakhā Dharma*, Santiniketan: Vidya Bhavan, 1951, p. 198.

appears to be jarring to these scholars. Yet my study of the *santha* literature from a philosophical perspective convinced me that the best way to present such a novel and radical theory is to use the epithet "Bauddha Vaiṣṇavism." My entire discussion on the philosophical concepts of this form of Vaiṣṇavism may finally convince the readers why I opted for such a designation. The philosophical tradition, that was initiated by the famous *santha*-poet Sāralā Dāsa sometime in fifteenth century CE by identifying Buddha with Jagannātha, reached its culminating point in the philosophical speculations of Pañcasakhā, five great *santha*s in sixteenth century and was sustained by the subsequent *santha* philosophers up to nineteenth century. This form of Vaiṣṇavism though Brāhmaṇical in affiliation is in no way degraded by absorbing some of the important components of Buddhism. Such assimilation rather makes this philosophical tradition rich and interesting. Orissa being a cradle of Buddhism in different phases of its history must have been exposed to its multiple forms of beliefs and ideas. As long as archaeological evidences were scanty one could have overlooked the impact. But now that it is proved beyond doubt that the whole of Orissa was exposed to the multiple schools of Buddhism throughout centuries, there should not be any hesitation in accepting the fact that there could be fruitful assimilation of what is apparently taken to be opposing philosophical trends. Thus, there is nothing wrong with presenting a tradition without any sectarian bias. I feel it reflects the true spirit of philosophy.

It is unfortunate that this rich philosophical tradition has not received the attention which it deserves. Most of the important works dealing with the philosophico-cultural trends of India are silent about this tradition. My avowed task in this work is to focus on the central concepts of this novel philosophical tradition comparing notes with other traditions on the issue. It must be admitted that these *santha*s were not academic philosophers, so their ideas are often not presented systematically. However, it can be gleaned from the voluminous materials available in print and in the form of manuscripts that they believed sincerely in what they preached. It is not possible to discuss all their theories in detail. Some of them are obscure and full of esoteric symbolism; while some other parts are philosophically not very stimulating. But we must remember that though *santha* philosophy is centred on the cultural motifs symbolizing Jagannātha cult, it is not a form of religion. Despite being the part of *bhakti* movement their philosophy reflected the basic concern of the classical Indian philosophy, i.e., release from *saṁsāra* and *duḥkha*. Therefore, the Orissan *santha*s raise their philosophy above the narrow concerns of religion.

The Task Ahead

Before I conclude this chapter, I would like to say a few words about the method I have followed. No doubt, the work aims to unravel and explore the metaphysical theories of Bauddha Vaiṣṇavism. But I have decided to devote the first section of the book to the delineation of the cultural milieu of Orissa. So I plan to present a brief outline of the philosophico-cultural history of this land with special reference to Buddhism and Vaiṣṇavism that had a definite role in the evolution of Orissan Vaiṣṇavism. I also include a chapter on the Jagannātha *Dharma*, as the philosophy of the Oriyā *santha*s is mostly centered on this cult. As I have stated earlier, philosophy of a land cannot be segregated from its culture and society. Philosophy may not be linked to history in the way politics is. But a philosophy removed from its socio-cultural backdrop is as abstract as a painting without a canvas. The second section of this book exclusively deals with the philosophical theories of Bauddha Vaiṣṇavism. In this section I have made an attempt to cover all possible sources that can serve as the conceptual backdrop of the theories of the Vaiṣṇavism of Orissa. Finally, this work is not intended as an excavation of a dead past but an exploration of a living faith that continues to inspire a sizeable section of the people of this land.

Part One
The Cultural Milieu

1

The Cultural Heritage of Orissa

ORISSA is situated on the eastern coast of India. It is enclosed by West Bengal on the north-east, Jharkhand (old Bihar) on the north, Chattisgarh on the west, Andhra Pradesh on the south, and a long coast line in the east opening to Bay of Bengal. What is now known as Orissa has a chequered history and was never the name of a unitary political unit. The state and boundaries of modern Orissa dc not correspond to the ancient political divisions of which we have some knowledge from epics, Purāṇas and the inscriptions. The most famous names that are associated with Orissa in the ancient period are Kaliṅga, Oḍra, Utkala, Toṣala, Koṅgoda and Kośala. We find reference to Kaliṅga in several chapters of the great ancient epic, *Mahābhārata*.[1] If we go by the story of the war fought at Kurukṣetra then among the major kingdoms that supported the Kauravas the name of Kaliṅga figures prominently. But the "Vana Parva" of *Mahābhārata* gives us some idea about its location. During Yudhiṣṭhira's pilgrimage Lomaśa Muni informs that Kaliṅga is the land of the river Godāvarī. The geographical limits of Kaliṅga can however be guessed from the rock-edicts of Aśoka. The Kaliṅga during Aśoka's time covered almost the entire region now known as Orissa. It had seen the days of glory as well as that of decadence. The names

1. *Mahābhārata*, Karṇa Parva, XL, Droṇa Parva, IV.122 and also Udyoga Parva, XIVII, p. 70.

Oḍra, Uḍra and Uḍraka were equally famous. Bharata in his *Nāṭyaśāstra* refers to a distinct form of language known as "*Uḍra-Māgadhī*." This shows that Uḍra or Ouḍra had a distinct identity during first century BC. The name Utkala appears in the *Mahābhārata* in association with the countries like Oḍra, Kaliṅga and Āndhras.[2] In early Buddhist literature[3] like *Vinaya Piṭaka* we also come across the name Utkala. During seventh century this territory was known as Toṣala or Toṣāli. It was divided into two parts — Uttara and Dakṣiṇa Toṣala. Later on we come to know of a further subdivision called Koṅgoda. The Chinese traveller Hiuen Tsang had recorded his visit to this territory. Kośala, the western part of Orissa also finds mention in the *Mahābhārata*, with Uttara Kośala standing for Ayodhyā and adjacent portions; and Dakṣina Kośala consisting of a portion of modern Orissa.

Like any other part of India, Orissa too never had a systematic history of its own. But there are enough archaeological, epigraphic and literary evidences to help us form an idea about its religio-cultural past. Wherever there are gaps, often, they are filled by popular anecdotes. From this brief geographical account it is obvious that the land had undergone many changes. The name Orissa was most probably derived from the word "Oḍra rājya" used by the Gajapati King Kapileśvara Deva. In his proclamation of 1436 inscribed on the walls of Jagannātha temple of Purī and Liṅgarāja temple of Bhubaneswar it is stated that his territory be named as Oḍra Rājya. Sāralā Dāsa, the fifteenth-century *santha* in his Oriyā version of *Mahābhārata* referred to Kapileśvara's kingdom (the then king of Orissa) as "Oṛisā Rāṣṭra." This is how the modern Orissa later on came to be known as Orissa.

Culture of a land is determined by the beliefs, practices, religion and language and ways of thinking cultivated by the

2. *Mbh.*, Droṇa Parva, UV.122. Also Bhīṣma Parva, IX, p. 348.
3. *Majjhima Nikāyā*, III.78. Also *Vinaya Piṭaka*, I.3.

human community. In this sense culture is closely associated with history. But in the absence of well-recorded documents of events, as in the case of Orissa, the history is reconstructed on the basis of architecture, archaeology, epigraphs and edicts of the ruling dynasties. So, ultimately, one finds that the culture of the land is to be deciphered from the history of political dynasties and the patronage extended by them to varied religious orders that swept the land. Naturally, the religious survey of this part of India is mostly related to the political power. The religious affiliations of the common people mostly remain unrecorded. But some of these religious trends patronized by the rulers left indelible marks on the social psyche and got assimilated to form a culture that we now refer to as the Oriyā culture. The most prominent among them are Buddhism, Vaiṣṇavism and Śaivism. These religio-philosophical trends sometimes came on collision path with one another, but fortunately for Orissa, the common attitude of tolerance led to a wonderful syncretism that encompassed many more world-views apart from the major religious trends, including Tantra and the religious faiths of the aborigines.

Kaliṅga entered in the realm of recorded political history during the reign of the imperial Nandas of Magadha. The power and glory of Kaliṅga is evident from the bloody battle Aśoka fought to conquer this land. The Aśokan rock-edicts located in the foothills of Dhauli Hillock stand as a mute witness to the embittered battle fought between Aśoka and the people of Kaliṅga. The anecdote says that the river Dayā that flows down the hill turned into a river of blood. The name Kaliṅga is thus always brought whenever history refers to Aśoka's transformation from the cruel warrior king (Caṇḍāśoka) to the champion of peace (Dharmāśoka). With the Aśokan conquest of Kaliṅga the land was officially exposed to the tenets of Buddhism.

The dynasty that rose to power not long after the Maurya rule is the famous Cedī dynasty that later on adopted the epithet Meghavāhanas. Khāravela, its illustrious ruler, left imperishable records of his rule on the rock inscriptions of Udayagiri and Khaṇḍagiri hills located in the close vicinity of modern Bhubaneswar. Khāravela was a great champion of Jainism in Orissa. People of this land still are proud of Khāravela and his attempts to make Kaliṅga a land of peace and religious tolerance. The period following the Meghavāhana rule till the rise of the Śailodbhava dynasty in the sixth century CE is somehow lost in obscurity. But the recent excavations and epigraphic evidences indicate that towards the later half of fourth century the Māṭhara dynasty assumed power and united a greater part of the land from the river Mahānadī to Godāvarī. This dynasty played a great role in the spread of Brāhmaṇical religion in this land. The rulers of this dynasty were staunch Vaiṣṇavas.

However, during the sixth and seventh centuries we come to know about another dynasty known as Śailodbhavas that ruled over a tract of Kaliṅga known as Koṅgoda. But the political stability was short-lived as Kaliṅga and other regions of the then Orissa witnessed the struggle between three great powers, i.e., Śaśāṅka of Karṇasuvarṇapura, Harṣavardhana and Pulkeśin II towards the beginning of seventh century. Śaśāṅka and Harṣavardhana, each kept Orissa under its subjugation for a while. Śaśāṅka was a Buddhist baiter and Brāhmaṇism got an upper hand during this period. But Buddhism also retained its own identity. The Chinese traveller Hiuen Tsang visited Wu Cha (Orissa) during the reign of Harṣvardhana in CE 638. From his account we get some vital clue about the religio-cultural scene of the period. He wrote: "In the south-western part of the country is the *Pussi-po-killi* monastery in a mountain, the main *stūpa* of which exhibited supernatural light." He also mentions about a second such *stūpa* emanating similar light. Historians like Prabhat Mukherjee[4] and

4. Prabhat Mukherjee, *Lalitagiri, Udayagiri & Ratnagiri*, Madras: Sangam Books, 1984, p. 2.

Mahatab[5] conjecture that Hiuen Tsang was referring to the renowned Buddhist establishments at Udayagiri, Ratnagiri and Lalitagiri. The excavation of this complex has thrown new light on the unknown facet of the history of this land. Now the historians are almost unanimous that Hiuen Tsang's *Pussi-po-killi* is modern Puṣpagiri. During the rule of Harṣvardhana Mahāyāna was the most popular form of Buddhism. The extensive remains and the topographical features of the site support the view that three monastic establishments forming a university complex became a great centre of Buddhist religion and philosophy. The excavation at Ratnagiri has unearthed terracotta seals bearing the inscription — *ratnagiri mahāvihāra ārya vikṣu saṅgha*. But after the death of Harṣvardhana Orissa crumbled into pieces and a number of principalities raised their head.

The next significant chapter of ancient Orissan history begins during the rule of the Bhaumakaras and Somavaṁśīs (eithth to eleventh century). At one phase the former were ruling over the Utkala part and later the Kośala part. The Bhaumakaras were Buddhists. The early rulers of this dynasty used such titles as *parama saugata* and *parama tathāgata* that authenticate their Buddhistic affiliation. Historians now confirm that during their rule the Tāntric sects of Buddhism became very popular in the kingdom of the Bhaumakaras. With the adequate royal support these sects of Buddhism immensely influenced the culture of the land. It is claimed that in 795 the Chinese emperor Tse Tsong received the last section of the Buddhist text *Avataṁsaka* as a gift from Śubhaṅkara I, the Bhaumakara king of Oḍra country, "who had deep faith in Sovereign Law and who followed the practice of Mahāyāna."[6] These rulers of Bhaumakara dynasty were

---

5. H.K. Mahatab, *Oṛisā Itihāsa*, p. 48.

6. *Epigraphica Indica*, vol. XV, qtd. in P. Mukherjee, *The History of Medieval Vaiṣṇavism in Orissa*, New Delhi: Asian Educational Services, 1981, p. 15.

not only the scholars of Tāntric Buddhism but made every effort to make the new sect take its roots in the soil. It is now obvious that they must have taken all care to nurture the Puṣpagiri complex of Mahāyāna Buddhism. The presence of a large number of statues of gods and goddesses of Vajrayānī order proves the conjecture. Besides, according to the archaeologists, this is the complex where we have the greatest concentration of Buddhist sculptures in India. Again they built many such *vihāras* and complexes, including the Bauddha *vihāras* at Aragarh, near Bhubaneswar. These sites of Buddhist antiquities bear memories of a glorious past. Defying the ravages of time and centuries of neglect they depict the rise and fall of a new school of Buddhism. The contributions of the Bhaumakara dynasty in shaping up the assimilative trend of this land also deserves special mention. Since the later rulers of this dynasty Tribhuvana Mahādevī and Daṇḍī Mahādevī were Vaiṣṇavas and also encouraged Tantra school of thought, a great assimilation among Vaiṣṇavism and Buddhism and Tantra was heralded during the period. The Sixty-four Yoginī temple located at Hīrāpur of Purī, was built during this phase. The rule of Bhaumakaras for a period of more than four centuries can be taken as a milestone in the cultural history of Orissa. This will become explicit when I come to the philosophical speculations of the medieval *santhas*.

When we come to the Somavaṁśī dynasty we face a paradoxical situation. There are very few archaeological and epigraphic records to prove the details of the dynasty. Yet, a large number of Śaiva temples built in and around Bhubaneswar (including the famous Liṅgarāja temple) are traditionally ascribed to them. The architects of this land had given a distinct turn to the art of temple building during the Somavaṁśīs, otherwise known as "Keśarīs," that later on came to be known as "Kaliṅga order." On the basis of some copper-plates and inscriptions Binayaka Mishra[7] reconstructs that the

7. Binayak Mishra, "Dynasties in Orissa," cited in H.K. Mahatab, *Oṛisā Itihāsa*, p. 89.

Somavaṁśīs who ruled over the Kośala part of ancient Orissa later on extended its suzerainty over Utkala, Kośala and Kaliṅga also. Though Śaiva by faith the Somavaṁśī rulers encouraged all other religious beliefs including Buddhism. Some of the Buddhist shrines like the one situated in Solamapura of Cuttack were built during the period.

But the historians face a real challenge when *Mādāla Pāñji*, the Jagannātha temple chronicle, comes up with the legend of Yayāti Keśarī of this dynasty. *Mādāla Pāñji* says: In his eleventh *aṅka* he asked the *saṁnyāsī*s and brāhmaṇas, "where existeth Jagannātha, the tutelary deity of the kings of Orissa?" They replied that from beyond the seas came the Moguls. The Lord was taken to Sonepur but we know not where hath He secreted. Then the king repaired to Sonepur and elicited from enquiry that the images might have been buried under a banyan tree, which was revered by the ancestors of the people. The king caused the tree to be cut down and unearthed the images. Forthwith the images were taken back to Purī, and duly installed in a newly constructed temple.[8] This account of the *Mādāla Pāñji* (including the names of the ancestors of Yayāti Keśarī) seems anachronistic and leaves us with many unanswered questions. Also there are no historical records to prove that there was such a king with Vaiṣṇavite affiliation who built the famous Jagannātha temple. Yet, it is not very easy to dismiss the legend of Yayāti Keśarī, as *Mādāla Pāñji* has a special value for the common mass of Orissa. Certain uncertainties prevail in locating this Yayāti Keśarī in the history of Orissa. Some historians like Mahatab and Binayak Mishra believe *Mādāla Pāñji* most probably referred to Mahāśivagupta Yayāti Keśarī II,[9] who was a scion of Somavaṁśī dynasty and ruled over certain parts of Orissa during CE 795 to 840.

8. Translated from *Mādāla Pāñji* by P. Mukherjee, *The History of Medieval Vaishanavism in Orissa*, New Delhi: Asian Educational Services, 1981, p. 12.

9. Mahatab, p. 94.

Whatever may be the historical fact the entire episode, though anomalous, is helpful in creating an impression that in Orissa Śaivism is not seen as a rival of Vaiṣṇavism.

The cultural history of Orissa reaches its culminating point with the advent of the Gaṅga dynasty. It was Ananta Varmana Coḍagaṅgadeva of this dynasty who united the whole Kaliṅga between the Ganges and the Godāvarī and turned Kaliṅga into a powerful empire. He was initially a Śaiva, but later turned into an ardent follower of Vaiṣṇavism under the influence of Rāmānuja. It was Coḍagaṅgadeva who built the great temple at Purī as the abode of the Jagannātha triad. With this Vaiṣṇavism got a permanent foothold in Orissa. Though other sects were not exactly neglected by the Gaṅga dynasty great changes occurred in the religio-cultural scene of Orissa. The Gaṅga period is marked by the steady augmentation of Vaiṣṇavism with the gradual decline of Śaivism. At the same time varied sects of Buddhism, that continued to register its presence in Orissa, were gradually losing their hold with the upsurge of *bhakti* movement espoused by the Vedāntin Vaiṣṇavas. Yet the influence of Buddhism cannot be said to be totally erased. Buddhism could have declined during the phase but Buddha had assumed a new identity, i.e., Buddha-Jagannātha, as is evident from the front door panel of the temple. The panel depicting the *daśāvatāra* of Viṣṇu places Jagannātha as the Buddha *avatāra*.

After the downfall of the Gaṅga dynasty the Sūryavaṁśīs gained control over Kaliṅga. The rulers of this dynasty are also famous as the Gajapati Kings. Though initially adherents of Śaivism they soon turned into staunch Vaiṣṇavas. Thus, the dominance of Vaiṣṇavism continued unabated. Historians regard this phase as the golden age of Oriyā culture. Orissa could create a landmark in the sphere of language, literature, philosophy and art during the rule of Gajapati kings. First epic in Oriyā language in the form of Oriyā rendering of *Mahābhārata* was undertaken by Sāralā Dāsa, the first *santha* poet of Orissa during the rule of Kapilendradeva, the first ruler of this dynasty. This was no ordinary translation; Sāralā Dāsa very smoothly blended many local legends and philosophical ideas with the original story of the *Mahābhārata*. With this work not only Oriyā language established its own identity, the work also served as a platform for expression of the indigenous form of Vaiṣṇavism that was already taking shape centering on the cult of Jagannātha. This was the beginning of a new trend. Within a century Oriyā, the language of the common people replaced Sanskrit, the language of the elites. This ultimately brought literature out of the clutches of Sanskrit. The famous Pañcasakhā provided a new verve to this language of the people by pouring out serious philosophical thought in simplest lyrical forms. The cultural developments received a further boost with the arrival of Śrī Caitanya in the land of Jagannātha. The entire land was swept by the flurry of cultural activities.

But it seems that certain amount of tension continued to exist regarding the implicit Buddhistic influence on the thought and philosophy of the Oriyā *santha*s, who under no circumstances were prepared to embrace the traditional conception of God. This may seem obvious from the following anecdote confirmed by *Mādāla Pañji*. The Buddhists, it has been stated, lived in the rock-cut caves during the reign of Madana Mahādeva, a ruler of this dynasty. Though the king was a supporter of Brāhmaṇism the queen espoused the cause of the Buddhists. Once during a heated discussion between them over the matter it was decided to have a formal trial of their respective strength as the men of science and magic. With the help of a certain trick the brāhmaṇas won. This enraged the king further and he ordered the massacre of the Buddhists.[10] This same episode is narrated in the works of Īśvara Dāsa, a seventeenth- century *santha* in his work *Caitanya Bhāgavata*[11] with slight variation. He identifies the king as Anaṅgabhīma Deva, the third Gajapati king; whereas the

10. Cited in Mukherjee, pp. 52-53.

11. Īśvara Dāsa, *Caitanya Bhāgavata*, III.

famous historian Sterling[12] feels that the event must have occurred during Pratāparudra Deva's reign. Since the anecdote has its origin in the *Mādāla Pañji*, it may be concluded that those who maintained the temple chronicle did not favour the Buddhistic leaning of a certain section of Vaiṣṇavas, especially the *santhas*. The autobiographical accounts provided by these *santhas* (Pañcasakhā) may give some credence to such an anecdote. Some of these *santhas* had to face the wrath of the priestly class for deviating from the path of religious faiths recommended by the Brāhmanical orders and also for insisting on *nirākāra upāsanā* (the worship of the formless). But it seems that the stories about the persecution by the king seem to be blown out of proportion for, these *santhas* were revered by the royalty as well as the common people. Curiously enough Buddhism was not totally effaced from the land despite the unprecedented supremacy of Vaiṣṇavism. We come to know from the Tibetan work *Pog Som Jon Zang* that "Mukunda Deva (Dharmarāja) the king of otivisa (Orissa) who favoured Buddhism, became powerful. . . . He, too, did some service to Buddhism."[13] The accounts available about the reign of Gajapati dynasty proves that the Jagannātha *dharma* became the centre of Oriyā identity. But the influence of other cults, including Buddhism, continued to give an interesting shape to the Jagannātha *dharma*. But with the ascendance of cultural and religious power there was the decline of political power. The Muslim invasion of Orissa saw the period of internecine strife and bloodshed. Despite frequent attack on Jagannātha temple the cult as well the culture that grew around Jagannātha continued to dominate Orissa.

From the above sketch about the cultural life of Orissa it becomes clear the land was exposed to some of the distinct

12. *Sterling's Orissa* ed., 1904, pp. 80-81, cited in N.N. Vasu, *Modern Buddhism and its Followers in Orissa*, Dehli: Gyan Publishing House, 1986, pp. 68-69.

13. Qtd. in Vasu, p. 70.

life-views espoused by the major religious trends like Buddhism, Vaiṣṇavism and Śaivism. It is obvious that by twelfth century CE there was Vaiṣṇavization of Jagannātha *dharma*. But this should not mean that it was or is exclusively Vaiṣṇavite. Some popular cults had also registered their presence. The predominance of Tantra and indigenous tribal religions of *śavaras* could be taken as the cases in point. Most interestingly, both the Āryan and non-Āryan cults at some or other point of time lost their individuality and got absorbed in the culture of the land which ultimately found expression in the Jagannātha *dharma*. This is evident from the peculiar rites and rituals followed in Jagannātha worship till date. I shall cover the interesting dimensions of Jagannātha cult in the next chapter. This fact can be taken as a living example of cult-fusion that had become a regular phenomenon of Oriyā culture.

Before I conclude this chapter I would like to say a few words about the cultural pattern of Orissa that has incredible potentiality for a syncretism. The way it has assimilated and accommodated divergent viewpoints and religious systems is amazing. Here I may draw attention to two such instances of cult-fusion. I have already stated that Śaivism once upon a time was very popular in this land. At first glance this seems to be a very usual religious phenomenon. Śaivism too was very popular in the southern part as well as in other parts of India. But we also know that Vaiṣṇavism and Śaivism were seen as rival religious cults in certain parts of India. But in Orissa these two cults were assimilated to give rise to a cult popularly known as "Hari-Hara" worship. The composite image of Hari and Hara can be found in the earliest surviving Śaiva temples of Orissa. T.E. Donaldson, who has done extensive works on iconography of different religious cults of Orissa, feels that this may be due to the influence of the Paśupata sect of Śaivism that espoused Hari-Hara concept.[14]

---

14. T.E. Donaldson, *Iconography of Vaiṣṇava Images of Orissa*, New Delhi: D.K. Printworld, 2001, p. 49.

At the same time it is noteworthy that in no other part of India has such syncretism assumed the amount of importance that it has in the case of Orissa. This can be discerned from the practice of the joint worship of Viṣṇu and Śiva in the famous Liṅgarāja temple of Bhubaneswar. The *liṅgam* in the temple has a natural line running vertically along the surface that is invoked as both Hari and Hara by the priests. On the top of the temple the symbols of both the deities, i.e., half *cakra* (discus) and a *triśūla* (trident) are placed. Again, the rites of the temple include both Vaiṣṇavite and Śaiva worship. Similarly, the blending of Śāktism with Vaiṣṇavism can be discerned in the joint worship of Durgā and Mādhava. There are innumerable temples dedicated to "Durgā-Mādhava" in which Durgā, the embodiment of *śakti* is placed next to the image of Mādhava (Viṣṇu); and worshipped both according to the Śākta rites as well as the Vaiṣṇava rites. This again is a rare religious phenomenon seldom noticed in Brāhmaṇical forms of worship of other regions of India. This trend of cult syncretism has culminated in Jagannāthism. This peculiar trend of Orissan culture finds its true expression in the thought and works of the *santha*s. Had the people of Orissa not been acquainted with the culture of assimilation the literature of the *santha*s would not have enjoyed popularity among masses.

2

The Jagannātha Dharma

THE *santha* philosophy of Orissa is inextricably connected with Jagannāthism. G.C. Tripathi, the famous Jagannāthologist, very righly observes, "the development of the concept of Jagannātha is also the history of the development of philosophical speculation in Orissa."[1] Jagannātha not only is the most revered deity of the land, but he is also regarded as the real sovereign Lord of Orissa. However, the apparently grotesque and very unusual form of the deity has been the real source of puzzlement to many. Famous Oriyā historian and literateur H.K. Mahatab cites one such example to which Pundit Jawaharlal Nehru drew his attention. I quote here the observation by Edward Thompson in his article "Making of the Indian Princes":

> Notorious shrine of Jagannath, the uncouth temple where an incomprehensible people reverenced ugliness as the personification of divine attributes and Brahminism seem to flaunt its difference from all other religions of the modern world.[2]

Here Edward Thompson not only denigrates the religion centred on Jagannātha, but also puts the blame on the whole

1. G.C. Tripathi, "Jagannātha: The Ageless Deity of the Hindus," *The Cult of Jagannātha and the Regional Traditions of Oṛissa*, ed. A. Eschmann, *et al.*, p. 480.
2. Edward Thompson, "The making of Indian Princes," in *Thorn Memoir of the War in India*, Cited in H.K. Mahatab, *Oṛisā Itihāsa*, 1.

Brāhmaṇical religion for accommodating such a deity in its fold. The remark though cruel, can be forgiven because it comes from a mind utterly fanatic by disposition. But in the next sentence H.K. Mahatab tells us that Nehru too entertained similar thoughts about the iconography of Jagannātha and was inquisitive as to how such a grotesque God could be worshipped by the people of Orissa. This may appear more shocking. But Nehru and many more persons inquisitive like him should have known that this ugly deity has drawn the maximum attention from the greatest minds of India who have been responsible for making the Indian culture proud. Right from Śaṅkarācārya to Kabīr, Nānak to Caitanya saw His ugly form and they were won over. Name any religious cult and one is likely to find a permanent establishment of that order in this land of Jagannātha. The deity called Jagannātha definitely is ugly, for He has no shape or size that may remotely resemble any creature on earth — neither a man nor a beast — an oversized head with two stump-like hands protruding from the head-cum-trunk, with two wheel-like eyes but without ears or legs or belly. Yet it is claimed to be the Jina of the Jainas, Ādi Buddha of the Buddhists, Rudra of the Śaivas, Bhairava of the Śāktas, Viṣṇu of the Vedāntin Vaiṣṇavas and the beloved Kṛṣṇa of Caitanya. Jagannāthism absorbed varied and sometimes antagonistic religious trends within its own form and gave this land a philosophy of grand synthesis; and also a new cultural identity.

The Iconography of Jagannātha

The origin and development of Jagannāthism is shrouded in mystery. Volumes have been written to trace its origin and map out its possible links with all possible religious traditions that flourished in this land, both Hindu and non-Hindu, including the indigenous tribal religions of Orissa. Despite all such attempts the history of this cult continues to be as inexplicable as ever. At the centre of all the mystery stands the peculiar iconography of the Jagannātha as it flouts all the accepted norms of iconography in India. The standard rules of iconography of the Hindu gods and goddesses prescribe that the images should resemble human forms though there may be certain variations, for example, there can be idols with three eyes and sometimes with eight/four/ten arms. Accordingly most of the deities of the Hindu pantheon have human forms with youthful appearances, heavily ornamented and holding different objects in their hands. Surprisingly, the Jagannātha triad, occupying the *sanctum* of the temple does not conform to this standard norm of the Hindu iconography. Nor can these images be said to be the symbolical representation of any Hindu deities. Here too the norm of Hindu iconography is grossly flouted. There are certain standard practices prescribed by the Purāṇas. For example, Śiva is represented by *liṅgam*, Śakti is represented by *yantra*s (the mystical figures) Viṣṇu is represented by *śālagrāma* stones, obtained from the river Gaṇḍakī. In case of the deities of Purī this does not happen.

On the *sanctum sanctorum* of the Jagannātha temple one finds three such huge deities and a post-like form representing Jagannātha, Balabhadra, Subhadrā and *sudarśana cakra*. The Purāṇic sources like *Skanda Purāṇa*, *Brahma Purāṇa* and *Nārada Purāṇa* that can be dated as late as tenth century refer to the glory of this cult. Surprisingly, all of them depict the deities as having human forms. The Utkala Khaṇḍa of *Skanda Purāṇa* that exclusively deals with the Jagannātha/Puruṣottama cult narrates that Viṣṇu manifested himself in four forms — Jagannātha/Viṣṇu/Kṛṣṇa, Bala (Balabhadra), Subhadrā and Sudarśana. But the deities are described in the most ornamental way that comes closest to the images of gods found in other Hindu temples. The *Purāṇa* describes the unveiling of the Jagannātha idols in the following way:

> He [king Indradyumna] unveiled the great altar. At that time all of them saw Lord Kṛṣṇa, the son of Vāsudeva; Rāma, Subhadrā, and Sudarśana. . . . All the idols were charming in their features with unguents smeared and the *limbs* duly adorned. He saw Lord Kṛṣṇa with a kind and beaming face.

> The chest was broad and projecting forward. *He had long and brawny arms* capable of lifting the poor. His eyes resemble full-blown lotuses. . . . He was seated in the lotus posture.[3] (emphasis supplied).

But the images that we see in the temple have no limbs, no lotus-like eyes, no lotus-like postures. So the question that is likely to bother us is wherefrom such odd iconographic features emerged? Is the Jagannātha trinity originally Hindu? Or is the Vaiṣṇava form imposed on the deities worshipped by some other religious cults? The questions are not yet answered and perhaps will never be answered.

This is not the end of the novelty of this cult. On the *sanctum* of the temple Jagannātha is worshipped alongwith his brother Balabhadra and sister Subhadrā. In no other Hindu temple brother and sister are worshipped together. Whenever a deity is placed with a female figure it is taken to be its consort or *śakti*. According to the Brāhmaṇical and Tāntric practices the god is conceived as *śaktimat* (embodiment of power); and usually is placed with His *śakti* (power) who is often viewed as the consort. So in our tradition Kṛṣṇa is jointly worshipped with Rādhā, Viṣṇu with Lakṣmī and Śiva with Pārvatī. Nowhere a brother and sister are placed side by side. This unusual phenomenon leads to further bewilderment. The Utkala Khaṇḍa of *Skanda Purāṇa* tries to sort out this issue by depicting Subhadrā as sister as well as the consort.[4] Such depiction is more confusing, for in Orissan culture sister can never be imagined as the consort. Of course, it has been generally accepted that Subhadrā is another name for Ekānaṁśā the tribal Goddess of the Vṛṣṇi clan to which Kṛṣṇa belonged. So an attempt has been made to solve the problem with

---

3. *Skanda Purāṇa*, Part V, II.ii.19. 35-41a.

4. *Skanda Purāṇa*, Part V, II.ii.19. 17, The *Purāṇa* states that, "His sister Śrī is glorified in the form of his *śakti*." Also refer the same text, II.ii.19. 45-47.

reference to Varāhamihira's *Bṛhat Saṁhitā* (50.37-39). A chapter on iconography of this book prescribes that Ekānaṁśā should be flanked by Baladeva and Kṛṣṇa. Accordingly it is assumed that Subhadrā is placed in the middle. But in this work the Goddess Ekānaṁśā is depicted having four arms, whereas the Subhadrā of the Jagannātha temple has no arms. Besides, Ekānaṁśā is often depicted as the dark Goddess, but the Goddess of Jagannātha trinity is yellowish in colour. Such unusual features pave way for the speculation that the trinity is not exactly representation of any of the gods of the Hindu pantheon. Rather it is the representation of *triratna* (Buddha, Dharma and Saṁgha) of Buddhism since *dharma* in this tradition is represented by the female figure. Again some Orissan poet-philosophers try to resolve this puzzle by presenting Jagannātha, Bhalabhadra and Subhadrā as Viṣṇu, Śiva and Brahmā, respectively. Others interpret the trinity as Jagannātha, Śiva and Durgā on the basis of a panel found near the famous sun temple at Koṇārka. So the presence of a female God in between two male Gods continues to remain an unsolved riddle.

Another striking feature of the iconography is noted in the material used in the making of the idols of the Jagannātha temple. The substance used for the deities is *nīma* wood. That is why Jagannātha is often known as *Dāru Devatā* (the wooden God). Though the idea of the wooden deity is not unknown in our tradition, definite evidences are not available about the existence of such wooden deities in Hindu and Brāhmaṇical temples. May be such wooden deities were not very popular as it required a lot of care for its maintenance. As the idols of Jagannātha triad are made of wood, the idols are renewed approximately every twelve years. Besides, the images are covered with layers of silken threads, clothes, and incences like sandalwood paste, *kastūrī*, gums and oil, technically known as *saptāvaraṇa* (seven layers). These layers are stripped every year and new sets are applied to avoid damage. The worship of the wooden idols is largely responsible for the speculations about the autochthonous origin of the deities. In tribal religion the anthromorphic deities are rare. They usually worship wooden logs, pieces of stone or earthen pots as their deities. In Orissa among the tribals of *śavara* group there exists the practice of worshipping the wooden logs or tree as the God (the *śavara*s call it the "Kituṅg"). "Jagaṅta" another revered God of the *śavara*s is regarded as a manifestation of "Kituṅg." Therefore, it acts as a pointer to the autochthonous origin of the Jagannātha cult. It has been argued by many scholars that the "Jagaṅta," the tribal God was later on accepted within the Brāhmaṇical fold and came to be known as Jagannātha.[5] This hypothesis cannot be dismissed as a wild conjecture. We also notice that Puruṣottama Mahātmya section of the *Skanda Purāṇa* places the story about the genesis of Jagannātha worship to its autochthonous origin. It is stated that Jagannātha was originally worshipped in the form of Nīlamādhava by the chieftain of the *śavara*s named Viśvāvasu in the deep woods. King Indradyumna, the ruler of Mālava sent his minister to trace the deity, as he wanted to construct a temple for Viṣṇu. But by the time the deity was traced and the king reached the spot the God had vanished; and later on the God reappeared in the form of the wooden log out of which the Jagannātha images were carved. The association with the autochthonous element does not end with this anecdote. The autochthonous elements are very much a part of the Jagannātha worship in its present form. A section of the non-brāhmaṇa servitors of the Jagannātha temple, called *daitā*s claim themselves to be the descendants of the *śavara* chief and are involved in certain important rituals of the temple.

Origin of the Cult — The Nature of Controversy

The strange iconography of the Jagannātha idols and strange practices of worship raise interminable debates. All the controversies can ultimately be narrowed down to one basic

5. B.M. Padhi in his work entitled, *Dāru Devatā* (1964) elaborates on this thesis. Cited in "The Vaiṣṇava Typology of Hinduisation and the Origin of Jagannātha," *The Cult of Jagannātha*, p. 101.

issue, i.e., the religious source of the Jagannātha *dharma*. History is almost silent on the subject; hence the scope for conjectures broadens. Interestingly, the origin of this cult is traced back to every possible religious cults ranging from Jainism[6] to Nṛsiṁha worship[7] to tribal form of worship of the wooden posts.[8] Within the limited pages of this chapter it is not possible for me to discuss the claims and the counterclaims in detail. So I shall concentrate on two popular views about the origin of the Jagannātha cult. The study of the origin and nature of this unique cult reveals that the scholars are sharply divided in their opinion on the issue – some fervently supporting its Brāhmaṇical and specifically the Vaiṣṇava origin and while others standing by its Buddhistic origin. Some eminent scholars like M.N. Ganguly,[9] P. Mukherjee,[10] S. Misra[11] G.C. Tripathi[12] espouse that Jagannātha is primarily Vaiṣṇavite in its form and origin. They mostly rely on the use of the term *puruṣottama* as an appellation of Jagannātha as well as Viṣṇu. The word also appears in the *Śrīmadbhagavad-Gītā* to designate Kṛṣṇa. In Vaiṣṇava theology and Āgamas, Puruṣottama generally stands for Viṣṇu in one of His aspects like Mādhava, Nārāyaṇa, etc. Later on in the *Śāradā Tilaka* the term came to stand for the erotic aspect of Viṣṇu.[13] In this work he is mostly

---

6. Nilakantha Dasa, *Śrīmadbhagavad-Gītā* (Oriyā) Pīṭhikā Section, Cuttack: New Students Store, 1980, pp. 37-50.
7. A. Eschmann, H. Kulke and G.C. Tripathi, "The Formation of Jagannātha Triad," *The Cult of Jagannātha*, pp. 169-88.
8. B.M. Padhi, *Dāru Devatā*.
9. M.M. Ganguly, *Orissa and her Remains* (1912) cited in *Medieval Orissa and Cult of Jagannātha*, Baba Mishra, New Delhi: Navarang, 1995, p. 47.
10. Prabhat Mukherjee, *History of Medieval Vaisnavism in Orissa*, New Delhi: Asian Educational Services, 1981, pp. 1-22.
11. S. Mishra, "Jagannātha Mandira" (Oriyā), *Sahakara*, vol. XVI.7, p. 30,
12. G.C. Tripathi, *The Cult of Jagannātha*, p. 31.
13. *Śāradā Tilaka*, XVII.

depicted in his *Śrīkara* aspect as the consort of Lakṣmī. But the Jagannātha that is worshipped in the temple at Purī has Subhadrā, not Lakṣmī on his left side. This leads the scholars to conjecture that originally there were two deities, viz., Puruṣottama and Lakṣmī on the pedestal and the idol of the third deity — Balabhadra was incorporated at a later stage, most probably during thirteen century.[14] Even if we purchase this thesis one question remains unanswered — When and how the Puruṣottama-Viṣṇu assumed this unusual form? No Hindu scripture provides any clue about the iconographic peculiarities of the Jagannātha idols. The same logic can be applied to Mukherjee's alternative claim. According to him the Saṅkarṣaṇa-Vāsudeva worship that was prevalent during pre-Gupta period was modified and they were worshipped as Balabhadra and Jagannātha in Orissa. Subhadrā was a later addition to this creed due to the influence of Śakti cult in post-Gupta period.[15] He also relies on certain scriptures like *Viṣṇudharmottara* in support of his theory.

Another curious phenomenon that goes against the purely Vaiṣṇavite interpretation of the cult can be noted in the context of the use of the word "Jagannātha." The title Jagannātha signifying "Lord of the universe" is not exclusively applicable to Viṣṇu alone. It is a general appellate used with reference to Buddha and Śiva also. Interestingly, the designation Jagannātha was seldom used with reference to the Viṣṇu temple at Purī. It may be noted that the scriptures including the Puruṣottama Mahātmya of the *Skanda Purāṇa* prefer to use the title "Puruṣottama" more frequently. Two other important works that refer to the temple located at Kaliṅga are, *Anargharāghava Nāṭaka* of Murari Misra and *Prabodha Candrodaya* of Krishna Misra, composed sometime in ninth to eleventh century. Surprisingly in both the works the word Jagannātha

---

14. G.C. Tripathi, "On the Concept of 'Puruṣottama' in the Āgamas," *The Cult of Jagannatha*, p. 56.

15. Mukherjee, pp. 4-7.

is conspicuous by its absence. The land therefore was more famous as Puruṣottama-kṣetra (the land of Puruṣottama), from which the place Purī derives its name. Inscriptional sources reveal that the use of the appellation Jagannātha to Viṣṇu with reference the temple at Purī occurs for the first time in the inscriptions of Bhānudeva II in 1309 in Śrīkurmam temple of Andhra. On the other hand, the word Jagannātha is more frequently used in the works of Indrabhūti and Anaṅga-vajra, the famous *siddha*s of the Vajrayāna branch of Buddhism. Indrabhūti is believed to be the King of Sambala (present Sambalpur) of Orissa. This atypical use of the word Jagannātha with reference to the temple at Purī gives credence to the thesis that the present forms of deities of the temple at Purī have nothing common with the images of Puruṣottama and Lakṣmī narrated in the oft-quoted scriptures.

Monier-Williams,[16] Hunter,[17] R.L. Mitra,[18] and Mahatab[19] are some of the eminent scholars who think that Jagannātha cult is primarily Buddhist in origin. They also provide certain valid grounds in support of their inference. I plan to discuss their arguments in detail in the fourth chapter on the role of Buddhism in the formation of the *santha* philosophy of Orissa. But at this point it should be noted that those scholars who support the Vaiṣṇavite origin of the Jagannātha cult do not deny the fact that Buddhism had exerted some influence in the evolution of this cult.

Whatever may be the root of this controversial cult of Jagannātha; whatever may be the reason behind such strange iconographic features, there is no doubt that the predominantly Brāhmaṇical society of the period must have felt quite uncomfortable about this peculiar Hindu God, especially in

---

16. Monier-Williams, *Buddhism*, Latest edn., New Delhi: Munshiram Manoharlal, 1995, pp. 165-66.
17. Qtd in Tripathi, *The Cult of Jagannatha*, p. 480.
18. R.L. Mitra, *Antiquities of Orissa*, Calcutta: 1875, vol. II, p. 180.
19. H.K. Mahatab, *Oṛisā Itihāsa*, pp. 433-75.

the context of a Vaiṣṇavised deity. So we come across several anecdotes and legends about the shapeless forms of the deities. But such accounts are neither sustainable by history nor by scriptures. Whatever may be the reason for such iconographical features it at least allows us to imagine that Jagannātha is not the property of a particular religious sect, rather the entire cult is a process of gradual evolution that has step by step absorbed components from varied ideologies and ideas championed by different cults and sects that flourished here from time to time. But at the same time it cannot be denied that both Buddhism and Vaiṣṇavism played greater roles in the formation of Jagannāthism. Nobody is sure whether Buddha became Jagannātha or Jagannātha turned into Buddha. But the element of syncretism is definitely palpable.

3

Vaiṣṇavism in Orissa

Vaiṣṇavism in Orissa has a chequered history. Its consistent growth in this land was often thwarted by the predominance of Buddhism and Śaivism. Yet at a later stage, especially after the Vaiṣṇavisation of the Jagannātha worship during the twelfth century it stood as the most predominant form of religious faith. The *santha*s of Orissa in consonance with the syncretic culture of the land provided a distinct metaphysics to this religious faith that made the Orissan Vaiṣṇavism unique in every respect. Before I go into the details of the development of this cult in Orissa I deem it fit to devote some passages to the evolution of Vaiṣṇavism in India.

The Origin of the Cult

Viṣṇu, the central figure of Vaiṣṇavism appears to have evolved from the syncretism of three god-concepts — the Vedic God Viṣṇu, the cosmic-God Nārāyaṇa and the man-God Vāsudeva Kṛṣṇa. However, why and how these three distinct trends assimilated is a matter of historical debate. Literary and epigraphic sources reveal that Viṣṇu was worshipped in the Vedic period along with the worship of other gods such as Varuṇa, Soma, Indra and Agni, etc. Vedas also eulogize Viṣṇu as the sun-God.[1] Gradually he was accepted as the chief among the popular triumvirate of Hinduism — Brahmā, Viṣṇu and

1. *tad viṣṇoḥ paramaṁ padaṁ sadā paśyanti sūryah. diviva cakṣurātatam. Ṛgveda,* I.164.4.

Maheśvara. Nārāyaṇa, who has often been identified with Viṣṇu in the Purāṇic age, is believed to be a non-Vedic God. His name occurs for the first time in two passages of the *Śatapatha Brāhmaṇa*.[2] In these passages Nārāyaṇa is stated to be the Lord supreme and is immanent in all beings. Puruṣa Sūkta, the Vedic hymn that describes the primeval Lord as the thousand-headed, thousand-eyed being, is said to be his litany.[3] It seems that in the Brāhmaṇa portions of the Veda, Nārāyaṇa was seen as the cosmic God. In the subsequent period Viṣṇu with his supreme power was taken to be synonymous with Nārāyaṇa and Bhāgavata. The rise of Vāsudeva cult is believed to be associated with Sāttvata royal family ruling over Sūrasena-maṇḍala of northern India. These rulers belong to Yādava dynasty where Kṛṣṇa was born. This dynasty in course of time left northern India and came to the south. As a result Bhāgavatism spread to the south. Identification of Kṛṣṇa with Vāsudeva and the subsequent rise of Kṛṣṇa cult are of much later origin. There is no reference to the cowherd Kṛṣṇa in the early Vaiṣṇava literature. In some Purāṇas like *Vāyu, Harivaṁśa* and *Bhāgavata* we come across the reference to Kṛṣṇa as the killer of Kaṁsa. So it is not clear how the name Kṛṣṇa became an important part of the Vaiṣṇava cult. But with the advent of the Purāṇic age and the composition of Purāṇas Viṣṇu-Nārāyaṇa-Vāsudeva-Kṛṣṇa was exalted to the status of the primal deity; and the worshippers allied to Nārāyaṇa-Viṣṇu-Kṛṣṇa worship came to be known as Bhāgavatas, Sāttvatas, Ekāntins, and Vaiṣṇavas.

It is a general impression that the concept of *bhakti* owes its origin to Bhāgavatism that was centred on Viṣṇu-Kṛṣṇa worship. This is again a matter that cannot be settled without generating controversies. Many scholars are of the opinion that though the origin of *bhakti* has been traced to the *Ṛgveda* it took a definite form with the advent of the Bhāgavata cult.

---

2. *Śatapatha Brāhmaṇa,* XII.3.4 & XII.6.

3. *Śatapatha Brāhmaṇa,* XIII.6.2.

Suvira Jaisawal for example throws some interesting light on this concept by analysing the significance of the word Nārāyaṇa in the context of the concept *Pañcarātra sattra* that is very frequently referred in the *Pañcarātra* (a sect of Viṣṇu worshippers) Āgamas. According to her,

> Nārāyaṇa, who represented the entire tribal settlement was the *Bhagavat*, the owner and dispenser of communal wealth and was closely associated with agriculture. Similarly, *bhakta* was originally sharer of the communal wealth mainly consisting of food, and as a member of the tribe, he belonged to Nārāyaṇa. In course of time, the gulf between the all-powerful body of the tribe and the individual member widened, and *Bhagavat* Nārāyaṇa became a trascendental supermundane god and *bhakta* his devotee.[4]

Jaiswal believes that, with the break up of tribal society and its assimilation with Brāhmaṇism *bhakti* became a major religious concept in the post-Buddhist period. But a large section of scholars may not agree with her. According to them the identification of three distinct gods — Nārāyaṇa, Viṣṇu and Kṛṣṇa, later on led to the notion of Bhāgavatism; and the culminating point was reached in syncretic trend presented in the Kṛṣṇa-Vāsudeva worship of the *Bhagavad-Gītā*. Therefore they argue that this treatise provides the foundation of the theory of *bhakti* that was further systematised in the *bhakti* works like the *Nārada-Bhakti-Sūtra* and the *Śāṇḍilya-Śūtra*. The literary evidences convince us that in the subsequent period *bhakti* concept (especially Kṛṣṇa-*bhakti*) found its fullest expression in writings of the Tamil devotees known as *āḻvār*s. So a more convincing and uninterrupted tradition of the passionate devotional attitude, which originated in the Vedic literature, gradually reached its zenith in the songs of twelve Vaiṣṇava mystics and saints, known as *āḻvār*s. *Āḻvār* in Tamil, means a man deeply immersed in the love of God. The *āḻvār* movement came to be recognised as a distinctive religious

---

4. Suvira Jaiswal, *The Origin and Development of Vaisnavism*, New Delhi: Munshiram Manoharlal, 1980, pp. 229-30.

trend during fifth to ninth centuries. They were wandering singers, mad after God. One of them was a king, another a beggar, a third a woman, a fourth an untouchable. They staunchly propagated that God is accessible to all only by intense love and complete self-surrender irrespective of rank, caste or even culture. Their devotional songs became popular under the name of *Vaiṣṇava Veda* (the scriptures of the Viṣṇu cult). Most probably, after the *āḷvār*s we find the same passionate devotional attitude saturated in the bulk of Purāṇas. The *Bhāgavata Purāṇa* is the culmination of that attitude. In the *Bhāgavata Purāṇa*, prominence is given to the intense lovability of Kṛṣṇa, as a superb child, a youthful lover being God Himself. The erotic dimension of *bhakti* superbly expressed in the *Bhāgavata Purāṇa*, became the most potent factor in stimulating an intensely erotic devotional attitude towards Bhagavān Kṛṣṇa and it continues to stand as the main source of inspiration for the bulk of devotional literature in India. The Bhāgavatism continued to predominate the religious scene of certain parts of India for quite some time.

Though the *āḷvār*s of south India kept the interest of the people alive in the cult of Vaiṣṇavism and in the tradition of *bhakti*, Hinduism in other parts of the land was bogged down under renewed emphasis on intricate rituals and practices. As a result common people found Buddhism more attractive and more accessible. During eighth-century Śaṅkarācārya arrived on the scene with an ardent mission of revitalising Hinduism in its struggle against Buddhism. In comparison to Hinduism, Buddhism was a much more definite and unified religion. So Śaṅkarācārya tried to pinpoint the ideological unity of all *āstika* systems by emphasizing on the Upaniṣadic philosophy of non-dualism. Though this great spiritual leader never discarded *bhakti* he did not also give much importance to *ekāntin bhakti* or the idea of passionate attachment to the God. In Śaṅkara's philosophy there was hardly any scope for interpreting *bhakti* in terms of the soul's longing for a personal God, and the emotional bond between the devotee and God. Thus, the non-dualistic teaching of Śaṅkara could not quench the religious thirst of the masses. So we notice the great revival of *bhakti* movement in twelfth century CE in the form of the Vedāntin Vaiṣṇavism. There arose four new Vaiṣṇava schools, namely Śrī, Brahma, Rudra and Sanakādi headed by Rāmānuja, Madhva, Viṣṇusvāmī and Nimbārka, respectively. This group of Vaiṣṇavas cannot be classed as *bhakta*s in the sense the *āḷvār*s were. They were primarily *ācārya*s and were interested in providing a metaphysical basis of the theory of *bhakti*. So their task was not to stick to the Purāṇic literature but to provide the metaphysical superstructure to the theory of *bhakti* on the basis of alternative interpretations of the *Brahma-Sūtra*. These Vaiṣṇavas transformed the supreme Reality from an impersonal non-dualistic absolute principle to a concrete and determinate *Brahman-Īśvara* who positively responds to the love and adoration of the individual souls. He as the supreme principle was no longer viewed as impersonal but a personal God accessible by devotion and who could grant his benedection on his devotees. Though there were doctrinal differences in the theories of these four sects of the Vaiṣṇava Vedāntins, yet all of them were unanimous about projecting the highest Reality as *saguṇa Īśvara*. Thus, they revived the idea of worshipping the God as a person, i.e., *saguṇopāsanā*. As a philosophical corrolary they exalted the status of *bhakti* as the primary mode of *mukti*. The impact of this new form of Vaiṣṇavism served as the turning point in the religio-philosophical history of Orissa as well as India.

The wave of *bhakti* as well as *santha* movement that swept India during fourteenth to nineteenth century can be said to have its roots in the new philosophical interpretation of these Vedāntins. Rāmānujācārya identified the highest Reality *Brahman* with Viṣṇu and depicted Śrī or Lakṣmī as his power and consort. This cult got further support from the works of the Vedāntin Vaiṣṇavas like Nimbārka and Madhva. Madhva was a great exponent of dualistic Vaiṣṇavism and a representative of the Brahma Vaiṣṇava sect. According to this sect pure devotion to Kṛṣṇa is the only path of liberation. The next important preacher was Nimbārka. Though hailing from the south he had made Vṛndāvana the centre of his activity. His religious school is known as Sanaka Sampradāya. Nimbārka believed that salvation was achievable by taking refuge at the lotus feet of Kṛṣṇa. No liberation could be possible without the grace of God. It was Nimbārka who introduced the idea of *madhura bhakti* and also introduced the idea of Rādhā.

The history of Vaiṣṇavism took a new turn with the appearance of Śrī Ċaitanya on the socio-cultural scene of India. Though the centre of his religious activity was Purī, the land of Jagannātha, yet he took initiatives to spread the message of his neo-Vaiṣṇavism to other parts of India by asking his disciples to make Vṛndāvana the centre of this new sect.

Vaiṣṇavism and Orissa

The origin and the forms of Vaiṣṇavism that prevailed in Orissa are very difficult to trace. Yet it must be noted that Vaiṣṇavism was not entirely unknown to Orissa. Though the impact of this sect was not that spectacular in the early part of the Orissan history the presence of innumerable temples devoted to Viṣṇu in his different forms proves its populariry at certain points of time. Mādhava images popularly known as Mādhavānanda are found in large numbers in Prachi Valley. *Skanda Purāṇa* and *Brahma Purāṇa* also refer to Kṛṣṇa as Mādhava made of blue sapphire that was worsipped at Purī. Some images of Viṣṇu in the form of Nārāyaṇa and Gopīnātha are also found in other parts of Orissa. However, all these forms of Viṣṇu have no iconographical similarity with the Jagannātha trinity. In most of the places the image of Viṣṇu has four arms holding conch, discus, mace and lotus.

A few modern scholars have traced the presence of Vaiṣṇavism in Orissa during the reign of Khāravela of the first century BC.[5] But Steincorn very rightly points out that

---

5. P. Mukherjee, *The History of Medieval Vaisnavism in Orissa,* New Delhi: Asian Educational Services, 1981, pp. 4-5.

"from the archaelogical remains and inscriptions available at present, it appears that up to tenth century Vaiṣṇavism occupied a relatively subordinate position in Orissa."[6] There are no epigraphic records to prove that Viṣṇu worship was popular in Orissa during the pre-Gupta period. But Vaiṣṇavism seemed to have entered Orissa during the Gupta dynasty and was popular in certain parts of Orissā. The earliest reference to Vaiṣṇavism *alias* Bhāgavatism in Kaliṅga is found from the copper-plate inscriptions of the Māṭhara kings of Kaliṅga,[7] who used the title *paramabhāgavata*. The worship of Nārāyaṇa as *Bhagavān* by Prabhañjanavarman, a Māṭhara king is known from his Niñgoṇḍi plates.[8] After the Māṭharas, Kaliṅga passed to the hands of early Gaṅgas. Hastivarman, a ruler of this dynasty patronized Vaiṣṇavism and it was popular in Kaliṅga at least up to CE 578.[9] After Hastivarman we find no epigraphic record in support of Vaiṣṇavism. Though Śaivism replaced Vaiṣṇavism in Kaliṅga during the sixth century. Vaiṣṇavism gained popularity in the western parts of Orissa when the Pāṇḍuvaṁśī kings of Dakṣiṇa Kośala adopted it as their official religion. The royal title of some of the rulers of this dynasty was Paramavaiṣṇava. It is believed that this dynasty was in power in the sixth and seventh centuries.[10] But the subsequent rulers of this dynasty patronised Śaivism. Thus, the influence of Vaiṣṇavism was on the wane.

I have stated earlier that the Bhaumakara kings who ruled over a part of modern Orissa from CE 738. were originally the

6. H.V. Stietencorn, *Advent of Viṣṇuism in Orissa*, qtd. by J. Padhi in *Śrī Jagannātha of Puri*, Puri: S.G.N. Publications, 1993, p. 57.

7. S. Rajguru, ed., *Inscriptions of Orissa*, 4 vols., Bhubaneswar: Orissa State Museum, 1958-66, vol. I Part II, p. 44.

8. R.C. Mazumdar, ed., "Narasimhapalli plates of Hastivarman," *Epigraphica Indica*, vol. XXIII, pp. 62-67ff. qtd. in B. Rath, *Glimpses of Vaisnavism in Orissa*, Berhampur: Kalyani Prakashan,1983, p. 96.

9. Rajguru, vol. I, Part II, pp. 24-29.

10. Rajguru, vol. IV, pp. 18-32.

followers of Buddhism. But the later rulers like Tribhuvana Mahādevī, Pṛthvī Mahādevī and Daṇḍī Mahādevī changed the religious affiliation of their ancestors and adopted the title, *Paramavaiṣṇavī*.[11] That was the precise time when the Vaiṣṇava cult assimilated certain elements of Mahāyāna sect of Buddhism and also of Tantra. A sort of compromise between the Buddhists and Vaiṣṇavas took place in this land when Daṇḍī Mahādevī was the queen. The *santha* literature of medieval Orissa perhaps can be said to be the reflection of this composite type of religion and philosophy.

From our discussion it is clear that Vaiṣṇavism could not make inroads into Orissan culture, in the true sense of the term, till the twelfth century. But the religious scenario changed once the later Gaṅgas established their suzerainty over Orissa. Anantavarman Coḍagaṅgadeva, the first ruler of this dynasty, though initially a follower of Śaivism, turned into a great Vaiṣṇava under the influence of Rāmānujācārya. To prove his attitude of religious tolerance towards all the prevalent Hindu sects he adopted the titles *Paramamaheśvara*, *Paramavaiṣṇava* and *Paramabrāhmaṇya*. But his Vaiṣṇavite predilections could be judged from the fact that he not only constructed a temple for Jagannātha, but also saw to it that Vaiṣṇavite rites were introduced in the Jagannātha worship. With Vaiṣṇavisation of Jagannātha *dharma* the foundation was laid for Vaiṣṇavism in Orissa. Most probably the Vaiṣṇavism adopted by the Bhaumas at the time of Daṇḍī Mahādevī also merged into the newly adopted Śrī Vaiṣṇavism of Rāmānuja, and the Jagannātha cult ultimately.

The royal patronage that Rāmānuja received paved the way for the advent of other sects of Vedāntin Vaiṣṇavism in Orissa. Some of these great Vaiṣṇava *ācārya*s visited the Puruṣottamakṣetra or Purī and were successful in bringing about a great change in the cult and culture of Jagannātha.

---

11. Vinayaka Misra, *Inscriptions of Bhaumakara kings*, qtd. in Rath, p. 97.

Most of these sub-sects of Vaiṣṇavism also established their religious centres (*maṭhas*) at Purī. Jagannātha gradually came to be known as Nārāyaṇa and Kṛṣṇa. But it was Śrī Caitanya who revitalised Vaiṣṇavism after he visited Lord Jagannātha at Purī sometime in the sixteenth century. He was no philosopher, no *ācārya* nor a *santha*, but a great *bhakta*. In Lord Jagannātha he saw his beloved Kṛṣṇa. His esctatic singing and chanting of the name of Kṛṣṇa created such an impact in the minds of the people that he became a cult figure in Orissa as well as India. I shall discuss about the philosophical basis of his Vaiṣṇavism a little later.

The Major Trends of Vaiṣṇavism in Orissa

As I have shown in the previous section, Vaiṣṇavism is primarily based on the *ekāntin* (sole devotion), *bhakti* theory centred on Viṣṇu or any of His forms. However, in the development of Vaiṣṇavism across the ages one can notice distinctively two different trends. First, the Vaiṣṇavism growing around the Puarāṇic account of the deity depicts Kṛṣṇa as the pastoral youthful hero indulging in love-play with the cowherd girls of Vṛndāvana. The second strand draws its inspiration from the *Mahābhārata* and *Gītā* where Kṛṣṇa is presented as the philosopher and the warrior king. In this aspect he is mostly seen as Viṣṇu or Nārāyaṇa. In case of Orissa, it seems to be more acquainted with the latter form that extols Viṣṇu in its Nārāyaṇa aspect. So the influence of *Bhāgavata Purāṇa* was not very conspicuous. At the same time the other form of Vaiṣṇavism was not totally unknown to the people of Orissa as is evident from the popularity of *Bhāgavata* in Oriyā. But as far as the Oriyā *santha*s were concerned they claimed to owe allegiance to Vaiṣṇava Vedāntins like Madhva, Nimbārka and Viṣṇusvāmī. That clearly reveals that they were more influenced by the Vedāntic version of Vaiṣṇavism than the Purāṇic version. The idea of an amorous and playful Kṛṣṇa constantly engaged in love-dalliance with either the *gopī*s or Rādhā was never very popular in Orissa till Śrī Caitanya preached the theory of *prema bhakti* in Orissa. Curiously enough, despite their proclaimed loyalty to Vedāntin cults the Orissan Vaiṣṇavas never followed them as far as the philosophical principles were concerned. Their brand of Vaiṣṇavism was definitely very distinct from both, the Vedāntin as well as the Purāṇic. For a true assessment of the neo-Vaiṣṇavism of the Oriyā *santhas* it may be helpful if we discuss in nutshell the basic metaphysical position of both the forms of Vaiṣṇavism that left its foot marks on Orissa.

Vedāntin Vaiṣṇavism

Śrī Vaiṣṇavism of Rāmānujācārya played a very crucial role in providing final shape to the cult of Jagannātha. Not only his philosophy helped the process of Vaiṣṇavisation of this cult, he also played a greater role in providing a true philosophical basis of the theory of *bhakti*. The broad-based metaphysical geography remained intact, though subsequent Vaiṣṇava *ācāryas* incorporated certain minor conceptual alterations. Thus, the journey from the Advaitic non-dualism to a subtle form of dualism between the individual self and the divine self started; and with this the *bhakti* theory got a true philosophical anchorage. Rāmānuja offered a monistic interpretation of Vedānta. The faith he adhered to is known as Viśiṣṭādvaitavāda. Following the tradition of Vedānta he accepted *Brahman* as the highest Reality. But unlike Śaṅkara he left no conceptual gap between the *Brahman* and *Īśvara*. With this the *nirguṇa Brahman* of Upaniṣads turned into a *saguṇa Īśvara* (with positive and divine qualities). So there was no problem in conceiving the *Īśvara/Brahman* as the repository of all perfections, free from all defects. He was delineated as the principle that pervades all living and non-living beings, is the inner controller of all, is possessed of the auspicious qualities of knowledge, power and he is the creator, protector and destroyer of the world. He is stated to possess a wonderful celestial body of unsurpassable beauty and has for his consorts Lakṣmī (Śrī), *bhū* (earth) and *līlā* (sport). In his highest mode of existence he is known as *parā-Brahman*, *parā*-Vāsudeva and Nārāyaṇa. He is imagined to be four-armed, heavily ornamented and holding celestial weapons like conch and discus. Rāmānuja's conception of a *saguṇa Brahman-Īśvara* became a permanent feature of Vedāntin Vaiṣṇavism. *Brahman* was no longer conceived as an abstract principle, but a personal God though the subsequent Vedāntins preferred to ascribe different epithets to the same Lord Supreme. Madhva called Him Nārāyaṇa Viṣṇu, who is endowed with six divine powers, viz., *jñāna* (knowledge), *śakti* (power), *bala* (prowess), *aiśvarya* (wealth), *vīrya* (virility) and *teja* (energy). Nimbārka preferred to call Him Kṛṣṇa. He also introduced the character of Rādhā as the consort of Kṛṣṇa. He says:

> There is no salvation without except the lotus-like feet of Kṛṣṇa. . . . Who at the desire of the devotees, assumes a form easy of meditation and whose essence is unthinkable and whose essence cannot be comprehended.[12]

He also talks of Vraja as the abode of God.

With the gradual personification of the highest Reality the ontological gap between the individual self and the divine self was introduced to facilitate *bhakti* as a mode of *mukti*. Though Rāmānuja was a non-dualist he maintained a subtle distinction between the two. To explain the relation between the individual self and the *Īśvara-Brahman* he conceived a threefold scheme of eternal principles (*tattva trayī*) viz., *cit* (consciousness) and *acit* (matter) and *Īśvara* (the supreme soul). He then presented the supreme soul (*Īśvara*) as the inner controller of the other two. The individual soul (*cit*) and the matter (*acit*) constitute the body of the *Īśvara/Brahman*, who in turn is their soul. Accordingly the relation between the conscious *jīva* and the *Brahman* is viewed as that of the part (*aṁśa*) and the whole (*aṁśī*). These changes incorporated by him in the interpretation of the *Brahma-Sūtra* facilitated the theory of *bhakti* that could be seen as a philosophically-anchored theory. Interestingly enough, Rāmānuja considers

12. Nimbārka, *Daśa Ślokī*, IX.

soul to be atomic and dependent on *Īśvara*. So the soul has a natural tendency to seek the final deliverance. Madhva moved one step forward to present a dualistic interpretation of *Brahma-Sūtra* by introducing the primacy of *bheda* (distinction). Accordingly he conceives the essential difference between God and man, and God and the world. According to him, all knowledge springs from the *paramātman*. The real knowledge is the knowledge of difference. He argues, if the individual self is non-different from *Brahman* then there would be no urge on the part of the *jīva* to attain *mokṣa*. Individual souls, though sharing the nature of the *Brahman* are not identical with him. They are mere reflections of the *Brahman* just as there are reflections of one sun in the different sheets of water.[13] Nimbārka, on the other hand, advances the theory of *bhedābheda* (both identity and difference) to explain the relation between the *jīva* and *Brahman*. The relationship between the *jīva* and *Brahman* is that of difference and unity. For him the matter and soul are not the attributes of the *Brahman* but the power of *Brahman* yet they are different from the *Brahman*, as they possess different natures. According to him, there is a distinction between the independent reality of the Puruṣottama (*Īśvara*) and the dependent reality of the *jīva*. Here comes the importance of *bhakti* as a mode of self-realisation.

Once the conceptual as well as ontological breach between *jīva* and *Brahman* is admitted the door for the emotional explanation of *bhakti* is flung open. So the emphasis on *jñāna* as the mode of *mukti* gave way to *bhakti*. Rāmānuja, of course, tried to maintain some sort of balance between *jñāna* and *bhakti* by defining *bhakti* as constant meditation of God (*drūvān smṛtiḥ*). But the influence of the Tamil *āḷvār*s becomes conspicuous when he makes a distinction between *prapatti* and *bhakti*. *Bhakti*, according to Rāmānuja requires *jñāna* or the knowledge of the Vedas and *karma* (the following of the

13. Madhva, *Brahma-Sūtra-Bhāsya*, II.3, p. 18.

sacrificial rites). But this would disqualify the lowest castes as they were denied the rights to follow these acts. As a result, they were denied the right to pursue the path of *bhakti*. For such people Rāmānuja prescribes *prapatti* or taking refuge in God by completely surrendering to Him. The word *prapatti* is derived from the root *prapad* that means "to take refuge in" or "to piously resign." So *prapatti* entails an attitude of complete self-surrender to God. The introduction of this concept brings all classes of people to the fold of God-realization. Besides, Rāmānuja also accommodates the concept of God's grace (*prasāda*) in the process of self-realization. Rāmānuja while offering a primary status to *bhakti* has tried to assimilate *jñāna* and *karma*, but Madhva clearly indicates that the ultimate path of liberation does not consist in knowledge but only in *bhakti*. Knowledge may be one of the conditions of release but it is *bhakti* that leads to *mukti*. Bondage for him is due to the will of God and *bhakti* is also to some extent, due to his grace. He defines *bhakti* as "the attachment of heart towards him with the full knowledge and belief that He is the best thing."[14] Nimbārka adds further dimension to this concept by stating that an individual has an inherent desire for *mukti* (*mumukṣu*). But the *mukti* is not possible without the grace of God. *Bhakti* for him is a special kind of love for God. But the most important concept introduced by Nimbārka was the idea of *mādhurya pradhāna bhakti* (the sweet and romantic attachment). This idea played a very crucial role in later theories of Vaiṣṇavism. With this new interpretation, the word *bhakti* acquired a new connotation. *Bhakti* was no longer understood simply in terms of service to God or just the love for God, but it primarily signified passionate longing of a beloved for the object of his love. Thus, we find that the connotation of the term *bhakti* gradually shifted from a state of meditation to an intense emotional state. Rāmānuja had conceived *bhakti* as constant remembrance of God (*upāsanā*). But ultimately

---

14. *Madhvabhāṣyam* on *Bṛhadāraṇyaka Upaniṣad*, I, p. 4.

Nimbārka transformed it into a form of attachment experienced between a man and woman while in love. Again the chief characters in the scheme of *bhakti* also went on changing. Rāmānuja talked of Nārāyaṇa with Lakṣmī as his consort. But Nimbārka gave exclusive prominence to Kṛṣṇa and his mistress Rādhā, attended by thousands of his female companions (*gopīs*). Therefore, many scholars feel that Nimbārka inspired Gauḍīya Vaiṣṇavism. Nimbārka's speciality lies in the fact that he espoused the idea of the worship of Kṛṣṇa with Rādhā as his companion. According to him the *Brahman*, i.e., Kṛṣṇa, for the sake of *līlā* has divided himself into two — Rādhā and Kṛṣṇa. They are in fact inseparable. At the same time Nimbārka depicted the relation between the two as that of *svakīya prīti* (conjugal love) rather than *parakīya prīti* (adulterous love). By the end of fourteenth century the Vedāntin Vaiṣṇavism assumed the form of a full-fledged *bhakti* theory.

Prema-Bhakti Tradition of Śrī Caitanya

Prema-bhakti tradition is associated with the name of a great spiritual leader Śrī Caitanya. The simple, yet the effective method of a God-oriented life preached by Śrī Caitanya, made it the most popular form of religious sect in India. During the medieval period, he created a new genre of God-consciousness equating spiritual realisation with love and absolute surrender. His message was simple and straightforward. It was Kṛṣṇa-*bhakti* alone that could overtake all other forms of spiritual realisation. Caitanya practically wrote nothing nor did he preach any philosophy. So whatever knowledge we have of his philosophical attitude can only be gleaned from his biography entitled *Caitanyacaritāmṛta* written by Kṛṣṇadāsa Kavirāja. This work is regarded as the most authentic work on the life and times of Śrī Caitanya. Kavirāja gives a vivid account of Caitanya's encounter with two of the great persons of Orissa. The first was a philosopher and the second was a *bhakta*. The first person he met was Vāsudeva Sārvabhauma, the staunch Advaitin, at Purī. His dissonance from the Advaitic conception of *Brahman* and the path of *jñāna* comes out very transparently in this work. Dismissing the position of the Advaita Vedānta Caitanya is found to argue that *Brahman* cannot be indeterminate (*nirviśeṣa*) in nature. Elaborating his own position on the issue he says that Upaniṣads describe *Brahman* as *nirguṇa* in the sense that as *Brahman* or *parama Īśvara* (God) he does not possess any phenomenal qualities. But in the ultimate sense he has all possible non-phenomenal powers and these powers are threefold in nature. They are, *Viṣṇu śakti*, *kṣetrajña śakti* and *avidyā śakti*. The *Viṣṇu śakti* may further be conceived from three points of view — *hlādinī*, *sāndhinī* and *saṁvit*. These three powers stand for *sat*, *cit* and *ānanda*. *Kṣetrajña śakti* stands for the power of manifestation of the God as souls of individuals. So it is also known as the *jīva śakti*. *Avidyā śakti* is the power by which the world of appearance is created. God creates the world by his unthinkable power.

We also come to know about Śrī Caitanya's theory of *bhakti* from *Caitanyacaritāmṛta*. This is presented in the form of a dialogue between him and Ray Ramananda, the Governor of Rajahmundry. He was a royal employee of the King Pratāparudradeva of Orissa and the second person of Orissa, Śrī Caitanya encountered. Śrī Caitanya met him during his southern sojourn; and it is well known that he inspired the master. The book makes it clear that Caitanya was not satisfied with the ordinary interpretations of *bhakti*. He always felt that *bhakti* should not have anything to do with philosophical knowledge. He was convinced that the only knowledge required for pure *bhakti* was the wisdom regarding the intimate relationship between the individual soul and God. This inalienable love between man God highlighted by Caitanya came to be known as *prema bhakti*. According to him, this love is fivefold: *śānta* (peaceful love), *dāsya* (servant of God), *sākhya* (friendship with God), *vātsalya* (filial attitude towards God) and *mādhurya* (love of God as one's lover). Out of these five kinds of relationship between man and God, the sweet and amorous longing for the union with God scores over the other modes of love. It is the intensity of love that makes the lover lose his identity. The love of the cowherd girls of *gopa* (*gopī*) and particularly the love of Rādhā for Kṛṣṇa exemplifies this sort of highest love. Thus, the intensity of devotion is made to depend on the intensity of emotion. But it should not be confused with ordinary passion (*kāma*) of an individual for a phenomenal entity. It transcends all such phenomenal boundaries. So it is emhasized that a true *bhakta* must have all the qualities of heart like truthfulness, tenderness, magnanimity, selflessness, etc. Love of Kṛṣṇa is innate in human nature as it is the manifes-tation of the *hlādinī* nature of God. It remains dormant and can be aroused only under positive conditions.

One is not sure to what extent the neo-Vaiṣṇavism of Śrī Caitanya influenced the people of Orissa during his lifetime. But the warmth that Caitanya received in Orissa, and the way he was extolled by his contemporaries, especially the Pañcasakhā, prove that he was revered by the masses. Śrī Caitanya was never called a *santha* or *ācārya* but *Mahāprabhu* (the great master) as he was more or less deified by his followers. The Orissan *santha*s loved to depict him as the incarnation of Jagannātha as well as of the Buddha. His stay at Purī for long fourteen years must have brought Śrī Caitanaya closer to the Oriyā Vaiṣṇavas. But Gauḍīya Vaiṣṇavism, as Śrī Caitanya's philosophy was designated later, did have little impact on Orissa at least for a century.

From our discussion so far it follows that Vaiṣṇavism played an important role in the religio-cultural life of the people of Orissa. At the same time it should be noted that Vaiṣṇavism could truly entrench itself in the minds of people only after the Vaiṣṇavisation of Jagannātha cult. Interestingly enough, despite immense royal support the common people of the land could not accept either the Vedāntin Vaiṣṇavism or the Gauḍīya Vaiṣṇavism without certain reservations. The form of Vaiṣṇavism indigenous to Orissa continued to rule the hearts and mind of the people. The *santha*s of Orissa, especially Pañcasakhā espoused the typically Orissan form of Vaiṣṇavism in which the amorous form of *bhakti* had no significance. Similarly Śrī Caitanya's conception of Rādhā as the paradigm of *bhakti* was taken in a negative sense. Therefore, though Jagannātha was identified as the Kṛṣṇa, yet Rādhā was never given any status within the main temple as his illustrious beloved. Similarlly, the anti-monistic attitude of Śrī Caitanya had virtually no impact on the philosophical position of the Orissan *santhas*. Instead the highest Reality was considered as the formless (*nirākāra*), indeterminate (*nirviśeṣa*), one and unique *Brahman*. He continued to remain the *Śūnya Puruṣa*. Summing up the nature of their philosophical pursuit Santha Divākara Dāsa very significantly advises: "Respect all the sects of Vaiṣṇavism, but never compromise with your own stand; be friendly with all the forms of spiritual discipline but be firm on your own principles."[15] Thus, we are forced to conclude that despite the steady impact of Vaiṣṇavism in its multiple versions, it could never serve as the true model for the metaphysical speculations of the Vaiṣṇavism of Orissa. So we have to look beyond traditional Vaiṣṇavism if we want to truly understand the basics of the Orissan *santha* philosophy. Hence, in the next chapter I shall concentrate on the impact of Buddhism to trace the philosophical roots of the unique Vaiṣṇavism of Orissa.

---

15. *samasta vaiṣṇava pūjiba, āpaṇā sūtra na chāḍiba.*
samasta saṅge prīti heba, nija bhāvare dṛḍha thiba.
— Divakara Dasa, *Jagannātha Caritāmṛta*, I, pp. 21-24.

4

Buddhism in Orissa

THE Jagannātha cult of Orissa and the *bhakti* movement centred on it bear strong traces of Buddhism. Like many other parts of India, Orissa too witnessed the strong presence of Buddhism in its multiple sectarian forms. But nowhere were the Buddhistic ideas so smoothly amalgamated into Brāhmaṇism as in the case of the *santha bhakti* theory of Orissa. My basic intention here is to explore and examine the extent to which the culture of Orissa was associated with various branches of Buddhism. This exploration is significant in more than one sense. First and foremost, there is a felt necessity to set the record straight about the role of Orissa in nurturing Buddhism, especially its Tāntric versions, as most of the scholars on Tāntric Buddhism maintain an inexplicable silence on this matter. So I plan to go into the details of archaeological, literary and historical evidences that may convince the readers that Orissa has all along been a cradle of Buddhism. The metaphysical and religious ideas of varied forms of Buddhism, in turn, have played an important part in the life and culture of the people. Therefore, the exploration I intend to undertake is all the more important for, without understanding the basic metaphysical presuppositions of Tāntric Buddhism it may not be possible to understand the extent of its impact on the *santha* philosophy of Orissa.

I

Buddhism and Orissa

For a true assessment of the impact of Buddhism on Orissan

philosophy we need to dwell at some length on the close links between Buddhism and the culture of this land. A philosophy with mass appeal cannot grow overnight, unless it is deeply rooted in the social psyche. Of all the religious creeds that influenced Orissan history, Buddhism seems to have played a predominant role. Though the history of Orissa is not recorded very systematically, we can glean the accounts of Buddhistic association with Orissa through innumerable archaeological evidences, literature, rituals and practices and, above all, through some important Buddhist scriptures. Buddhist treatises like *Pāg Sām Zong Zāng*, Lama Tāranāth's *History of Buddhism*, the travel accounts of Hiuen Tsang and Fa-Hien offer us glimpses of the story of the growth and development of Buddhism in Orissa. In these works we find frequent references to Kaliṅga, Oṭiviśā/Oḍeviśā, Uḍra, Oḍra, Uḍḍiyān, etc. *Mahāsattārikā* of *Majjhima Nikāya* records that Vassa and Bhañña, two tribes of Utkala Deśa, discarded their previous religious belief after recognizing the merits of Buddha's teachings.[1] Similarly, the Pāli text *Aṅguttara Nikāya* furnishes interesting details about two merchant brothers named, Tapassu and Bhallika, who became the first lay disciples of the Buddha. The two brothers paid reverence to the Blessed One on the eighth week of his enlightenment and offered him rice cakes and lumps of honey.[2] Besides, another work entitled *Ḍāthavaṁśa* recovered from Ceylon records that a molar tooth relic of Buddha was worshipped in Dantapura the capital of Kaliṅga.[3] On the basis of this work Sir Monier-Williams even goes to the extent of claiming that a relic of Buddha's burnt body was placed inside the body of Lord Jagannāth of Purī; and He actually is a Buddhist deity.[4] Some of these accounts may be discarded as simple myths. But we must not forget that the myths are rooted in the cultural milieu of the land.

---

1. *Majjhima Nikāya*, III, p. 78 cited in N.K. Sahu, *Buddhism in Orissa*, Bhubaneswar: Utkal University, 1958, p. 8.
2. *Aniguttara Nikāya*, I.26, Cited in Sahu, p. 9.
3. B.C. Law, *Ḍhātavaṁśa*, Introduction. Cited in Sahu, p. 14.

→

The first historical evidence of Buddhism in Orissa is related to Aśoka's conquest of Kaliṅga and his subsequent conversion to Buddhism. Orissa, under his rule, must have come under the impact of Buddhism. During Kaniṣka's time, when Buddhism was split into two distinct schools, viz., Hīnayāna and Mahāyāna, both the sects had spread their roots in Orissa. We know from Tāranātha's account that Poṣāḍha, a great scholar of Hīnayāna school (Sarvāstivāda), propagated his faith in this land. The presence of this sect during the first century CE can be established on the basis of a *Bodhi stūpa* in Bhubaneswar, of which a few railing posts are preserved in the State Museum of Orissa.

After Kaniṣka's reign Mahāyāna rose into prominence. From Hiuen Tsang's account it appears that Parimalagiri (Po-lo-mo-lajd-li), Surabhagiri and Bhora Śaila of Orissa were important centres of Buddhist learning.[5] It is believed that Bhora Śaila was the abode of the famous dialectician Diṅnāga[6]; and the place is named Delānga after him. In one of the inscriptions located at Nāgārjunakoṇḍa we come across the

---

4. M. Monier-Williams, *Buddhism*, New Delhi: Munshiram Manoharlal Publishers Pvt. Ltd., 1995, pp. 165-66.

   In this book the author provides an interesting account of the synthesis of Buddhism and Vaiṣṇavism. He records:

   "Buddhism, in fact, could never have maintained itself in India till the twelfth and thirteenth century of our era, had it not gradually and to a great extent through interaction with Vaiṣṇavism and Śaivism, dropped its unnatural pessimistic theory of life and its unpopular atheistic character, and accommodated itself into the system. . . . This indeed, is the best explanation of what has happened at Purī in Orissa, where a temple once dedicated to Gautama Buddha, and supposed to contain a relic of his burnt body was afterwards dedicated to the Jagannāth form of Kṛṣṇa . . ."

5. Sahu, p. 110.

6. Sahu, p. 110.

reference to a *mahāvihāra* at Puṣpagiri.[7] It may be identified with *Pussi-po-killi* of Hiuen Tsang's travel account. Historians believe that this *mahāvihāra*s could be located at the complex excavated at Ratnagiri, Udayagiri and Lalitagiri. The complex consists of a series of monasteries, *stūpa*s and *caitya*s. Very recent excavations carried out in the Lāṅguli hillocks near Jājpur, also confirms the existence of a similar *mahāvihāra*. It is well known that the Buddha was elevated to the status of God by the Mahāyāna school. Therefore, it is not surprising that innumerable statues of Buddha in different postures were worshipped in different parts of Orissa. Even the modern district of Orissa called "Bauddha," is said to be named after Lord Buddha. Besides, the Padmeśvar temple dedicated to Padmapāṇi Avalokiteśvara along with the images of Tārā and Prajñāpāramitā prove the strong presence of Mahāyāna Buddhism in Orissa. I have stated in the second chapter that during the rule of the Bhaumakaras some sort of assimilation between Buddhism and Vaiṣṇavism was already taking shape. When the Buddha was admitted into the Hindu fold as an *avatāra* of Viṣṇu, Orissa was socially and culturally prepared for such a syncretism. This new trend found expression in the temple art of Orissa. So the icon of Buddha could always be noticed on the outer carvings of the temples, whether dedicated to Viṣṇu, Śiva or Śakti, from the eleventh century onwards. This significant feature of temple art proves that despite the onslaught of other religious movements Buddhism never could be effaced from the life and culture of this land.

Tāntric Buddhism and Orissa

During the eighth century Tāntric form of Buddhism emerged as a strong force. Tāntric Buddhism may be said to be a popular development of Mahāyāna Buddhism, which rose into prominence between the eighth to the twelfth century. How and when Tāntricism crept into this highly metaphysical and

7. Sahu, p. 46.

ethical trend of thought is a matter of controversy. Tradition holds Asaṅga, the great exponent of Yogācāra school of Buddhism, to be the first philosopher to introduce the Tāntric elements into Buddhism. Others, on the other hand, hold that Nāgārjuna was the real founder of Tāntricism. There are also scholars who go to the extent of claiming that Tantra was not absolutely new to Buddhism and that, in fact, Lord Buddha had himself given instructions concerning *ṛddhi*s, *mudrā*s, *maṇḍala*s and *tantra*s for the less advanced disciples interested in worldly prosperities.[8] However, it seems clear that the Tāntric elements were explicitly incorporated into Buddhism at a much later period of its history. It is plausible that strict moral principles advocated by Buddha did not suit some Buddhists, so there must have been certain secret conclaves known as *Guhyasamāja*. They advocated many Tāntric practices that were transmitted in the most secret manner through an unbroken chain of *guru*s. Later on it came out into the open during the eighth century.

Vajrayāna, one of the important branches of Tāntric Buddhism, played a crucial role in the development of both Jagannāthism as well as the Orissan Vaiṣṇavism. The central concepts of Orissan Vaiṣṇavism owe their conceptual origin more to Tāntric Buddhism than any other systems of philosophy, including Vaiṣṇavism. Unfortunately, the role of Orissa in the development of this cult is seldom admitted. Most of the works on Tāntric Buddhism maintain a baffling silence about Orissa's contribution in nurturing this important branch of Buddhism. Therefore, I intend to devote a little more space to the discussion on the development of Vajrayāna and the allied sects in the backdrop of Orissa.

8. B. Bhattacharyya, "Tāntric Culture among the Buddhists," *The Cultural Heritage of India*, vol. IV, ed. Haridas Bhattacharyya, Calcutta: Institute of Culture, Ramakrishna Mission, 1983, p. 261.

Uḍḍiyāna Pīṭha

According to the sacred scriptures of Tāntric Buddhism Uḍḍiyāna was one of the primary centres of Vajrayāna. In *Sādhanamālā*, an important work of Vajrayāna order, we find mention of four *pīṭhas* or sacred spots of the Vajrayāna, viz., Kāmākhyā, Sirihaṭṭa, Pūrṇagiri and Uḍḍiyāna.[9] *Hevajratantra*, another work of equal importance, reaffirms the status of Uḍḍiyāna as a *pīṭha*.[10] *Pāg Sām Jon Zāng*, a work of Tibetan origin, too identifies Uḍḍiyāna as the place of its origin.[11] About the identification of the first two spots there is little scope for controversy. Kāmākhyā is in modern Assam and Sirihaṭṭa in modern Sylhet, a part of Bangladesh. The exact location of Pūrṇagiri is not yet settled (some scholars identify it as Poona). However, there seem to be a lot of debate over the exact location of Uḍḍiyāna. Historians like, L. Waddel,[12] Sylvain Levi,[13] P.C. Bagchi[14] and others suggest that Uḍḍiyāna refers to the Swāt valley of Kabul. Haraprasad Sastry, B.B. Bhattacharya,[15] Nick Douglas[16] and N.K. Sahu,[17] on the other hand, identify Uḍḍiyāna as Orissa. Each side has its own

---

9. B. Bhattacharyya (ed.), *Sādhanamālā*, vol. II, Baroda: Gaekwad Oriental Series, No. 26 & 41. 1925-28, Preface ixxviii ff.
10. D.L. Snellgrove, *The Heavjra Tantra*, vol. I, p. 141, cited in R. Mishra, *Sahajayana: A study of Tantric Buddhism*, Calcutta: Punthi Pustak, 1991, p. 41.
11. Cited in B. Bhattacharyya, *An Introduction to Buddhist Esoterism*, Delhi: Motilal Banarsidass, 1980, p. 45.
12. L.A. Waddel, *Tibbetan Buddhism*, 26. Cited in Sahu, p. 143.
13. Sylvain Levi, *Journal Asiatique*, (1915) pp. 105 ff. Cited in Sahu, p. 143.
14. P.C. Bagchi, *Indian Historical Quarterly*, vol. VI, pp. 576 ff. Cited in Mishra, pp. 41-42.
15. For H.P. Sastri's views refer B. Bhattacharyya, *An Introduction to Buddhist Esoterism*, Delhi: Motilal Banarsidass, 1980, p. 44.
16. Nick Douglas (ed.), *Tantrayoga*. Cited in Mishra, p. 41.
17. Sahu, pp. 141-79.

arguments in support of their presupposition. According to P.C. Bagchi there are two sets of names often found in Tibetan works — (1) O-rgyan, U-rgyān, O-ḍi-yā na; and, (2) O-ḍi-visā, Uḍra and Oḍra. Bagchi is of the opinion that the first set of names, as well as Wi-tch'ang and Yue-ti-yen, mentioned by the Chinese writers are different forms of the same name, i.e., Uḍḍiyāna, that is locatable in Swāt valley. But the second set of names (which is also mentioned as Ut-tcha) refers to Uḍra or Uḍraviṣaya (Orissa).[18] Contradicting this B. Bhattacharyya argues that these two sets of names are seldom distinguished in the Buddhist literature of the Tāntric period and the words Oḍa, Oḍra, Uḍra, Oḍivisā and Oḍiyāna are used as variants of Uḍḍiyāna.[19] It is interesting to note that in the work *Sādhanamālā*, Uḍḍiyāna is mentioned as Oḍrayāna. So Uḍḍiyāna stands for Oḍra or Orissa. Another evidence in support of the claim that Uḍḍiyāna was but Orissa can be gathered from the frequent reference to Indrabhūti, a great *siddha* of Vajrayāna School of Buddhism, and the king of Uḍḍiyāna. There are no historical evidences to prove that there was any such king by name Indrabhūti in the Swāt valley. On the contrary, there are enough indications of his being the king of Oḍivisā or Orissa. *Caturāsiti Siddha Pravṛtti* mentions Indrabhūti as the king of Oḍivisā.[20] Again, P. Cordier in his *Bsṭāñ-ḥgyur* catalogue gives sufficient indications of his being the king of Orissa.[21] However, the most crucial evidence against Uḍḍiyāna being located in Swāt valley can be drawn from the literature of the *siddhas* of this order. Many of the *siddhas* of Tāntric Buddhism like Sarahpā, Luipā, Sabaripā, according to

---

18. P.C. Bagchi, "Reviews on *Sādhanamālā*," *Indian Historical Quarterly*, vol., VI, p. 576, fn. Cited in Sahu, p. 143.
19. Bhattacharyya (ed.), *Sādhanamālā*," Intrd. xxxvii. fn.
20. This work is preserved in Tibetan in Bstanhgyr, p. 86.1. Cited in Sahu, p. 144.
21. *Bsṭāñ ḥgyur*, p. 86.1 and *Cordier Catalogue*, p. 39 and 96, Cited in Sahu, p. 144.

the Tibetan sources, belonged to Uḍḍiyāna. They composed a large number of religious songs or *dohās*. According to H.P. Sastri and B. Bhattacharyya, some of the eminent writers of these *dohās* like Sarahpā, Luipā, Minapā, Jālandhripā, Kṛṣṇācārya, Tāntipā, etc., were either born in Orissa or spent a considerable amount of time in Orissa.[22] The language of these songs these *siddhas* composed seems to be drawn from the parent stock of modern Oriyā, Bengali and Maithilī.[23] If Uḍḍiyāna should have been located in Swāt valley then the *siddhas* would have obviously used the language prevalent in the north-western part of India. But this is not the case. So it should be presumed that Uḍḍiyāna was located somewhere in the eastern zone of India. Moreover, no Vajrayānī images of any importance have yet been recovered from the Swāt valley whereas they are abundantly found in Orissa. Such facts may add credence to the claim that Uḍḍiyāna was located in this land.

It is more unfortunate that those scholars who had vociferously argued about the identification of Uḍḍiyāna with Orissa earlier, seemed to change their position and claim rather vaguely that Uḍḍiyāna should have been a part of Bengal. Bhattacharyya, for example, mysteriously changes his version in a later work[24] and claims that Uḍḍiyāna must have been located somewhere in Bengal though he never specifies it. It is regrettable that the subsequent scholars have relied more

22. B. Bhattacharyya, *An Introduction to Buddhist Esoterism*, Delhi: Motilal Banarsidass, 1980. p. 44 (The view of Haraprasad Sastri cited therein).

23. The language used in these songs continues to be a matter of great debate. Mm. H.P. Sastry claims it to be in Older Bengali, whereas, the Oriyā scholars like, K.K. Kara tries to prove that it is an archaic form of Oriyā, again, the Maithilī scholars claim it to be in their own language. The most plausible explanation seems to be that these three languages belonged to the same parent stock.

24. B. Bhattacharyya, *An Introduction to Esoteric Buddhism*, Delhi: Motilal Banarsidass, 1980, p. 46.

on Bhattacharyya's later version and have been repeating this claim without ever checking the facts. The only historical fact they place in support of their hypothesis is about the royal patronage Buddhism received from the Pāla dynasty of Gauḍa (Bengal). These eminent authors conveniently overlook much publicized archaeological findings as early as 1869 at Ratnagiri, Lalitagiri and Udayagiri of Orissa. These and many other archaeological discoveries tilt the scale in favour of Orissa being the cradle of Vajrayāna. There are abundant evidences to show that Uḍḍiyāna was in fact a part of Orissa. I cite here a few of them. First and foremost, according to Vajrayānic texts, Uḍḍiyāna was associated with the worship of the deities like Māricī, Kurukullā, Lokeśvara, Urdhvapadā Vārāhī, etc. These deities are still traceable in Orissa. According to N.K. Sahu, the famous scholar who had worked extensively on the history of Buddhism in Orissa, the goddesses Kurukullā and Vajravārāhī who are described in the Tāntric literature as the presiding deities of Uḍḍiyāna[25] are found in no other part of India, except in Orissa. Besides, the images of Dhyānī Buddhas, Mañjuśrī, Padmapāṇi, Jāmbhala, Heruka, Tārā, etc. (the gods and goddesses of Vajrayāna sect) are found all over Orissa, in large numbers. (A list of such Buddhist sites and the icons discovered from such sites is provided in Appendix II of this book that may help the readers in assessing the pervasive impact of Mahāyāna Buddhism, including its Tāntric branches on this land). In contrast, there are very negligible archaeological evidences to support the view that Tāntric Buddhism was most active in Bengal under the royal patronage of the Pāla dynasty. Certain anomalies regarding this claim are brought out by the historians like R.C. Mitra and P.C. Bagchi. Here I would like to quote Bagchi's observations on the matter. He says,

> The patronage of Pālas no doubt gave an impetus to Buddhism and saved the religion from the fate which

25. *Sādhanamālā* II, Intdr. XXVII, Cited in Sahu, p. 154.

> overtook it in the rest of India, but does not seem to have materially affected the dominant position of Brāhmaṇical religion. For it is worthy of note that by far the large majority of images and inscriptions which may be assigned to the period between 750 and 1200 AD are Brāhmiṇical and not Buddhist. . . .[26]

It seems that historians and scholars seldom look at the role of Bhaumakara dynasty in nurturing Buddhism during that period. I have already indicated that the rulers of Bhaumakara dynasty were staunch Buddhists. The Bhaumakaras not only developed *mahāvihāra*s at Ratnagiri, Udayagiri and Lalitagiri, but also built many temples devoted to the gods and goddesses of the Vajrayānī order. Besides, recent excavations at Ārāgarh near Khurda district have brought to light the existence of Buddhist *caitya*s apart from the Lalitagiri and Puṣpagiri complex. Experts are of the opinion that this *caitya* might have been constructed by Śubhaṅkar Deva II of Bhaumakara dynasty for the use of the monks of Vajrayāna order. So, it is unfortunate that the historians have often jumped to hurried conclusions that Pāla dynasty was the only dynasty to foster Vajrayāna and the allied sects.

The genesis of such biased hypotheses may have its root in H.P. Sastri's discovery of the *caryā* poems and the Buddhist *dohā*s from the royal library of Nepal. He claimed that these songs of the Buddhist *siddha*s were composed in archaic Bengali. So the speculation about the presence of Tāntric Buddhism in certain parts of Bengal needed some historical support. The sympathetic attitude of the Pāla dynasty towards Buddhist cults naturally came handy in establishing the hypothesis as foolproof. Very often in our scholastic effort to establish the supremacy of a regional culture we tend to forget that during the ancient and medieval period the states and

26. R.C. Majumdar (ed.), *History of Bengal*, vol. I, Dacca, pp. 425-26 qtd. in K.L. Hazra, *The Rise and Decline of Buddhism in India*, New Delhi: Munshiram Manoharlal, 1995, p. 369.

kingdoms were not determined on linguistic basis. Bengal, Orissa and Bihar being contiguous States have sometimes been under the same suzerainty. The geographical boundaries expanded and receded from time to time. So there is no harm in giving its due to what the culture of a region deserves.

When Buddhism was losing its base all over India during the Mohammedan rule, it continued to flourish in this part of India. The famous historian Kern is of the opinion that the later Buddhists took shelter in different parts of Orissa after the Mohammedan invasion of Gauḍa (Bengal and Bihar) in CE 1200. He writes, "Many emigrants from Magadha rejoined their brethren in the South and founded colleges on a modest scale, in Vijayanagara, Kaliṅga and Koṅkaṇa."[27] Kern's claim finds further support in the account of Buddhagupta Tathāgata Nātha, a Tibetan pilgrim, where he mentions of his visit to Utkala towards the later half of the seventh century CE. He talks about the existence of old *caitya*s, *stūpa*s and various relics of the Buddhistic faith which once had a stronghold upon the minds of the people residing there. Such records offer sufficient indications about the popularity of this cult in Orissa as late as the seventeenth to the eighteenth century CE. In fact, Orissa is one of the few places in India, where Buddhism is not yet a matter to be relegated to the pages of history. It still survives in certain parts of the state. N.N. Vasu's pioneering work *The Modern Buddhism and its Followers in Orissa,* perhaps, for the first time brings into limelight the strong bond that the later forms of Buddhism could establish with the culture, literature and society of Orissa. He, in this work, provides a detailed account of the rituals and practices of the Bathuri tribe of Mayurbhanj and Keonjhar districts of Orissa, who continue to be Buddhists by faith. There are still a great number of people of the weaving community, popularly called "Bauddha tanti," settled in Badamba (of Cuttack district) who, as the name

27. *Manual of Buddhism*, qtd. in N.N. Vasu, *The Modern Buddhism and Its followers in Orissa*, Delhi: Gyan Publishing House, 1986, p. 13.

suggests, are practising Buddhists. Till date, Buddhist Gods are worshipped by the local people at Kendrapara, in the Mahākāla temple during Buddha Pūrṇimā. The name Mahākāla itself suggests that the icon must be of Vajrayāna order. Similarly, in the western part of Orissa people follow many rituals and practices, which suggest a longstanding influence of Tāntric Buddhism. But the strongest evidence regarding the impact of Tāntric Buddhisim can be traced in the worship of Lord Jagannāth of Purī. The use of *yantra, mantra, maṇḍala,* and *upacāra,* in the daily rituals suggest the influence of Buddhist Tantra.

Tāntric Buddhism as Presented in the Santha Literature

However, the strongest evidence of the impact of Buddhism on Orissan culture can be gleaned from the *bhakti* literature of the medieval *santha*s. The famous *santha* Acyutānanda Dāsa, in his famous work *Śūnya Saṁhitā,* provides certain crucial clues about the presence of Buddhism during his time. He refers to at least three sects of Buddhism, viz., Nāgāntaka, Yogāntaka and Vedāntaka.[28] Nāgāntakas were the followers of Nāgārjunapāda, the famous *siddha* of Tāntric Buddhism; Vedāntakas were the followers of the Sautrāntika School of Buddhism and Yogāntaka obviously refers to the Yogācāra School of Buddhism. He also mentions the names of Tāntric *siddha*s like, Gorakṣanātha, Vīra Singha and Lohī Dāsa. Among them Vīra Singha was a confirmed Buddhist. He is believed to have composed the work entitled *Vīra Singha Cautiśā*. In the concluding line of the manuscript he refers to himself as a Buddhist.[29] The Buddhist theory of *Śūnyavāda* forms the very basis of this work. The temple chronicle *Mādāla Pāñji* records that Pratāparudradeva the then king of Orissa was the worst persecutor of Buddhism. As a result Vīra Singha was believed to have taken shelter in Daṇḍakāraṇya forest. Thus,

28. Acyutānanda Dāsa, *Śūnya Saṁhitā*, Ch. III.

29. *Ibid*. Also *Caitanya Bhāgavata* of Īśvara Dāsa, Ch. XII.

Acyutānanda's account of Vīra Singha, the Nāgāntaka, is not a figment of his imagination. It was during the rule of this king that the famous five proponents of Orissan Vaiṣṇavism (Pañcasakhā) championed a *śūnya*-centric philosophy, which in many respects is an extension of the Vajrayānic vision of truth, Reality and God. In fact, the impact of Buddhism has been so great that it formed the very basis of a neo-Vaiṣṇavism of the Orissan *santhas* that held its own in the face of orthodox Brāhmaṇism, on the one hand, and the onslaught of Śrī Caitanya's Vaiṣṇavism (with royal support), on the other.

The Buddhistic strain of metaphysics did not lose its hold on Orissan culture till the nineteenth century. The Mahimā cult that came into prominence during the second half of the nineteenth century pursued the same type of metaphysics championed by the Pañcasakhā. Rather, this new cult reached the culminating point of *śūnya* theory by getting rid of the extra baggage of Vaiṣṇavism. Mahimā Dharma is a Hindu reformist movement, which largely draws its metaphysical theory from the Pañcasakhā tradition. The modern Mahimā followers may deny it, but the impact of Buddhism stands out prominently in the works of Bhīma Bhoi, the most prominent *santha* of this cult. N.N. Vasu, in his work mentions two rare books of Mahimā Dharma, viz., *Aḷekha Līlā* and *Yaśomatimālikā*, that are based on the happy belief, handed down from generation to generation, that the Buddha would appear in flesh and blood for the diffusion of true knowledge. This clearly establishes that Vajrayāna, which had lost its moorings almost from the rest of India, continued to hold its predominance in religio-philosophical literature of Orissa, at least at a conceptual level.

Vajrayāna and Jagannāthism

From the above discussion we may have a glimpse of the strong bearing Buddhism had on the life and culture of Orissa. Therefore, it is very natural that the scholars find it reasonable to claim a Buddhist genesis of the Jagannātha cult. While discussing about Jagannātha *dharma*, in the second chapter of this book, I have already indicated that the peculiar iconography of the deity has often led to such inferences. I shall like to draw the attention to some of the important arguments of the side supporting the Buddhistic origin of Jagannātha *dharma*.

One of the most important arguments here has its genesis in the worship of three deites Jagannātha, Balabhadra, the two brothers, and Subhadrā, the sister in the middle. As I have pointed out earlier, this is something very unusual in Hindu tradition. So historians like William Hunter, Cunningham, R.L. Mitra, Monier-Williams, H.K. Mahatab and many others advocate that the Jagannātha temple, prior to its Vaiṣṇavisation in the ninth century, was a Buddhist shrine. Hunter says, "Jagannāth represents, with unmistakable clearness that coalition of Brāhmaṇa and Buddhist doctrines, which forms the basis of Viṣṇu worship."[30] Cunningham,[31] on the other hand speculates that the Jagannātha triad represents the Buddhist triad — Buddha, Dharma and Saṅgha — of which Dharma is always represented as female. Mahatab and Mitra also lend support to this claim. However, S.B. Dasgupta[32] adds an interesting dimension to this thesis. According to him, the key Mahāyānic concepts of *śūnyatā* and *karuṇā* were re-understood in terms of *prajña* and *upāya* by Vajrayāna. Further, they interpreted these two concepts as static and dynamic, as male and female principles. *Upāya* as the male principle was identified with Buddha, and *dharma* became *prajñā* or the female principle; finally, *saṅgha* was interpreted as the phenomenal world produced through the union of *prajñā* and *karuṇā*. So the Jagannātha triad, he argues, in all probability

30. W.W. Hunter, *The Indian Empire*, 1883. Qtd. in J. Padhi, *Śrī Jagannāth at Puri*, Puri: S.G.N. Publications, 2000, p. 40.

31. Qtd. in Padhi, p. 40.

32. S.B. Dasgupta, *Obscure Religious Cults*, Calcutta: Firma KLM. Pvt. Ltd., 1976, p. 277.

represents *triratnas*, viz., Buddha, Dharma and Saṅgha, transformed as *upāya, prajñā* and their son. "In the esoteric Buddhist literature the epithet Jagannātha (i.e., the Lord of the world) is widely used as a prefix to Buddha or rather the Lord Supreme, and it is also a well-known adjective used before the Lord Supreme of the Hindus, and thus, through the medium of the epithet Jagannātha, the first of the three jewels could easily be Hinduised and the Hinduisation of the other two was but a matter of course."[33] This hypothesis finds confirmatory support from certain archaeological findings. A stone of Aśokan polish with Buddha, Dharma and Saṅgha at the top has been found in Bhubaneswar and is preserved in the Asutosh Museum in Calcutta. On this panel the three images bear resemblance to the three deities of the Purī temple.

Mahatab's argument in support of the Buddhistic genesis of the Jagannātha triad is also closer to this theory. He very validly argues that the pedestal where the three deities are installed is called the *ratna vedī,* which is believed to be the abbreviated form of *triratna vedī* — referring to the three *ratnas* of Buddhism.[34] It is indeed very peculiar that the *vedī* (pedestal) made of unembellished stone of the *sanctum* of the Jagannātha temple is called the *ratna vedī* (the bejewelled throne). With this, Mahatab tries to reconstruct the evolution of this cult by providing a happy synthesis between the Buddhist, Vaiṣṇavite and autochthonous claims, regarding the genesis of Jagannāthism. He believes that during the reign of Aśoka the aborigine *śavaras* of Orissa were converted to Buddhism. In course of time, when the Buddha was deified, the simple-minded people started worshipping the *triratna* as the symbol of one deity called Jagannātha. He further argues that Jagannātha is another name of the Buddha; and the term has a Buddhistic root. Later on Jagannātha was identified with

---

33. Dasgupta, p. 277.

34. H.K. Mahatab, *Oṛiyā Sāhityara Itihāsa,* Bhubaneswar: Sāhitya Akademy, 1958, p. 118.

Viṣṇu when the Tāntric ideas predominated in the land. Thus, he comes to the conclusion that the Buddhist shrine was turned into a Vaiṣṇavite temple in course of time.

Another oft-repeated argument in this regard is based on the frequent use of the term "Jagannātha" in the treatises of two important *siddhas* of the Vajrayāna order, viz., Indrabhūti and Anaṅgavajra. They wrote *Jñānasiddhi* and *Prajño-pāyaviniścaya Siddhi,* respectively. In both the works Jagannātha is invoked as the Lord Supreme. Both these works are composed in Sanskrit and deal with matters of philosophical and esoteric significance. In the opening verse of *Jñāna-siddhi* it is stated that "Lord Jagannātha, who is the same as all Buddhas, and who is as all pervading as sky, is worshipped by all wise men."[35]

Similarly, Anaṅgavajra describes Jagannātha as *śūnyagarbha,* the embodiment of all knowledge and beyond all conceptualisations. Since Indrabhūti is believed to be the king of Orissa, the reference to Jagannātha appears to be very significant. So, it is argued that Jagannātha was originally the Vajrasattva of the Vajrayānīs. It may not be totally out of context to hold that in some of the important works recovered from Nepal Jagannātha has been identified with the Ādi Buddha. Again, there are as many as eight Jagannātha temples situated in Kathmandu (the capital of Nepal) and its vicinities. This cannot just be wished away as a matter of coincidence. Nepal being a Hindu state, there may not be anything unusual about having the temples of Jagannātha, the Hindu God. But out of so many gods of the Hindu pantheon why this predominance was attached to Jagannātha remains as inexplicable as ever. So we find that there is some sort of link between these two concepts — Buddha and Jagannātha. On this basis it has been argued that the very name Jagannātha

35. *praṇipatya jagannāthaṁ sarvajīnavarārcitaṁ,*
sarva buddhamayaṁ siddhi vyapinaṁ gaganopamam.

Indrabhūti, *Jñānasiddhi,* ed. B. Bhattacharya, Baroda: Gaekwad Oriental Series, no. 44, 1929, p. 31.

owes its origin to the frequent use of this term by the *siddha*s of the Vajrayāna order. The enigmatic nature of the genesis of the Jagannātha worship gives further credence to this conjecture. I have stated earlier that there are conflicting accounts about the exact nature of the Jagannātha cult before the twelfth century. The famous deity at Purī, for a long time, was known as Puruṣottama. It came to be known as Jagannātha only during the fourteenth century. So it is possible that Indrabhūti, the king of Uḍḍiyāna, made this name popular. Therefore, it may be presumed that this change of nomenclature may be due to the influence of Vajrayāna.

It is well known that by the eleventh century the Buddha has been admitted into the Hindu pantheon and he had been given the status of the ninth incarnation of Viṣṇu, in such works as the *Bhāgavatam* (1.3.24), Kṣemendra's *Divyadāna Kalpanā* and Jayadeva's *Gīta Govinda*. But in Orissa, Jagannātha has been called "Bauddha Jagannātha" and is placed as the ninth incarnation instead of the Buddha. The iconography of Jagannātha temple bears strong evidence to this fact. The ten incarnations are found on the frieze over the main gate of this temple. Here, we find Jagannātha in place of Buddha, the ninth incarnation. Similar carvings can be observed in the interior walls of the *Nātamaṇḍapa*, inside the Jagannātha temple. What is most interesting about this iconography is that in both the places the Jagannātha is presented as having a complete form with both hands and legs intact.

This age old association between Buddha and Jagannātha ultimately finds the theoretical support when the famous Oriyā *santha* poet Sāralā Dāsa used the word Buddha-Jagannātha in his Oriyā transcreation of the *Mahābhārata*. He in his Oriyā rendering of *Mahābhārata* says: "Jagannātha, you are present here as Buddha for the delivernce of the world."[36] Pañcasakhā and the subsequent *santha* philosophers like Caitanya Dāsa,

36. *saṁsārajanaku taribā nimante,*
buddharūpe bije hoi acha jagannāthe.

— Sāralā Dāsa, *Mahābhārata*, Sabhā Parva

Divākara Dāsa, Arakṣita Dāsa and Īśvara Dāsa followed the trend.

Our perusal of some of the substantial arguments in favour of the Buddhist genesis of the Jagannātha cult reveals that they are not just wild speculations. One may or may not agree with such interpretations but the close association between later Buddhism and Jagannāthism cannot be simply wished away.

II

An Outline of Vajrayāna Philosophy

In the previous section I have tried to scan the relation between Buddhism and the Orissan culture from a historical angle. Keeping these facts in the background we come down to explore how the Oriyā *santha* philosophers expound their theories about the nature of the phenomenal world, the highest Reality and liberation by introducing certain key Buddhistic, especially Vajrayānīc, concepts. Earlier, I have discussed in brief about the history and ethnography of this sect of Buddhism in relation to Orissa. Let me now concentrate on its metaphysical presuppositions.

I have claimed earlier that Orissan Vaiṣṇavism is largely inspired by Vajrayāna. Therefore, it is necessary for us to have a brief acquaintance with the metaphysical theories of this sect. It is a general impression among the intellectuals that Tāntric Buddhism, as such, is a perverted form of Buddhism that is just the miss-mass of esoterism and sexo-yogic practices. This is gross injustice to a system of thought which had a great hold on a sizeable section of Indian mind, once upon a time. And it continues to be popular in many parts of the world, including Tibet and Nepal. It would be a travesty of truth to say that Vajrayāna has no metaphysics of its own. A look into such treatises as *Jñānasiddhi* of Indrabhūti, *Prajñopāya viniścaya Siddhi* of Anaṅgavajra and *Advayavajra Saṁgraha* of Advaya Vajra convinces us about its rich philosophical contents. In the true sense of the term Vajrayāna is an extension of the Mahāyāna philosophy. Mādhyamika concepts like *śūnyatā, nirvāṇa, karuṇā* and *prajñā,* on the one hand, and the Yogacārī concepts like *vijñāna* and *abhūtaparikalpa,* on the other hand, form the metaphysical basis of this sub-sect. But it makes certain necessary modifications to transform the highly abstract philosophy into practical and living faith. The most important conceptual transformation is with regard to the idea of *śūnyatā.* This concept is now identified with *vajra,* from which the sect derives its name. *Vajra* literally means "diamond" and also thunderbolt. It also means that which is adamantine in nature. *Vajra* refers to that aspect of the Reality, which is absolute and indestructible, in contrast to the fickle fictions, a man usually entertains about the world. According to them, *śūnyatā*-nature of the world is its ultimate immutable nature, as immutable as *vajra* (thunderbolt). *Advayavajra Saṁgraha,* an important text of this sect says, "*śūnyatā,* which is firm, substantial, indivisible, impenetrable, incapable of being burnt and imperishable, is called *vajra.*"[37] Padma Vajra, another *siddha* of this order defines Vajrayāna as the path of non-substantiality. In other words, it is a method of the realization of *śūnyatā,* for *vajra* itself is *śūnyatā.*[38] In the next step Vajrayāna conceives *śūnyata/vajra* as the *vajra-sattva,* the supreme deity. *Vajra* here stands for *śūnyatā* and *sattva* for quintessence. Another important concept that was introduced by Mādhyamika is *karuṇā. Nirvāṇa* has all along been a key concept in Buddhism. But in Mahāyāna Buddhism we come across a novel interpretation of the term. For Buddha, *nirvāṇa* has to be realized through one's own effort. But Mahāyāna adds an altruistic tinge to this idea by incorporating the lofty ideal of *karuṇā,* i.e., universal compassion. *Nirvāṇa* for them means

---

37. *dṛḍham sāram asauśrīyam accedya abhedya-lakṣaṇam,*
adāhi avināśīca śūnyatā vajram ucyate.

Advaya Vajra Saṁgraha, ed., H.P. Sastry, Baroda: Gaekwad Oriental Series, No. 40 1927, p. 37.

38. *Guhyasiddhi,* M.S. p. 6 (A) qtd. in S.B. Dasgupta, *An Introduction to Tāntric Buddhism,* Calcutta: University of Calcutta, 1974, 71.ff.5.

compassionate identification with the whole humanity, lying in the vortex of suffering, misery, birth and death. So personal liberation is not the goal. *Sūtrālaṁkāra* very succinctly put it: "There is no *pūṇya* if you feed yourself, but when you feed others. Similarly, there is no greatness in personal liberation, it must be liberation for one and all."[39] This ideal is encapsulated in the example of Avalokiteśvara — the all-compassionate — who refuses *nirvāṇa* until all the creatures of the world obtained freedom from the worldly suffering. Vajrayāna along with *śūnyatā* also absorbs the idea of *karuṇā* within its fold. In Mahāyāna texts we find that *śūnyatā* is identified with *prajñā,* i.e., perfect knowledge of non-essentiality of the self and the *dharmas*; and *karuṇā* is called *upāya,* i.e., the means for the attainment of the highest knowledge. In Mahāyānic texts like *Saddharmapuṇḍarīka*[40] *upāya* has also been explained as missionary woks prompted by universal compassion for the suffering beings. Vajrayāna transform these twin concepts, i.e., *prajñā* and *upāya* into male and female principles. *Prajñā* is conceived as absolutely passive and the negative aspect of the reality; and *upāya* as the dynamic and active aspect of the reality. *Upāya* is believed to bring into existence the phenomenal world, the possibility of which lies in the *prajñā* or *śūnyatā*. Unlike in Sāṁkhya philosophy, here the passive aspect is conceived as female and active aspect as the male. But in the ultimate sense, *śūnyatā* and *karuṇā, prajñā* and *upāya* — all these four principles refer to the Ultimate non-dual (*advaya*) reality. In this connection we must take note of the concept of *advaya* and the allied concept *yuganaddha*. Both these concepts imply the same meaning, i.e., unity or non-duality. *Prajñopāyaviniścaya Siddhi* states: "when there is

39. *yathā puṇyaṁ prasavate pareṣāṁ bhojanaṁ dadāt,*
na tu svayaṁ sa bhunjāḥ tathā pūṇyamahodayaḥ
— *Sūtrālaṁkāra,* v.72

40. *Saddharmapuṇḍarīka* Ch. II, *Bibliotheca Buddhica Publication*, pp. 28-58. qtd., in Dasgupta, *Obscure Religious Cults*, p. 28.

the union of *prajñā* and *karuṇā* the result is *nirvāṇa*. In this state the mind is neither aware of *śūnyatā* or *aśūnyatā*. Again there is neither the rejection of *śūnyatā* nor *aśūnyatā*, for the thought of *śūnya* or *aśūnya* may lead to conceptualized discrimination. In the state of *prajñā* mind becomes as expansive as the sky. As the sky merges with the sky, similarly, in the state of *prajñā* there is no discrimination between the subject of knowledge and the object of knowledge. There is no duality between the action and the agent. This knowledge of non-duality is *vajra* or *śūnya*.[41] Besides Vajrayāna also incorporates certain basic principles from the Yogācāra, another branch of Mahāyāna. Asaṅga and Vasubandhu, the eminent exponents of this sect introduced the elements of Yoga in their philosophy. Besides they accredited ultimacy to *vijñāna* in place of *śūnyatā*. Vajrayāna drew support from this doctrine to claim that mind or inner experience is the source of energy. Mādhyamika had already shown the identity between *śūnyatā* and *karuṇā*. Vajrayānīs now add the idea of *vijñāna* to the fold. Interestingly, to this three-fold identity they add a fourth one, i.e., *mahāsukha* (supreme bliss). This concept is an important innovation of Tāntric Buddhism, which evolved from the idea of *nirvāṇa* delineated in earlier Buddhism. In Buddhist literature that we come across, there exist certain disagreements over the question whether *nirvāṇa* is a positive state at all. However, there are sufficient indications in many Pāli texts about its being a state of infinite bliss.[42] Vijñānavāda also shares this opinion. But Vajrayāna modifies this concept further and identifies bliss with *nirvāṇa* and calls it *mahāsukha*. They

41. *na śūnya bhāvanāṁ kuryāt nāpica aśūnyabhāvanāṁ,*
na śūnyaṁ santyajed yogī nācaśūnyaṁ parityajed.
aśūnya śūnyayorgāhe jāyate ananta kalpanā,
nirvikāro nirasaṁgo niskānkṣagata kalpanā ṣaḥ,
ādyāntaḥ kalpanāmukto vyomavad bhavayed buddhaḥ.

B. Bhattacharyya (ed.), *Prajñopāya Viniścayasiddhi*, Baroda: Gaekwad Oriental Series, p. 44. 1929, IV.5.8.

42. *Sutta-nipāta*, 933. qtd. in Dasgupta, *Obscure Religious Cults*, p. 33.

conceive of *mahāsukha* as the ultimate reality absorbing within it, both existence (*bhāva*) and extinction. *Mahāsukha* is sometimes identified with the Lord Vajrasattva who is of the nature of the unity of *prajñā* and *upāya*. This is how Vajrayāna absorbs some key concepts from Mahāyāna and transforms them into a new philosophy.

Critics and scholars love to indulge in hot debate over the nature of Orissan Vaiṣṇavism. But even the worst critic of the "Buddhistic orientation" theory cannot but admit the significance of Buddhism here. When we come to the theories of the Orissan Vaiṣṇavas, one may find it very difficult to accommodate them in the broad framework of Vaiṣṇavism. Some of their philosophical viewpoints are so off the beaten track that one may be confounded about the genesis of such ideas. One may or may not agree with N.N. Vasu[43] in claiming that the great *santha*s of Orissa were Buddhists, concealing their true affiliations apprehending prosecution of the priestly class as well as the king. But the fact remains that their philosophy absorbs a great deal from the later forms of Buddhism.

---

43. Vasu, p. 130.

5

The Orissan Santha Tradition

THE *santha* philosophy of Orissa is, in every respect, the product of the soil. The culture of amalgamation that has become the most prominent feature of Orissan culture is mirrored in the works of the *santha*s. These *santha*s transformed the religious syncretism of Jagannātha *dharma* into a form of philosophical synthesis. They apparently were the followers of some or other *sampradāya*s or Vaiṣṇava sects, yet such affiliations virtually had nothing to do with their philosophical outlook. Their's was the voice of universalism. Love and compassion for the suffering humanity characterized their thought and action. So they were non-conformists in more than one sense. The Oriyā *santha*s never used the title "Gosvāmī" as was the practice among the Vaiṣṇavas. They had only one identity. They were "Dāsa" meaning "slave" or "the lowliest of the low." Sometimes they called themselves śūdra (lowest among four-fold caste order), to emphasize that in their heart and mind they were with the downtrodden and oppressed caste of the society. They stood by a philosophy of life that in many respects transgressed the dominant religious and spiritual faith of the elites.

Fifteenth century can be said to be a crucial phase in the religio-philosophical history of India. It was the period when Buddhism was losing its foothold all over India; and Vaiṣṇavism was rising in popularity. The Vedāntin Vaiṣṇavism had already left its imprints both in the south and north. This had resulted in a new form of Vaiṣṇavism spearheaded by the *santhas* like Rāmānanda and Kabīr who revolutionised the very conception of religion. *Bhakti* was the keyword for them but the term was stripped of its traditional significance. It now stood for a message of love that was free of meaningless religious trappings. The God continued to be the object of devotion but the God was portrayed as *nirguṇa* (transcending all positive and negative qualities). When the whole of India was witnessing the emergence of a religious and spiritual reawakening Orissa did not lag behind.

The philosophical and cultural reawakening of Orissa can be said to have started with the Oriyā rendering of the *Mahābhārata* by Sāralā Dāsa sometime in the middle of fifteenth century. This also heralded the beginning of a *santha* tradition that could be said to be truly Oriyā in spirit and form. *Santha* Sāralā Dāsa's Oriyā version of *Mahābhārata* is in no sense a mere translation of this great epic; on the contrary it is a new creation. The main story of *Mahābhārata* is kept as a skeleton around which he weaves many new ideas that might have been suppressed in the hearts and minds of the people. So this great work revolutionised the Oriyā culture in more than one sense. It represented a literature of protest: a protest against empty religiosities revolving round the presiding deity of the land, viz., Jagannātha; a protest against the supremacy of Sanskrit that had closed the doors of spirituality to the common and ordinary people. Sāralā Dāsa was successful in his mission. This is evident from the fact that Sāralā's *Mahābhārata* is still very popular in the villages of Orissa and recited in village congregations for the enjoyment of the people. According to the famous scholar of Oriyā literature C.R. Das, "Sāralā's *Mahābhārata* is perhaps the first of its kind in any Indian language. The Bengali *Mahābhārata* was about two centuries later. The *Mahābhārata* in Telegu took as many as three poets to complete and the entire thing was read only in the eighteenth century."[1]

1. Chittaranjan Das, *Glimpses into Oriya Literature*, Bhubaneswar: Orissa Sahitya Akademi, 1982, p. 66.

Bauddha Vaiṣṇavism

Sāralā Dāsa's *Mahābhārata* is not only the first epic in Oriyā language but it is also the first work to explicitly represent the philosophical and cultural fusion that was already fermenting in the soil of Orissa. This great poet-philosopher initiated the task of giving expression to this inclination. As far as the content was concerned Sāralā Dāsa followed the Vaiṣṇavite affiliation of the original *Mahābhārata*. But he very freely introduced certain local elements in his Oriyā rendering that cannot be called true to the Vaiṣṇavite spirit. G.C. Tripathi, the famous Jagannāthologist very rightly observes that Sāralā Dāsa "ingeniously combines *two* different traditions regarding the nature of Jagannātha — the one declaring him to be Buddha and the other to be Kṛṣṇa. The *substance* of the wooden statue of Jagannātha is Kṛṣṇa himself whereas its form is that of Buddha."[2] Yet Tripathi's conjecture about Sāralā Dāsa's motive behind such an unusual conglomeration does not appear very convincing. He argues that the typical iconography of the Jagannātha needed some mythological basis before he could present Him as the Kṛṣṇa. So Jagannātha's identification with the Buddha made Sāralā Dāsa's task easy. But before we accept Tripathi's hypothesis we must keep certain facts in mind. First, it has now been unanimously accepted by the historians that by the thirteenth century the Jagannātha cult had been fully Vaiṣṇavised. So Sāralā Dāsa's effort to present Him as Buddha, instead of making his task easier, would have made it rather difficult. Presenting Jagannātha-Kṛṣṇa as Buddha (perceived to be a non-Brāhmaṇical deity) would have offended the popular religious sentiment. So the most plausible reason for the identification of these two trends may be traced elsewhere. It is possible that Orissan culture was not totally unaccustomed to this spirit of assimilation of apparently opposite trends.

2. G.C. Tripathi, "Jagannātha: The Ageless Deity," *The Cult of Jagannāth and the Regional Tradition of Orissa*, ed. A. Eschmann, *et al.*, Delhi: Manohar, 1986, p. 481.

Further, defying the general trend of Vaiṣṇavism Sāralā Dāsa depicts Jagannātha as *nirākāra, nirguṇa, Aḷekha* and *nirañjana*. For him he is the *Śūnya Puruṣa*. As a result Kṛṣṇa of the *Mahābhārata* ultimately turned into the *Śūnya Puruṣa*-Buddha-Jagannātha. Thus, Vaiṣṇavism, Buddhism and Jagannāthism all were rolled into one to give rise to a new form of Vaiṣṇavism that was taken to its logical conclusion by the Pañcasakhās within one hundred years of the composition of his *Mahābhārata*.

Besides Sāralā Dāsa's transcreation of the epic serves in more than one way in gathering the philosophical ambience of the period. The work clearly indicates his impressions of the multiple sects that were very active in Orissa during the period. He takes help of certain original anecdotes to tell the story of Gorakṣanātha of the Nātha cult, Vīra Singha of Tāntric Buddhism and Sahaja Sundarī of the Sahajīyā Vaiṣṇavism. His acquaintance with these cults also is evident from his thorough knowledge of their metaphysical trends. The work also records his acquaintance with the seminal concepts of Orissan Vaiṣṇavism, including the theories of *jñānamiśra bhakti* and *piṇḍa-Brahmāṇḍa* identity. Thus, this work is of immense value for a proper understanding of the *santha* philosophy of Orissa.

This new form of Vaiṣṇavism launched by Sāralā Dāsa was given a philosophical structure by the five great *santha*s of sixteenth century, viz., Jagannātha Dāsa, Balarāma Dāsa, Acyutānanda Dāsa, Yaśovanta Dāsa and Śiśu Ananta Dāsa. They are popularly known as the Pañcasakhā or the five soul-mates. Their task in developing a radically different form of Vaiṣṇavism, in a certain sense, was more daunting as they had to keep the identity of their theory intact in the face of a contemporaneous Vaiṣṇavism preached by Śrī Caitanya. He had not only the necessary royal backing but people had started taking interest in Śrī Caitanya's ways of preaching Kṛṣṇa *bhakti*. It may appear paradoxical that these groups of five philosophers were never tired of proclaiming their

Vaiṣṇavite status. They not only openly pledged their allegiance to Śrī Caitanya but also were the self-proclaimed representatives of Vaiṣṇava schools. As far as their religious initiation (*dīkṣā*) was concerned, they belonged to typical Vaiṣṇava *sampradāya*s established by the Vedāntin Vaiṣṇavas like Rāmānuja, Madhva, Nimbārka and Viṣṇu Śvāmī. So sometimes they are called the Pañcaśākhā (branches) of the Orissan Vaiṣṇavism. Yet the moment we scan their writings we notice a thorough demolition of all that Vaiṣṇavism in general stands for. The philosophical theories propounded by them have virtually nothing to do with the *sampradāya*s they represented. Similarly, they were hesitant to share Caitanya's mistrust of the Upaniṣadic non-dualism. Rather, they very successfully reinterpreted the religious syncretism of the Jagannātha cult into a non-dualistic metaphysics that encapsulated the philosophies of Buddhism, Upaniṣads (as interpreted by Śaṅkara) and Yoga. This big gap between what they apparently claimed and what they actually espoused seems inexplicable. Many scholars ascribe this strange phenomenon to the fear of royal persecution. It is well-known that Pratāparudradeva, the then ruler of Orissa, was a passionate supporter of Śrī Caitanya. This may be one of the reasons why Pañcasakhā occasionally expressed their allegiance to this great Vaiṣṇava preacher. In their eagerness to avoid any unpleasant situation these five *santha*s even depicted Śrī Caitanya as the incarnation of both Jagannātha and Buddha. Such depiction also helped them to go on with their avowed task without inviting direct confrontation with the upcoming influence of Śrī Caitanya. But history proves that not only the philosophical trend established by the Pañcasakhā survived the onslaught of Śrī Caitanya's neo-Vaiṣṇavism, but it also flourished and flowered in the subsequent period through the works of *santha*s who followed, like Caitanya Dāsa, Dvārakā Dāsa, Divākara Dāsa, Mahādeva Dāsa and others. It almost took two hundred years for Gauḍīya Vaiṣṇavism of Śrī Caitanya to spread its roots in Orissa. The popularity of their poetic works might have waned with the spread of Western education. But simple metaphysical poems composed in the form of *bhajans* are still immensely popular in rural India. Interestingly, these people not only sing them but they too grasp their true implications, which the so-called educated often find difficult to delve into.

The Santhas and their Works

Following the trend established by Sāralā Dāsa these five famous *santhas* initially rendered the sacred books of the Hindus into the language of the people. Three of the most important works rendered into Oriyā by them are — *Jagamohana Rāmāyaṇa* by Balarāma Dāsa, *Śrīmad Bhāgavata* by Jagannātha Dāsa and *Harivaṁśa* by Acyutānanda Dāsa. However, these works were not mere translations. Like Sāralā Dāsa they let their creative genius a free play. The introduction of local elements made the common people understand the deep nuances of these sacred works without any effort. Besides they also wrote several versions of the *Gītā*. But it seems the term *Gītā* had a different significance for them. Any work dealing with the metaphysics was titled as *Gītā*. The theories they had to propound were presented in the form of dialogues between Kṛṣṇa and Arjuna (following the pattern of the original *Śrīmadbhagavad-Gītā*). These dialogues, therefore, encompass every possible metaphysical question right from the nature of the highest Reality to the creation of the world. In certain cases Śiva and Pārvatī are also used as the spokespersons in their versions of the *Gītā*. Along with the depiction of metaphysical principles in the simplest of language these poet-philosophers also stated many things that can be said to be purely esoteric. They also took help of words loaded with religious symbolism. However the popularity of their writings, especially *bhajans*, among the people of the rural areas clearly suggest that they are not truly non-decipherable symbols. Since the modern people are not acquainted with the culture they find it difficult to follow certain phrases and words. Despite such obscurities in most cases, their metaphysical presuppositions are expressed quite lucidly in the simplest of poetic forms. They were great poets. This is one of the reasons why they are known in Orissa more as great poets than philosophers. In the following passages I try to give a very brief account of their life and works.

Jagannātha Dāsa : One of the eminent members of Pañcasakhā group, Jagannātha Dāsa was born in 1487. He was the first among the five to have come in contact with Caitanya. The anecdotes about his life state that Śrī Caitanya met him for the first time in the Jagannātha temple while he was engaged in analysing the Śāstras in Oriyā. He was so impressed by his skill that he conferred on Jagannātha Dāsa the title *ati baḍi* (the great one). His chief contribution to Oriyā cultural life was his Oriyā transcreation of *Śrīmad Bhāgavatam*. Through this stupendous work he not only acquainted the common people with this great Purāṇa but he also used this work to propagate his philosophy of life. This work continues to be an integral part of the life of the common Oriyā. No village in this part of the country is complete without a congregation place for the regular recital of his *Bhāgavata*. This place is popularly known as the *Bhāgavata Tuṅgī*. Another work, *Tulā Bhiṇā* is philosophically very significant. The book is written in the form of verse followed by commentaries in prose. About the title of this work the author says that as *tulā* (cotton) is thrashed to make it clear and light, similarly he intends to thrash out the serious philosophical problems in the work. The other works of philosophical significance are: *Dāru Brahma Gītā, Artha Koiḷi and Bhūgola Ekādaśa Skanda.*

Balarāma Dāsa : Balarāma Dāsa, the seniormost of these five comrades, was born in 1472. It is believed that he initiated Jagannātha Dāsa into Vaiṣṇavism on the advice of Caitanya. He was affiliated to the Viṣṇusvāmī sect and the *mantra* he adopted is called the *ajapā mantra*. His voluminous transcreation of *Rāmāyaṇa* entitled *Jagamohana Rāmāyaṇa* written in *dāṇḍī* metre (*vṛtti*) is still very popular among the masses. He is revered and remembered by the Oriyā community for his famous interpretation of body as the temple of Jagannātha in his works *Brahmāṇḍa Bhūgola* and *Virāṭa Gītā*. He is also fondly remembered for his strength of conviction in the equality of human race in the matters of spirituality. He wholeheartedly challenged the Brāhmaṇical supremacy of the then society. He narrates a very eventful incident of his life in his work *Praṇava Gītā* that shows the attitude of the brāhmaṇas of his time. Once he was caught red-handed by the priests of the temple while deliberating on the scriptures in the temple premises. According to the tradition set by the priests of the temple a non-brāhmaṇa had no right to engage in such intellectual activity. The matter was brought to the notice of the king. Being challenged by the king for the deviation of the sacred rules of the temple he retorted:

> Listen oh king, God is nobody's exclusive possession. God belongs to him who is pious and good, be he a *cāṇḍāla* (low born) or a Brāhmin. On kind and merciful Jagannātha nobody has monopoly.[3]

This sort of bold answer can only come from a man who is truly convinced about the all-pervasiveness of the supreme spirit. Other than the works mentioned he has composed the following works of philosophical importance: *Gupta-Gītā*, *Vedānta Sāra Gupta-Gītā*, *Brahma Gītā*, *Amara Kośa-Gītā*, *Brahma Purāṇa*, and *Garuḍa-Gītā*.

Acyutānanda Dāsa : There is no unanimity among the scholars regarding the exact date of Acyutānanda's birth. But most of the scholars believe that he was born sometime around 1502. He claimed himself to be the follower of Nimbānanda or Nimbārka. His *mantra* was called *śūnya mantra*. He is the most

3. Balarāma Dāsa, *Praṇava-Gītā*, Ch. 1, Verses p. 5-72, qtd. in N.N. Vasu, *Modern Buddhism and its Followers in Orissa*, Delhi: Gyan Publishing House, 1986, pp. 65-68.

prolific among the five *santha* poets. According to his own admission he has composed thirtytwo Saṁhitās and seventyeight Gītās. No one is sure about the number of works he had composed. Some of his philosophically significant manuscripts have not yet been published. Again, there are many works that are passed in the name of Acyutānanda. Whatever it may be he wrote some of the great works of Orissan Vaiṣṇavism. *Śūnya Saṁhitā* is one of the finest works that centres on the theme of Śūnyavāda of the Orissan variety. This work also documents the history of his time as well as the influence of Buddhism during that period. The *bhajans* composed by him continue to be popular among the common people of Orissa. His cryptic style and profuse use of esoteric symbols may appear obscure to the readers not associated with this culture. But the so-called illiterate masses of Orissa find no difficulty in deciphering their true implications. Some of his other works of philosophical importance are: *Anākāra Saṁhitā, Śabda Brahma Saṁhitā, Guru Bhakti-Gītā, Jñāna Bhakti-Gītā, Chayāliśā Paṭala, Brahma Śāṅkuḷi, Tattva Bodhinī,* and *Śūnya Saṁhitā Causaṭhī Ṭīkā*. Besides he has also composed a version of *Śūnya Saṁhitā* in Sanskrit.

Yaśovanta Dāsa : Born in 1487, Yaśovanta Dāsa claimed himself to be a follower of Madhvācārya. His *mantra* is called *abanā mantra*. His famous work *Prema Bhakti Brahma-Gītā* very lucidly exposes the *śūnya*-centric theory of Orissan Vaiṣṇavism. He has also authored the important work: *Ātmā parace Gītā* and *Caurāśī Ājñā*.

Śiśu Ananta Dāsa : Born in 1486, Śiśu Ananta Dāsa belonged to the Rāmānanda sect and his *mantra* is called *ekākṣara mantra*. His interpretation of the mind or *citta* as the root of *saṁsāra* as well as Reality in his work entitled *Hetu Udaya Bhāgavata* is a noteworthy contribution to Orissan Vaiṣṇavism. His cryptic line, "Can there be a God outside your mind?" encapsulates his attitude to spirituality. Another work of philosophical significance is *Gupta Ṭīkā*.

Caitanya Dāsa : He is believed to be a contemporary of Pañcasakhā. He hailed from the western part of Orissa, therefore in his writings there is no direct reference to Jagannātha. But the metaphysical tenor is same as that of the other *santha*s of his period. His work *Nirguṇa Māhātmya* offers an excellent exposition of the theory of *Śūnya Puruṣa*. *Viṣṇu Garbha Purāṇa* is another important work composed by him. In certain sections of these two works he seems to be very bold as he makes an effort to take the theory of *Śūnya Puruṣa* to its logical conclusion. Interestingly Jagannātha does not figure prominently in his writings. He prefers to identify *Śūnya Puruṣa* with Viṣṇu.

Besides these *santha*s, others like Dvārakā Dāsa, Arakṣita Dāsa and Divākara Dāsa are the eminent *santha*s of this genre. Arakṣita Dāsa was a king turned into a mendicant. His *Mahimaṇḍala Gītā* records the philosophical position of the Oriyā Vaiṣṇavas in detail.

Part Two
Philosophical Concepts

6

Śūnya Puruṣa

THE theory of *Śūnya Puruṣa* can be said to be one of the most original contributions of the Oriyā *santha*s in the development of history of ideas. The concept cannot be put into the straight-jacket of any available philosophical mould, not even the prevalent *nirguṇa bhakti* theory of the medieval period. The theory of *Śūnya Puruṣa* is also unique in the sense that this metaphysical position was not taken up not as a matter of academic or intellectual deliberation; the concept had deep social and cultural implications. The *santha*s of Orissa, like other *santha*s of India, were mainly interested in practical philosophy that could offer direction to a society, torn apart in the name of religion dominant at that time, i.e., the so-called *sanātana dharma*. Its aim was to give new meaning to the concept of *bhakti* as well as God. Being a part of the *bhakti* movement these *santha* philosophers referred directly or indirectly to a God that could be an object of highest love and devotion. Taken in this sense the theory of *Śūnya Puruṣa* is a theory based on the idea of the God as *śūnya*. I have stated earlier that the *santha* movement of India shared certain common features, but in no other *bhakti* tradition God is so explicitly delienated as *śūnya*, excepting perhaps the Sūfī cult and the Dharma cult of Bengal. But these cults, unfortunately do not espouse a systematic *śūnya*-centric metaphysics as it is found in the case of the *santha*s of Orissa. I propose to make a comparative analysis of the theory of Dharma cult and the Bauddha Vaiṣṇavism of Orissa, in Appendix I of this book.

The idea of *śūnya* plays a pivotal role in Orissan culture and philosophy since the fifteenth century CE or even prior to that. The earliest Oriyā works like *Śiśu Veda, Vedānta, Śrī Gītā Sāra, Vīrasingha Cautiśā, Gorekha Hadipā Saṁvāda,* that are believed to be composed between thirteenth and fourteenth century frequently refer to the concept of *śūnya*. A thorough scanning of the Oriyā literature since thirteenth century reveals that the culture of this land is so much associated with the term *śūnya* that it is very difficult to trace its origin in Oriyā metaphysical writings. In other words, the word *śūnya* had so much been ingrained in the Oriyā psyche of the period, that nobody seemed to bother much about its origin. But by sixteenth century the theory of *Śūnya Puruṣa* had acquired a metaphysical status through the literature of the *santhas*. However, we may get some clue about its genesis from the famous transcreation of the *Mahābhārata* in Oriyā language by Santha Sāralā Dāsa. I have stated earlier that Sāralā Dāsa introduced two novel concepts in this work, viz., *Buddha Jagannātha* and *Śūnya Brahman*. In a sense Sāralā Dāsa takes the first step towards the evolution of a new tradition by identifying Jagannātha with the Buddha, as well as *śūnya*. This point of convergence takes a theoretical shape in the concept of *Śūnya Puruṣa* that was developed in the subsequent period by the five great *santhas*, popularly known as Pañcasakhā. They transformed Jagannātha, the presiding deity of the land, into the symbolic representation of the ultimate metaphysical principle, viz., *Śūnya Puruṣa/Śūnya Brahman*. The succeeding *santhas* like Caitanya Dāsa, Arakṣita Dāsa, Dvārakā Dāsa, Divākara Dāsa, Īśvara Dāsa and others adhered to the same philosophy till the nineteenth century. Mahimā cult, which gained prominence in Orissa during nineteenth and twentieth centuries, continued to focus on the concept of the *Śūnya Puruṣa*, but it subsequently got rid of the Vaiṣṇavite fervour that was associated with this term.

I

The Genesis of the Concept of Śūnya

The epithet *Śūnya Puruṣa* may appear a little queer. Why do these *santhas* combine *Śūnya* with *Puruṣa*? They also append the word *Brahman* to *Śūnya*. We do not know whether these *santhas* used such combinations consciously or not. They were no linguistic analysts like the modern philosophers. It is more probable that they must have followed a tradition that was taking shape under the influence of varied philosophical systems that had spread their roots and branches in this land. But there is no harm in trying to trace the causes of such new usages. Therefore, I venture to explicate and trace the source of these two interesting concepts, viz., *Śūnya* and *Puruṣa*.

Let us start with the term *śūnya*. But before I carry on a full-fledged discussion on the philosophical implications of this concept I need to draw attention to the etymological significance of the word *śūnya*. The most favoured translation of the word is "void." This may give rise to certain grave misconceptions about the whole theory based on the concept of *śūnya*. A look at any English dictionary will indicate that the word "void" stands for "empty," "unoccupied," "containing nothing," etc. But neither the orthodox tradition (*āstika*) nor the heterodox (*nāstika*) tradition use the term with such negative implications. Śaṅkarācārya, in his commentary on the *Viṣṇusahasranāma* explicates the meaning of the word *śūnya* as *saviśeṣa rahitatvat śūnyavat* (it is without determination, hence like *śūnya*). Similarly, Nāgārjuna, the first propounder of Śūnyavāda, talks of *śūnyatā* as the ultimate *tattva*, and *tattva* in turn is defined as that, "which can be directly realized, which is calm and blissful, that where all plurality is merged, that where all cries of intellect are satisfied. In other words it is the non-dual harmonious whole."[1] Thus, the term *śūnya* is

---

1. *aparapratyayaṁ śāntaṁ prapañcairaprapañcitam,*
nirvikalpam anarthāmṛetat tattvasya lakṣaṇam.
— *Mādhyamika Kārikā*, XVIII.9

not entirely negative in its implication. Rather we can get some clue about its connotation if we look at its etymological root. *Śūnya* is derived from the root *śvi* implying "to swell." The ancient Indian mathematicians used the term *śūnya* as a number signifying the infinite (*ananta*) thereby turning it into the matrix of all the numbers. Explicating the significance of *śūnya* as the number zero further, Varāhamihira stated that what makes all numbers swell is *śūnya;* and just as there is no change in the infinite, similarly there is no change in *śūnya* either by addition or subtraction. This mathematical implication of the term *śūnya* can provide very valuable clue to one's understanding of the Mādhyamika notion of *śūnya* as well as the concept of *Śūnya Puruṣa* of the Orissan *santhas*. I shall discuss the varied nuances of the term as we procced with our discussion.

The idea of *śūnya,* though not entirely unknown to the Upaniṣadic and Vedic culture, is also not a very popular concept in the Brāhmaṇical tradition either. Texts like *Śrībhāgavatam* and *Mahopaniṣad* describe *Parama Brahman* as *Śūnyavat.* Similarly in *Viṣṇu Sahasranāma,* one can notice the use of the term *śūnyavat* with reference to Viṣṇu. Yet none of the orthodox (*āstika*) schools of Indian philosophy prefer to use the epithet *śūnya* in the context of the highest Reality or *parama Īśvara.* So it seems that the concept, *Śūnya Puruṣa* may not have a direct link with the Upaniṣadic or Purāṇic sources. So let us explore its possible connection with the Buddhist theory of Śūnyavāda, propagated by the Mādhyamika branch of Mahāyāna Buddhism.

It is well known that Nāgārjuna was the first systematic propounder of Śūnyavāda. For him, Reality is *śūnyatā,* when viewed from the phenomenal standpoint because the distinctions like existence/non-existence, affirmation/negation, do not apply to it. Again, the phenomenal world according to him is *śūnyatā,* when viewed from the absolute standpoint, because all that is phenomenal fails to represent the real essence of the being. In Nāgārjuna's words it is *niḥsvabhāva* (without a determinate essence). Thus, *śūnyatā,* as we have noted earlier, is not a negative term. For Nāgārjuna it signifies the transcendental principle that eludes the conceptual nexus applied in human thinking. It is beyond any form of intellectual categorisation, for, intellectual process requires determination and discrimination. Any attempt to determine a concept through predication of a quality implies negation of its opposite. Such predication leads to limitation as well as discrimination and duality, whereas the Reality is non-dual (*advaya*). According to the Mādhyamika theory, it is *catuṣkoṭi vinirmukta*, i.e., it is beyond the fourfold forms of categorisation.[2] In other words *śūnyatā* signifies a principle about which neither existence nor non-existence, nor a combination of both nor the negation of both, can be predicated. What Nāgārjuna and the thinkers of Śūnyavāda want to highlight is that the Reality being above all categorial dualities is indeterminate, ineffable and non-describable principle.

At this point one may very validly ask: Does not the definition of *śūnyatā* sound very much like the Advaitic definition of the *Brahman*? It is interesting to note that Gauḍapāda, one of the first systematic expounders of the Advaita Vedānta, almost agrees with Śūnyavāda in certain respects and never conceals his admiration for Buddha and his philosophy. He even uses the term *koṭi* with reference to the forms of intellect and expresses Nāgārjuna's viewpoint in a positive note. According to him, the real nature of the Absolute Reality, is obscured by four-fold forms of intellect.[3] Thus, Gauḍapāda is not exactly unfavourable to Nāgārjuna's

---

2. *atastattvam sadasadubhāyanubhayātmaka catuṣkoṭi vinirmuktaṁ śūnyameva.*

   Sarva-Darśana Saṁgraha of Mādhavācārya (tr. with Sanskrit Texts) by E.B. Cowell & A.E. Gough, (ed) K.L. Joshi, Delhi: Parimal Publications, 1986, p. 30.

3. *Āgama Śāstra of Gauḍapāda,* IV.84.

   Qtd. in C.D. Sharma, *A Critical Survey of Indian Philosophy,* Delhi: Motilal Banarsidass, 1976, p. 250.

interpretation of Reality in terms of *śūnya*. But it was Śaṅkara who gave a final shape to the Advaita metaphysics, dismisses the theory of Śūnyavāda, though his theory of *Brahman* comes closest to Nāgārjuna's conception of *śūnyatā*. Śaṅkara in his refutation of Śūnyavāda takes the word *śūnya* in the ordinary sense, implying void. Therefore, he does not mind discarding Śūnyavāda as a form of *ucchedavāda* (a theory of annihilation). In his opinion Śūnyavādins invalidly negate all phenomenal practices without having some higher truth (*anyatattva*) at their disposal.[4] Therefore, Śaṅkara had little qualms about dismissing the theory off hand. Yet Śaṅkara's explication of the concept of *Brahman* is so close to Nāgārjuna's conception of *śūnyatā* that it earns for him the sobriquet, "crypto Buddhist" (*Pracchanna Bauddha*).[5] Very much like Nāgārjuna, he too holds that *Brahman* being the Absolute Reality is beyond categorial discrimination, therefore, indescribable (*avyakta*) and *nirguṇa* (transcending determination through ascription of qualities) and *nirvikalpa* (inconceivable). In this sense there is not much of a distinction between the concepts, *śūnyatā* and *Brahman*, propounded by two apparent philosophical opponents.

Due to this uncanny similarity between Śūnyavāda and Advaitavāda in their conception of the highest Reality scholars are divided in their opinion about the origin of the theory of *Śūnya Puruṣa*. It is easier for the modern scholars to interpret the concept of *Śūnya Puruṣa* in Upaniṣadic and Advaitic terms because there is but little conceptual gap between the Advaitic *Brahman* and the Mādhyamika *śūnya*. So there is a tendency on the part of many scholars to wish away the impact of Buddhism on Orissan *bhakti* movement. They prefer to interpret it purely in terms of Advaitism. This claim of course

---

4. Śaṅkarācārya, *Śārīraka Bhāṣya*, II.2.31.
5. *māyāvādamsacchāstraṁ pracchanaṁ bauddhamevatat*.
   Qtd. in H.P. Sastri, *Bauddha Dharma* (Bengali), Calcutta: Purvasa Ltd., undated, p. 31.

cannot be brusquely cast aside. The non-dualistic leanings in the *santha* metaphysics along with the frequent use of the term *Brahman* appended to *śūnya* give credence to their thesis. Therefore, it is not surprising that Mahimā *dharma* of Orissa that is entirely based on *śūnya*-centric metaphysics is interpreted by the modern exponents of this cult as an extension of the Upaniṣadic Advaitism. They now call it Viśuddhādvaitism. But it seems incongruous that the concept of *śūnya* that had already become a part of Oriyā culture since thirteenth-fourteenth century could have anything to do with a fully Sanskritised classical theory of the Upaniṣads. The *śūnya*-based theory that was espoused by Orissan *santha*s (including the *santha*s of the Mahimā *dharma*) seemed to be more inspired by the vernacular literature of the land than that of the Upaniṣads.

All the confusions about tracing the origin of the *śūnya*-centric non-dualistic metaphysics of the Orissan *santha* tradition can be cleared if we keep in mind the following fact. Neither Śaṅkara's *Brahman* nor Nāgārjuna's *śūnyatā* is an object of devotion. Śaṅkara introduces the concept of *saguṇa Brahman/ Īśvara* to accommodate the theory of *upāsanā* or *bhakti*. So it will be unjust to say that the Orissan Vaiṣṇavism is nothing but a replica of the non-dualistic philosophy of the Advaita. By the same logic we cannot say that the Oriyā Vaiṣṇavas were the followers of the Mādhyamika Śūnyavāda. Obviously, it points to some other source. I intend take up the issue a little later.

The Concept of Puruṣa and its Implications

Now it is my turn to draw attention to another crucial concept that has led to a lot of confusion about the interpretation of the Orissan *santha* metaphysics. This is about the use of the term *puruṣa* in conjunction with the term *śūnya*. We find that the term *puruṣa* has been normally used in the Saṁhitās and Brāhmaṇa literature in the sense of a person, a "human being."

But in the earlier Upaniṣads, the word has been used in the following senses:

1. A human being.
2. The individual soul.
3. The presiding deity of some elements or the personal God.
4. The impersonal or abstract cosmic soul (*Brahman*).

We may note that the Oriyā *santha*s use the term *puruṣa* in none of these senses exclusively. It neither refers to individual soul nor to these abstract *ātman-Brahman*. For them, though attibuteless and indeterminate, *śūnya puruṣa* is an object of devotion and in a certain sense, a personal God. In this context it will be relevant if we refer to the Puruṣasūkta of the *Ṛgveda*. In this *sūkta* the word *puruṣa* has been used to signify a cosmic person. Here *puruṣa* is identified with the *Jñāna Puruṣa* Viṣṇu. This identification of *puruṣa* of the *Ṛgveda* with Viṣṇu — out of whose body the whole creation emanates — leads to the development of the idea of *Viśvarūpa* of Kṛṣṇa as enunciated in the *Gītā*. In this treatise various phenomena of the universe are delineated to be different parts of the body of the immeasurable Viṣṇu. This interpretation of the Godhead comes closest to the *santha* philosophers' conception of the *Śūnya Puruṣa*. According to the *Gītā*, there are two types of *puruṣa*, the perishable one (body) and the imperishable one (soul). Since the Lord is conceived as transcending both these categories of *puruṣa*, He is known as *Puruṣottama*. So many scholars[6] jump to the conclusion that the idea of *Śūnya Puruṣa* owes its origin to the theory of the *Puruṣottama* of *Śrīmad Bhagavad-Gītā*. Interestingly enough, Lord Jagannātha is also popularly known as "Puruṣottama." In fact, the name "Jagannātha" with reference to this deity of Purī is of much

---

6. K.C. Mishra, *The Cult of Jagannātha*, Calcutta: Firma K.L.M., 1984, p. 177.

later origin. This may provide further strength to the claim of the scholars who argue that the word *puruṣa*, in case of the theory of *Śūnya Puruṣa* actually refers to the *Puruṣottama* of the *Bhagavad-Gītā*; and therefore the theory of *Śūnya Puruṣa* has nothing to do with the Buddhistic notion of *śūnyatā*.

There seems to be some amount of plausibility in the claim of the scholars who swear by exclusively Brāhamaṇical origin of the theory of *Śūnya Puruṣa*. But before we reach this conclusion we have to clarify certain perplexing issues. First, what was the need on the part of the Orissan *santha*s for introducing a new concept, viz., *Śūnya Puruṣa* when Jagannātha was already known as *Puruṣottama*? Had the theory of the Orissan *santha*s been entirely inspired by the *Gītā* they could have straightforward used the word *Puruṣottama* instead of *Śūnya Puruṣa*. The use of this word would have been more befitting. Besides, a deeper look at the theory of *Śūnya Puruṣa* may lead to another pertinent question. Did the Orissan *santha*s present the concept in the sense in which Śrīkr̥ṣṇa is presented in the *Gītā*? There are several factors that have to be sorted out before we ensure a positive answer to the question. First, why the epithet *śūnya* is attached to *puruṣa*? Such use is never found in the *Gītā*. Second, the Orissan *santha*s very frequently talk of *nirguṇa upāsanā*, which is alien to the philosophy of the *Gītā*. So we note that the Vaiṣṇavas of Orissa do not follow the conception of *puruṣa* as found in the *Bhagavad-Gītā*, on a dotted line. However, the most important fact that comes in our way of accepting the sole influence of the *Gītā*, or for that matter any Brāhmaṇical work in shaping of the theory of *Śūnya Puruṣa*, is the frequent reference to Jagannātha, the symbolic representation of *Śūnya Puruṣa*, as the Buddha. Two verses, one from Sāralā Dāsa and the other from Caitanya Dāsa may be taken here to prove the non-Brāhmaṇical shade in their theory.

Sāralā Dāsa states:

You are present in the grand temple
on the shore of *Mahodadhi*

You have appeared as Buddha in the *kaliyuga*
to save the sinners of the World.[7]

Caitanya Dāsa, a contemporary of Pañcasakhā, writes:

Hari, the wisest one,
is born in this world as Buddha,
to despise the path of rituals and fire sacrifices
and to eulogise the *Brahma jñāna*.[8]

These two verses clearly refer to Buddha, as he has been delineated in the history as well as in the Buddhist literature. In the Mahāyāna texts, Buddha has been regarded as the embodiment of *karuṇā* (compassion). It is stated that the Buddha was born and reborn for the deliverance of the humanity from the clutches of ignorance and suffering. The first verse quoted above seems to refer to this dimension of Buddhism. But the second verse, composed by Caitanya Dāsa, exposes more noticeably the Buddhistic leanings of these medieval *santha* philosophers. Here the line "to despise the path of rituals and fire sacrifices" clearly refers to Buddha's protest against the superfluous practices propagated by the Vedas. In fact, Caitanya Dāsa in his work *Nirguṇa Mahātmya* takes up the twelve *avatāra*s of Viṣṇu sequentially to expose the wrongs committed in each of His incarnations, including that of Kṛṣṇa. He accuses Kṛṣṇa of indulging in love dalliance with the cowherd girls of *gopa* (*gopī*) and extramarital relationship with his aunt (Rādhā). But Caitanya Dāsa spares Buddha and conceives this incarnation (which he prefers to

7. *mahodadhitīre baḍadeulare basi,*
daridra mānaṅka dukha deuacha dhvaṁsi.
bauddharūpare kaliyuge avatāra,
hoiṇa papījanaṅku karucha uddhāra.
— Sāralā Dāsa, *Mahābhārata* (Oriyā), Madhya Parva.

8. *prabuddha buddha avatāre hari janmile saṁsāre.*
yajña karmaku nindā kaḷe, brahma jñānaku praśaṅsiḷe.
— Caitanya Dāsa, *Nirguṇa Mahātmya* XVI

name as Buddha-Nārāyaṇa) as the most perfect. Lord Buddha is presented here as the champion of *ātmājñāna* and as a *yogī*.[9] These references clearly indicate that the word Buddha is not just an epithet. These *santhas* were referring to the historical persona called the Buddha, who was well known for his revolt against the meaningless rituals sanctioned by the Vedas. So it will be hasty on our part to conclude that the word *puruṣa* actually signifies the *Puruṣottama* of the *Gītā* or the *puruṣa* of the Upaniṣads. We find that the concept of *puruṣa* could have been easily allied to the theory of *Puruṣottama* of the *Gītā* or the concept of *puruṣa* as the personal God as presented in *Śvetāśvatara Upaniṣad*, had not the *santhas* of Orissa frequently referred to Buddha as the *avatāra* of Jagannātha.

In all probablity, the Oriyā *santhas* used the term *puruṣa* to suggest that the highest Reality is not just an abstract principle but a real presence; a potential ground of the cosmic existence. It also appears that the idea of *Śūnya Puruṣa* is not exclusively taken from any specific source. I have already indicated that there does not seem to be any strong discordance between Śaṅkara's conception of *Brahman* and the Buddhist concept of *śūnyatā*. Since both the ideas were not alien to Orissan *santhas* they did not have any compunction about using the term *Śūnya Puruṣa* or *Śūnya Brahman* with reference to the highest Reality.

Śūnya Puruṣa and Buddha-Jagannātha

Before I go into the details of how the Orissan *santhas* delineate the typical nuances of the idea of *Śūnya Puruṣa,* I intend to say a few words about the very strange concept that may be said to have few parallels in the Hindu tradition. It is the idea of Buddha-Jagannātha. Here one comes across a unique alliance of two Gods — Jagannātha, the revered deity of the Hindus: and Buddha, the revered God of the Buddhists. Such a coalition appears more perplexing in view of the fact that

9. *ātmājñānare thira mana rakhile buddhanārāyaṇa.*
— *Nirguṇa Mahātmya*, XVI

Buddhism has always been perceived as an opponent, throwing a great challenge for the sustenance of Hinduism. So the great *ācārya*s like Śaṅkara and Kumārila Bhaṭṭa had targetted this system for a merciless demolition at the conceptual level. Naturally it appears rather strange that a *bhakti* tradition centering on a purely Hinduised deity like Viṣṇu could identify Him with the Buddha. No doubt the Buddha had been accommodated within the Hindu fold as an incarnation of Viṣṇu during thirteenth century. But Vaiṣṇavas have never given him the same status as Viṣṇu. Rather, the Gauḍīya Vaiṣṇavism, (which was equally popular in Orissa during the Pañcasakhā period) had the choicest criticisms preserved for the Buddhist. Though Oriyā *santha*s regard Caitanya as the incarnation of Buddha,[10] in the famous biography of Caitanaya, entitled *Caitanya Caritāmṛta* it is stated, "he is a wretch who denies form to God; touch not, behold not that slave of death. The Buddhists are atheists for not reciting the Vedas."[11]

Though it is matter of constant debate, yet it remains a fact that we come across such an extraordinary combination of two terms, viz., Jagannātha and Buddha, for the first time in the *Jñānasiddhi* of Indrabhūti, the noted *siddha* of Vajrayāna School of Buddhism. While speaking about the history of Buddhism in Orissa. I have mentioned that Indrabhūti was the King of the Sambalaka region of Orissa. In the opening stanza of this book he writes:

---

10. (a) *baudha rūpare āmbhe hoibu prakāśa,*
āmbha kalā jai puṇi nadiyā dvīpare,
caitana rūpe āmbhe prakāśibu thare.
— *Śūnya Saṁhitā*, XI.230-31

(b) *caitanya viṣṇu avatāra bahile bauddha śarīra.*
— Īśvara Dāsa, *Caitanya Bhāgavata*, XV

11. *Caitanya Caritāmṛta*, tr. J.N. Sarkar, vol. II, qtd. in K.C. Mishra, *The Cult of Jagannātha*, Calcutta: Firma K.L.M., 1984, p. 191.

> My salutations to you, oh, Jagannātha, the object of worship of all wise people. You are as expansive as the sky, identical with Buddha and source of all power.[12]

Of course, this oft-quoted stanza has generated a lot of controversy among the scholars of religious history. The critics who swear by the total Brāhmaṇical interpretation of the Jagannātha cult dismiss the conjecture of any link between Buddhism and Jagannāthism on the basis of the use of the word Jagannātha by Indrabhūti. They argue that the term "Jagannātha" etymologically stands for "the Lord of the Universe." This term, therefore, is used in the Buddhistic literature to refer to Lord Buddha. So on the basis of the use of the term Jagannātha by Indrabhūti we cannot afford to claim his affiliation to the cult of Jagannātha. But there are other evidences to support the claim that Buddhism had a fair amount of influence on the Jagannātha cult. Let us for example, look at the following popular *mantra* of the Vaiṣṇavite treatise, *Nilādri Mahodayam*, a treatise believed to be composed in fourteenth century CE — *dārubrahma svarūpāya tasmai buddhātmane namaḥ*.[13] In this *mantra* Lord Jagannātha, the *dāru Brahman* (the *Brahman* in wooden form) is invoked as the Buddha. Here the identification of Jagannātha and the Buddha is more conspicuous. Similarly we come across a common *mantra* shared by both the Buddhists and Hindus of Orissa with slight variations. The Buddhist prayer is:

> *kśamasva man jagannātha sarvapāpa vināśanam,*
> *sarva kārya prāṇadevaḥ praṇamāmi sureśvaram.*[14]

---

12. *praṇipatya jagannāthaṁ sarvajīna-varārcitaṁ,*
sarva buddhamayaṁ siddhi vyāpinaṁ gaganopamaṁ.

Indrabhūti, *Jñānasiddhi*, ed., B. Bhattacharya, Baroda: Gaekwad Oriental Series, no. 44, 1929, p. 31.

13. *Nīlādri Mahodayam*, 6.22 b.

14. Sylvan Levi, vol. 67, Boroda: Gaekwad Oriental Series, 1933, qtd. in H.S. Patnaik, *Lord Jagannātha His Temple, Cult and Festivals*, New Delhi: Arya Prakashan, 1994, p. 15.

In the Hindu version of this *mantra* the word *nirākāram* is used in place of *vināśanam;* and the word *idam dehī* is used in place of *prāṇadevaḥ*. So it cannot be denied that there existed a close link between both the cults. The *santhas* of Orissa made this bond more pronounced and articulate.

Thus, the bond that had its roots in the religious and cultural history of the land finds a full-blooded expression in the works of the Oriyā *santhas*. If Indrabhūti pays obeisance to Jagannātha in several passages of his work, entitled *Jñānasiddhi*, then the Oriyā *santhas* do not waste time in responding with equal zest. The *santha* literature, right from the period of Sāralā Dāsa (fifteenth century) to Dinakṛṣṇa Dāsa (seventeenth century) are replete with references to the Buddha-Jagannātha. Acyutānanda's *Śūnya Saṁhitā*, Jagannātha Dāsa's *Dāru Brahma-Gītā* and Kṛṣṇa Dāsa's *Deula Tolā* give us different versions of the story of the manifestation of Viṣṇu/Kṛṣṇa as the Buddha. In *Śūnya Saṁhitā*, Acyutānanda claims to have received the following message from the *Śūnya Puruṣa*:

> Hear me, O Acyuta I shall reveal myself again as the Buddha in the *kaliyuga*. I shall keep my true form hidden and appear as the Buddha.[15]

Examples of this kind abound in the writings of these Vaiṣṇava *santhas*, who despite being the worshippers of Viṣṇu were inclined towards the Buddhistic ideals. I quote here the following lines from Dinakṛṣṇa Dāsa, a *santha* of post-Pañcasakhā period that may give us some idea about how the identification of the Buddha and Jagannātha is complete and foolproof. He elaborates:

> Śrī Jagannātha you have appeared as Buddha in the *Nilagiri*. O Bauddha — the Lord of the *Nīlādri* — you have taken the form of the wooden God. All the ten incarnations

15. *boile acyuta tumbhe śuṇa āmbha vāṇī,*
kaḷiyuge bauddharūpe prakāśilu puṇi.
kaḷiyuge buddharūpa nijarūpa gopya. . .
— Acyutānanda Dāsa, *Śūnya Saṁhitā* XI

> (of Viṣṇu) have emerged from you. Incarnations after incarnations may come and go but they ultimately arise from and dissolve in the Bauddha Jagannātha.[16]

We find that the unique alliance of Jagannātha and Buddha never appeared atypical to the common man of Orissa. So, the *santhas* could very freely bring about this wonderful amalgamation of apparently inimical religio-philosophical trends without disturbing the Vaiṣṇavite affiliation of the Jagannātha *dharma*. Thus, the concept of *Śūnya Puruṣa* cannot be interpreted solely in terms of the Upaniṣadic and Advaitic ideology as this theory cannot be segregated completely from Jagannātha *dharma* and the concept of Jagannātha cannot be detached from the notion of Buddha *avatāra*.

II

The Nature of Śūnya Puruṣa

Now let us see how the Oriyā *santhas* expound the theory of *Śūnya Puruṣa*. Acyutānanda Dāsa's *Śūnya Saṁhitā*, *Anākāra Saṁhitā* and *Śūnya Saṁhitā Ṭīkā*; Balarāma Dāsa's *Virāṭa-Gītā*, *Brahmāṇḍa Bhūgola* and *Sārasvata-Gītā*; Jagannātha Dāsa's *Tulā Bhiṇā*, Caitanya Dāsa's *Nirguṇa Mahātmya* and *Viṣṇugarbha Purāṇa*, Dvārakā Dāsa's *Parace-Gītā* and *Chatiśa Gupta-Gītā* and Bhīma Bhoi's *Stuti Cintāmaṇi* and *Brahma Nirūpaṇa-Gītā*, deal with the concept of *Śūnya Puruṣa/Brahman*. From these works we can garner the varied nuances of this concept.

---

16. *bauda rūpe nīlagiri, śrī jagannātha bije kari.*
baudha nīlādri gosāiṅ, basichi yogārūḍha hoi.
kāṭhā pāṣāṇa rūpa dhari, dāru brahmare bije kari.
keteheṅ yuga jāichi, bauda avatāra achi.
bauda prabhu nirākāra, hoile daśa avatāra.
jeteka avatāra śreṇī, bauhu ātajāta puṇi.

Bauddha-Brahma Likhana, qtd. in Pradhan, *Prācīna Oṛiyā Sāhityare Nirguṇa Dhārā*, p. 113.

For the *santhas* of Orissa *Śūnya Puruṣa* is the ultimate Reality — the one and unique principle. It transcends all names and forms that charactarise the phenomenal world. Neither the categories of thought nor the forms of speech can envelope it. In this sense *Śūnya Puruṣa* is non-conceptualisable, non-categorisable, and thus non-graspable and ineffable in nature. How do we describe such a Reality Supreme? Its indeterminateness (*nirguṇattva* and *nirviśeṣattva*) evades words. No description is enough to catch its essence. It has no name, nor identifying mark, no specific description can measure up to it. A man's helplessness to explain the nature of this sort of Reality is perhaps best expressed in the following lines of Acyutānanda:

> There is nothing but only *śūnya* and *śūnya*, as if it is endless. There is no mark or sign so that it can be recognised. How shall I explain it? With what illustration? For no description can fit it.[17]

He further adds:

> Most devout persons and even gods fail to know Him. How can they? For, He is nothing. He is just Himself, for He has no parallel. If at all we search for a parallel then He himself is his own parallel.[18]

But if we have to describe *Śūnya Puruṣa* at all, then we may follow *Santha* Balarāma Dāsa, one of the prominent *santhas* of

---

17. *śūnya śūnya boli aśeṣa śūnya,*
śūnyara nāhiṅ kichi cinha varṇa.
śūnyara upamā ki debi muhiṅ,
jete lakya dele ghaṭiba nāhiṅ.
From the poem "Śūnya śūnya boli," *Acyutānanda Granthāvalī*, Kavitā khaṇḍa, ed., R. Chainy, Nemala: Acyutānanda Smṛuti Sansada, 1989, p. 94.

18. *aneka tapī loka thile, īśvara ādi kehi na jāṇile.*
kāhuṅ jānime se nuhai kichi, kevala tāhā tahiṅ bhāva achhi.
tāhāku āna paṭāntara nāhiṅ, tāhā paṭāntara tāhāra tahiṅ.
— Acyutānanda, *Śabda Brahma Saṁhitā* I

the Pañcasakhā group. He very lucidly explains what exactly is implied by the word in the following verse:

> He has no form, no outline,
> He is *Śūnyapuruṣa*
> He is the *Brahman* and the *Śūnya*.
> How can He have any name? [19]

Acyutānanda Dāsa also reiterates this in the following manner:

> It has no shape, no colour,
> It is invisible and without a name.
> This *Brahman* is called *Śūnya Brahman*.[20]

Santha Balarāma Dāsa expresses this same idea in a straightforward manner in the dialogue of Kṛṣṇa; "*Mahāśūnya* is my abode, how can speech reach me. In fact, no name can be ascribed to me since I am the formless *Brahman*."[21]

The above-mentioned lines may remind one of the famous Upaniṣadic line "That from which all speech with mind turns away, not having reached it"[22] (Also *Kena* and *Māṇḍukya* reiterate the same idea). It appears that the tone and tenor of these *santha*s are very much in line with the Upaniṣadic and Advaitic theories of the *Brahman*. It is, thus, obvious that any philosophical system following this line of thought is bound to grope for the right expression to express the inexpressible.

However, such similarity does not ensure that these *santha*s were restating philosophy of the Upaniṣadic non-dualism. One

---

19. *jāhāra rūpa rekha nāhiṅ, śūnya puruṣa śūnyadehī.*
śūnyare bhrahma sinā thāi, āvara nāma thiba kāhiṅ.
— Balarāma Dāsa, *Virāṭa-Gītā* I

20. *nāhi tāhāra rūpa varṇa, adṛśa avarṇa tā cinha.*
tāhāku brahmā boli kahi, śūnya bramhati se bolāi.
— Acyutānanda, *Brahma Saṁhitā* IV

21. *mahāśūnyareti viśrāma sethāre kāhiṅ achi nāma,*
bevāre mora nāma nāhiṅ arūpa brahma mu aṭai.
— Balarāma Dāsa, *Virāṭa-Gītā* I

22. *yato vāco nivartante aprāpya manasā saha,*
— *Taittirīya Upaniṣad* II.9. 1

may note here how wonderfully the Buddhistic notion of *śūnya* and the Brāhmaṇical view of *Brahman* are amalgamated. Here these *santhas* expressly state that there is no conceptual distinction between the *Brahman* and the *śūnya*. It is obvious that these *santhas* had no problem in realising that there is virtually very little conceptual disparity between these two concepts. But this tone of amalgamation is further continued with the identification of *Śūnya Brahman/Śūnya Puruṣa* with the *Parama Īśvara* (the God or the highest Being). In Acyutānanda's own words *Śūnya Puruṣa/Brahman* is also *nirguṇa parama īśvara* (the non-qualitative highest Being). Thus, we find that all the apparently incompatible concepts like *Brahman, śūnya* and *parama Īśvara* merge into one to denote the same ineffable unique Reality. One must also note how two incongruent concepts, viz., *nirguṇa* and *Īśvara*, become inalienably one in the philosophy of the *santhas*.

However, the words *Brahman, Śūnya* and *Nirguṇa Īśvara* are not felt to be enough. This same predicament is faced by any philosophical system anchoring on non-dualism. So we find that most often Upaniṣads take recourse to negative predication or contradictory predication as the best way of overcoming this paradoxical situation. We come across such negative descriptions in the Upaniṣads like *Kaṭha*.[23] But the *Bṛhadāraṇyaka Upaniṣad* uses the most cryptic expression in the form of *neti neti* (not this not this). The famous Buddhist text *Prajñā Pāramitā Hṛdayagarbha* also uses the phrase *neti neti* with reference to the highest Reality. Śaṅkara too applies such words with negative implications as, *nirvikāra, anirvacanīya, nirviśeṣa,* and *nirvikalpa*. Nāgārjuna presents it as *niḥsvabhāva* and *niśprapañca*. The Vajrayānīs on the other hand prefer to use the expression *avināśī* and *adāhī*. The Orissan *santhas* face a similar predicament in describing the ultimate Reality. So they describe the *Śūnya Puruṣa* as *nirākāra/anākāra* (formless), *avyakta* (undescribable), *Aḷekha* (non-scriptable), *niḥśabda* (without an

---

23. *aśabdamasparśamarūpamavyayam.*
— *Kaṭha Upaniṣad* I.3.15

element of speeech), *nirañjana* (taintless) and *anādi* (beginningless). Perhaps any thinker who conceives the highest Reality as non-conceptualisable is bound to take recourse to such descriptions. Thus, we find Divākara Dāsa attempting to describe *Śūnya Puruṣa* in the following way:

He is without quality and non-corruptible,
He is eternal and all enveloping
Immutable and without change.
He is unmanifest, without activity.
Neither subtle nor gross, neither short
Nor long
Just know him to be
Without determination (*nirviśeṣa*).[24]

Again Jagannātha Dāsa writes:

God is *nirguṇa* without beginning and end
Neither has growth nor depletion.
He is one and eternal
Without ever limited by adjuncts (*upādhi*)
He is the eternal witness and all blissful
The phenomenal world is but a mental construct
That leads to the perception of varied forms.[25]

---

24. *brahma sccidānanda jāṇa, nirvikāra se je nirguṇa.*
nitya je puṇi śāśvata, akṣara avyaya sehita.
nisphala niskriya je śānta, niravadya nirañjana ta.
sthula nohe se aṇu nuhe, hrasva dīrgha se ta nuhe.
nāhiṅ tāhāra parimāṇa, kevala nirviśeṣa jāṇa.

Divākara Dāsa, *Jagannātha Caritāmṛta*, 182, qtd. in N.N. Pradhan, *Prācīna Oṛiyā Sāhityre Nirguṇa Dhārā*, Cuttack: Dharmagrantha Store, 1986, p. 366.

25. *nitya nirguṇa bhagavāna, se nuheṅ ādi abasāna.*
jāhāra kṣaya vṛddhi nāhi, alapa bahuta nuhai.
se nitya eka rūpe thāi, ādi upādhi jāra nāhi.
nitya ānandamaya sākṣi, saṁsāre ete mātra lekhi.
manara kalpanā jagata, je rūpa dekhi nānā mata.
— Jagannātha Dāsa, *Śrīmad Bhāgavata*, XI.4

Sometimes the Upaniṣadic absolutists take the help of contradictory predicates, such as, that moves (*tat ejati*), that moves not (*tat na ejati*) to describe the Highest Reality. This is believed to help them in expressing the all-inclusive nature of the Reality. Similarly, we find that the *santha* poets of Orissa sometimes prefer to describe this Reality in contradictory terms. Yaśovanta Dāsa, for example writes:

He is not fire yet burns
Not water still flows.
He has no feet yet moves far and wide.
No eyes, but sees all.
He has no ears, but listens to far off voices.
He has no knowledge, but wisest of all.[26]

Again in the absence of a clear-cut positive predicate the *Śūnya Puruṣa* sometimes has also been described in a very mystical manner. A very popular verse from *Śūnya Saṁhitā* can be taken for illustration:

Well did you ask
the mystery of the *śūnya puruṣa*.
Śūnya puruṣa is the prisoner
of the abode of *śūnya*.
Śūnya puruṣa creates all illusions,
yet remains detached from it.

x x x

---

26. *agni nuhai se jaluchi kāhiṅ,*
jala nuhai se kemante vahi.

x x x

pāda nāhiṅ kenhe dūraku jāi,
cakṣu nahi se samasta dekhai.
karṇa nāhi dūra ḍāka śūṇai
vidyā nāhi sehu jñāna aṭai.

Yaśovanta Dāsa, *Ātmā Parace Gītā*, qtd. in C.R. Das, *Santha* (*Bhakti*) *Sāhitya*, p. 316.

Śūnya Puruṣa is well-versed
in crafty devices;
so the author of all sorts of activities.
Śūnya Puruṣa is the killer,
Yet, the saviour[27]

In their attempt to fully explore the range of its comprehensiveness the *santha* philosophers sometimes question the very adequacy of the terms *śūnya* and *nirguṇa* themselves. Almost like the Mahāyāna Buddhists they are apprehensive about the very use of the term *śūnya* with regard to the highest Reality lest it leads to a form of determinism. Mahāyāna Buddhism expresses certain reservations about the use of the term *śūnyatā,* since by ascribing *śūnyatā* to the highest Reality one is likely to exclude that aspect of the Reality that may not come under the confines of this particular predicate. They want to be absolutely sure that the inconceivability of the highest principle is not diluted in any way. In their opinion even the use of the word *śūnyatā* may smack of some sort of determination. So Nāgārjuna clarifies that,

> *Śūnyatā* (as the highest *tattva*), can be stated neither as *śūnya* nor *aśūnya;* nor can it be described as *śūnya* and *aśūnya* both, nor a negation of both.[28]

In a similar vein the Vajrayānī treatise *Prājñopāya Viniścaya Siddhi* maintains that in the state of *nirvāṇa,* "there is neither the knowledge of *śūnyatā* nor *aśūnyatā,* for the very thought

---

27. *bhalā pacārilu gupata sandhi,*
śūnya-puruṣa śūnya ghare bandī.
śūnya puruṣa udāsare rahe,
śūnya puruṣa savu māyā bhyāeṅ.
— *Śūnya Saṁhitā* IX

28. *śūnyamiti na vaktavyaṁ aśūnyamiti na vyaktavyam,*
ubhayaṁ nobhayaṁ caiva prajñptyartha tu kathyate.
— *Mādhyamika Kārikā* XXII.11

of these concepts may lead to conceptualized distinctions."[29] In brief, for the Mahāyānīs the true core of *śūnya* as the highest Reality transcends all forms of contradictions, as well as, conceptual binaries. This same idea is echoed in the writings of Pañcasakhā, too. Yaśovanta Dāsa describes the highest Reality in the following words.

> He (the Highest Reality) can be described as neither of the nature of *śūnya* nor *niḥśūnya* neither pure form nor impure form, neither *rūpa* nor *arūpa*, but as pure *tattva*.[30]

Elaborating this idea further Acyutānanda says that the concept of *Śūnyapuruṣa*, in the true sense of the term, transcends all opposing descriptions like *rūpa* and *arūpa*, *sākāra* and *nirākāra*, *nirguṇa* and *saguṇa*. Only by looking at the seemingly opposites with an attitude of equanimity can one understand the whole range of truth.[31] Thus, both *rūpa* and *arūpa* merge in the *Śūnya Puruṣa*. Similarly, regarding the *nirguṇa* and *saguṇa* distinctions he offers an illuminating example. He writes:

> A bird can only fly with both the wings. It can have a perfect

---

29. *na śūnyabhāvanām kuryāt nāpica aśūnya bhavānām*
aśūnya santyajed yogī ñaca aśūnyam parityajed.
Ananga Vajra, *Prajñopāya Viniścaya Siddhi*, ed., B. Bhattacharyya Gaekwad Oriental Series, 44, 1929, IV.5.8.

30. *na śūnya rūpam na viśūnya rūpam*
na śuddharūpam na viśuddha rūpam.
rūpam virūpam na bhajāmi
kiñcit svarūpa rūpaka paramārtham.
— Yaśovanta Dāsa, *Premabhakti Gītā* 1.71

31. *arūparu rūpa prakāśa heba,*
rūpa jaiṅa arūpare miśiba.
rūpa arūpaku sama karithibu
samatā rūpare savu pāibu.
— Acyutānānda, *Tattvabodhinī* I

> vision with both the eyes. In the absence of one, it becomes one-eyed, and in the absence of both, it is totally blind. This is the essence of *saguṇa-nirguṇa* relationship.[32]

Here we come across a purely non-dualistic scheme in which God (*Īśvara*) is seen as *śūnya* and *śūnya* is described as God. In the process the Oriyā *santha*s display a certain amount of guts in defying the traditional tenets of Hindu theology. So they do not hesitate to dismiss all that is accepted as sacred and sacrosanct in the orthodox Hindu tradition. Even, in certain cases, their voice seems to have a non-Brāhmaṇical undertone. Not only they discard all forms of accepted rituals like pilgrimage, fasting, use of holy marks, etc., which were and are very much a part of orthodox Hindu religion, they even discard the practice of idol-worship. The following lines of *Santha* Dvārakā Dāsa may give us some hints about their boldness of approach as far as religion was concerned. He declares:

> All chanting, rituals, pilgrimages are meaningless, all the arrays of gods and goddesses are nothing but illusions.[33]

He offers the argument that the *Brahman* is to be realised within one's own self. A person who has realised this would see such idols as nothing but pieces of stone. This same dismissive attitude is found in the writings of Acyutānanda and Caitanya Dāsa too. They sometimes even discard the Vedas, the most sacred reference point of Brāhmaṇical thought. But what makes us sit up and take note of this unique form of

---

32. *dui je ḍeṇāre pakṣī uḍikari jāi,*
dui je cakṣure sehi saṁsāre khelai.
eka je na thile kaṇā dui gale anḍha,
eṇukari nirguṇa saguṇa sehi bheda.
— Acyutānanda, *Gurubhakti Gītā* II

33. *japa tapa tīrtha karma pūjā brata micha,*
devā devī patala ye māyāmāna tuchha.
— Dvārakā Dāsa, *Chatiśa Gupta-Gītā* XII

Vaiṣṇavism is their fortitude in pursuing their own philosophical stand. Despite being self-proclaimed Vaiṣṇavas they do not even spare Viṣṇu, understood as a sectarian Godhead. If *Śūnya Puruṣa* is ineffable and indeterminate, then He has to transcend the limited predicates attached to Viṣṇu, however perfect they may be. The following lines of *Santha* Caitanya Dāsa, a contemporary of the Pañcasakhā, is simply striking in its tone. While singing the glory of the *Śūnya Puruṣa* he states:

> Even a hundred thousands of Brahmā would not succeed in measuring the lower part of *śūnya*; nor can hundred thousands of Viṣṇu measure its upper portion. Mahādeva, too, would fail to gauge *śūnya*'s length and breadth. *Śūnya* and *Aḷekha* (non-scriptable/non-describable) are concomitant. Thus, *Aḷekha* is in the womb of *śūnya* and *śūnya* is in the womb of *Aḷekha*. Whoever is *Aḷekha puruṣa* He too is *śūnya*.[34]

In the above stanza Caitanya Dāsa uses the term *Aḷekha*[35] frequently. The term means "non-scriptable," or the indescrible

---

34. *lakṣe brahmā hele taḷa śūnyaku na kaḷiba,*
lakṣe viṣṇu upare śūnyaku kaḷi na pāriba.
dīrgha prati śūnyaku lakṣe mahādeva,
adyāpi bhramile se kaḷi na pāriba.
śūnyara prati dīrgha śūnya sthali jete,
Aḷekhara vistāra sthali aṭe sete.
śūnya garbhe Aḷekha Aḷekha garbhe śūnya,
Aḷekha puruṣa śūnya aṭai samāna.
— Caitanya Dāsa, *Viṣṇugarbha Purāṇa* III

35. The word *Aḷekha* is often confused with *alakha*. The word *alakha* is a colloquial expression for the word *alakṣya*, i.e., invisible. But the Oriyā *santha*s make it explicitly clear that *Aḷekha* is the antonym of *lekha* (scriptable). Caitanya Dāsa, for example, analyses the word in the following way:

"As it could not be made explicit through writing, that is why the Reality is called *Aḷekha*."

lekha karanteṇa jahuṅ prakāśa nohilā,
Aḷekha boliṇa nāma teṇu se bahilā.
— Caitanya Dāsa, *Viṣṇugarbha Purāṇa* IV.

Reality. Similarly Balarāma Dāsa conceives the trinity, viz., Brahmā, Viṣṇu and Maheśvara, who are offered the most exalted position in Hindu scheme of divinity, as evolutes of the *Śūnya Puruṣa*.[36] Though depicted as Vaiṣṇavas, these Orissan *santhas* are in no sense theological in their approach.

Śūnya Puruṣa and Jagannātha

From our discussion so far it may appear that we are heading towards a very consistent form of absolutistic metaphysical theory; something very much in the line with Śaṅkara's Advaitavāda or Nāgārjuna's Śūnyavāda. But this does not happen in the case of the Orissan *santhas*, for they not only talk of *bhakti* but also project Lord Jagannātha as the embodiment of *Śūnya Puruṣa*. He is not a pure abstraction or absolute void. As the receptacle of all that is there in the phenomenal world, *Śūnya Puruṣa* is an object of love and worship also. So in this context a valid question may be raised. If *Śūnya Puruṣa* is not identifiable with any of the popular gods, and not even Viṣṇu, then how come He is identified with Jagannātha? To this crucial question the Pañcasakhā have an interesting answer. In fact, Balarāma Dāsa raises this question in his *Virāṭa-Gītā* through Arjuna: He asks, "If you are formless *Brahman* then how do you bear so many names?" To this paradoxical question the Lord has a very characteristic answer. He says:

> In reality I do not have a name. My devotees are like my father. As a father gives names to his child out of love, similarly my devotees call me by different names.[37]

Once the importance of the *bhakta* (devotee) is introduced and his emotion and the devotion are highlighted the *santhas* do

---

36. Balarāma Dāsa, *Brahmāṇḍa Bhūgola* I.

37. *arūpa brahma tu bolāu, ete nāma kimpā bahu?*
In reply Lord says,
arjuna nāma mora jete bhakata dele toṣa citte.
— Balarāma Dāsa, *Virāṭa Gītā* II

not find any difficulty in incorporating the idea of a personal God. In case of the Oriyā *santhas*, Jagannātha (already accepted as the presiding deity of this land), is projected as the highest object of devotion. However, they take meticulous care in clarifying their position regarding such a paradoxical stand. So we find Acyutānanda explaining, "The Lord is definitely without a form. He acquires form only for his devotees."[38] He further elaborates:

> He is the *Brahman*
> One lettered (*auṁ*) taintless.
> But in devotee's devotion he appears
> as embodied wooden God Jagannātha.[39]

The above-mentioned passages, to some extent, assuage the feeling of discomfort arising out of accommodating non-conceptualisability of the *Śūnya Puruṣa* with that of the ideas associated with a personal God. But still the introduction of *bhakti* in the context of a hard-hitting theory of abstract non-dualism may not appear very consistent. One may still very validly ask — how such a radical theory delineating the Reality as non-categorisable principle could accommodate the element of *bhakti*? We know that both Śaṅkara and Nāgārjuna steer clear of such ideas as *bhakti* and *upāsanā* to remain faithful to their metaphysical stand. But the Orissan *santhas* take a different route to explain their metaphysical convictions without disturbing the very basis of their mass appeal. I have already stated that the *santhas* were no dialecticians or logicians. Their goal was to make spiritualism accessible to the masses. This mission would have failed without introducing the element of *bhakti*. This was not so novel in the

---

38. *nirākāra prabhu ākāra nāhi ākāra hoichi bhakata pāiṅ.*
— Acyutānanda, *Chaurāśi Yantra*

39. *brahma ekākṣara je āpe nirañjana,*
deharūpi jagannātha āpe dāru brahma.
bhakata bhāvare āpe dāru brahma rūpa,
Aḷekha bhavanu āsi druśya jyoti rūpa.
— Acyutānanda, *Śūnya Saṁhitā* III

case of the Oriyā *santha*s alone. Kabīr, Dādū and many other *santha*s of the medieval period have followed the same path. In such circumstances the only thing the Vaiṣṇava *santha*s of Orissa could do was to bring a new twist to the connotation of the term *bhakti*. They offer a distinctively different interpretation of the term by highlighting on self-realization as the first step towards *bhakti*. This new interpretation helps them overcome the apparent incongruity in their metaphysics. I shall discuss in detail the peculiarities associated with their theory of *bhakti* in the next chapter.

We have already noted that the theory of *Śūnya Puruṣa* is not exactly a fascimile of the abstract absolutism of Śaṅkara and Nāgārjuna. It is clear that the Orissan *santha* philosophy amalgamates the idea of a personal God, at some level or other, with the notion of an ineffable and non-qualified highest Reality. The contradiction that may arise in this context is sorted out with the help of the powerful element of the devotee's vision of God as the Being of beings. It is interesting to note in this connection that the rituals practised in Jagannātha temple also reflect this spirit of amalgamation of the *sākāra* with the *nirākāra*. While offering *pūjā* to God the priest meditates on him as a formless (*nirākāra*) being. So the question that is likely to bother a scholar of Orissan *santha* movement is about the possible source of such a unique theory. No other Hindu cult talks of such a personal God who has a form, yet it is not the real form, who is receptacle of all yet in reality an abstract principle. This peculiar concept of Godhead may draw our attention to a similar theory propagated by Vajrayāna. The Vajrayānic idea of Vajrasattva comes closest to the Orissan theory of Jagannātha as the *Śūnya Puruṣa*. The very concept of Vajrasattva combines the idea of *śūnyatā* with *bhakti* and *upāsanā*. So I intend to throw some light on certain interesting dimensions of this branch of Tāntric Buddhism. I strongly feel that there is enough justification in comparing notes with the Vajrayānic notion of the highest Reality, as this cult had a strong conceptual presence in the cultural life of Orissa.

Vajrayāna as a Tāntric version of Mahāyāna sticks to the original interpretaion of *śūnyatā* as the ineffable, incomprehensible highest Reality. But at the same time it epitomses *śūnyatā* in the form of the Vajrasattva. Not only this, they also project him as the ultimate object of meditation and devotion. Thus, Vajrasattva is a personal God too. Etymologically speaking, "*śūnyatā* is said to be *vajra*, and all manifestation in form is said to be *sattva*; so Vajrasattva implies the unity and identity of the two."[40] This school of Buddhism further believes that even if Vajrasattva is free from all existence and non-existence, he, nevertheless, is endowed with all forms and existence; and is embodiment of loveliness.[41] S.B. Dasgupta while analysing the genesis of such an interesting theory of personal God argues that this idea has evolved from the Mahāyānic notion of *dharmakāyā* of the Buddha. The early Buddhists conceived Buddha as a historical person. But the Mahāyāna Buddhism transformed Buddha into the ultimate principle — "the totality of things or the principle of cosmic unity." The highest principle is believed to have three aspects known as the *trikāyā*s of the Buddha, viz., *dharmakāyā*, *sambhogakāyā* and *nirmāṇakāyā*. In Mahāyāna texts the word *dharma* usually signifies entity, so *dharmakāyā* stands for that-ness (*tathatā rūpa*) of all entities. In other words, it is the *dharmadhātu* (primordial element) underlying all that exists. *Sambhogakāyā*, on the other hand signifies "the body of bliss." It manifests in the *bodhicitta*s or the enlightened persons; and *nirmāṇakāyā* refers to the historical personage of Buddha, or the body of transformation. The concept of *dharmakāyā* plays an important role in Tāntric Buddhism for the evolution of the theory of

40. *śūnyatā vajram ityuktam ākāraḥ sattvam ucyate,*
tādātmyamanyoḥ aikyaṁvajrasattva iti smṛtaḥ.

Jvālāvalī Vajramālā Tantra, qtd. in S.B. Dasgupta, *Introduction to Tāntric Buddhism*, Calcutta: University of Calcutta, 1974, p. 78.

41. *bhāvābhāva vinrmukto vajrasattvaḥ sucintitaḥ,*
sarvakāra varopetaḥ aśecanaka vigrahaḥ.
— *Pañcakrama*, Qtd. in Dasgupta, p. 79.

Vajrasattva. Thus, what is tacitly implied in Mahāyāna is fully developed by the Vajrayānīs into a monistic theism.[42]

This non-dualistic principle is the focal point of Vajrayāna metaphysics. Reality is described as transcending all conceptualisation, yet the subtle source of all creations. He is also called the *Bhagavān*. *Vyakta Bhavānugata Tattva Siddhi*, an important Vajrayānī text elaborates,

> Vajrasattva is the God unparalleled, all moving, omnipresent creator and destroyer of all, the sublime Lord of the universe and the revealer of all potential thoughts.[43]

He is the perfect embodiment of *śūnyatā* and *vijñāna*. Indrabhūti, one of the great *siddha*s of this order, articulates the nature of the Vajrasattva in the following way:

> He is the being without origination and destruction, the all good, the soul-substance of all, the enlightened one encompassing within him all that is static and dynamic. . . . He eternally belongs to all elements, to all beings — he remains pervading all bodies in the form of flow of consciousness; he is immutable, unthinkable, passionless, *śūnya* like the sky, free from existence and non-existence.[44]

We must note that Vajrayānic conception of Vajrasattva cannot be called a form of theism in the strictest sense of the term. They make a reconciliation between the incomprehensibility of God with that of the subtle presence of God. So Vajrayāna cannot be said to subscribe to a theory of personal God, in the ordinary sense of the term. This is evident from the following stanza from *Advayavajra Saṁgraha*:

> The deities are nothing but manifestation of *śūnya*; and wherever there is manifestation it must be *śūnya* in essence.[45]

---

42. S.B. Dasgupta, pp. 9-15.

43. Dasgupta, p. 80.

44. Indrabhūti, *Jñāna-siddhi*, qtd. in Dasgupta, p. 78.

45. *Advaya Vajra Saṁgraha*, qtd. in B. Bhattacharyya, *An Introduction to Buddhist Esoterism*, Delhi: Motilal Banarsidass, 1989 , p. 109.

The concept of *Śūnya Puruṣa* as enunciated by the Oriyā *santhas* seems to echo the Vajrayānic conception of the Vajrasattva. In the works of Pañcasakhā, as well as of the subsequent *santhas* Lord Jagannātha has been depicted as the incomprehensible principle; at the same time, He is conceived as the object of love and devotion. In this sense the *Śūnya Puruṣa* is a personal God, yet not a personal God in the ordinary sense of the term. He is often described as the savior, all-pervading being, the embodiment of existence, consciousness and bliss. In the words of Acyutānanda,

> He is formless *Brahman* unparalleled in its beauty. Though formless he pervades all that is placed in this limitless world.[46]

Do not these lines remind us of the Vajrayānic description of the Vajrasattva?

The God as Śūnya

In the preceding sections I have examined the closeness between the Vajrayāna concept of Vajrasattva and the santhic concept of *Śūnya Puruṣa* as Jagannātha. Both the theories highlight the idea of God as *śūnya*. However, it should not create a feeling that, in my eagerness to emphasize the role of Buddhism in the shaping up of the Orissan *santha* philosophy, I am presenting a distorted picture of a great religio-philosophical movement. It must be made clear at the outset that I do not intend to claim that the Oriyā *santha* philosophers were the followers of Vajrayāna, or for that matter, any branch of Buddhism. Nor can it be claimed that they were adventitiously concealing their Buddhistic affiliations under the garb of Vaiṣṇavism as is claimed by Nagendra Nath Vasu in his monumental work *Modern Buddhism and its Followers in*

---

46. *arūpa śūnya brahma dehi rūpare paṭāntara nāhiñ,*
aśeṣa pure jete sthāna vyāpichi aṇākāra brahma.
— Acyutānanda, *Chayāliśa paṭala.*

Orissa. I simply want to point out that the way the Oriyā *santha*s present God as the *śūnya* has perhaps has no parallel in Hindu classical philosophy. In many respects it is a unique move. In classical Indian tradition philosophers have struggled to bridge the gulf between the indeterminate (*nirviśeṣa*) *Brahman* and the personal God. This was the reason why Rāmānuja and his followers while introducing the notion of *bhakti* in their Vedāntic scheme of thought had to reinterpret *Brahman* as *saguṇa* (qualitative), *sākāra* (with a definite form) and *viśiṣṭa* (with determination). Śaṅkara, too, had to introduce the idea of a *saguṇa Īśvara*, to accommodate the component of *bhakti*. So in our orthodox tradition no such reconciliation could be achieved between *nirguṇattva* and *bhakti*. Interestingly, we notice such compromise in the *nirguṇa-panthī bhakti* theories of the medieval *santha*s. However, the Oriyā *santha*s go one step ahead and conceive the Supreme Being, not only as *nirguṇa* but also as *śūnya*. Now, one may argue that if a similar model was already existent in the medieval period, then why should not I relate it to the Orissan theory of *śūnya*? But I have certain justifications for hanging on to Vajrayāna as the possible source of this theory. First, the use of the term *śūnya* is not so new to *santha*s of Orissa. The reference to the term *śūnya*, in the Orissan metaphysical tradition is as old as thirteenth century CE. So the idea of *śūnya* was not alien to this culture. However, the most vital pointer to my presupposition about the impact of the Buddhistic influence on the Orissan *santha* theory is the use of the typical epithet Buddha-Jagannātha in their literature.

At this point I should make a little digression to sort out another important problem that may lead to an anomalous situation about the non-dualistic stance of the Oriyā *santha*s. I have already stated that the *santha* philosophy of Orissa is by and large Jagannātha-centric and it is also non-dualistic. But the iconic representation in the *sanctum sanctorum* defies non-dualism and also monotheism. The most interesting feature of Jagannātha cult is to be found in the conception of God manifesting himself not only as a single God but a combination of four forms or *caturdhā mūrti*, viz., Jagannātha, Balabhadra, Subhadrā and Sudarśana. This may lead to a suspicion that the Jagannātha cult is not non-dualistic in nature. I have already stated that on the *sanctum* of the temple, Lord Jagannātha is placed along with his brother Balabhadra and sister Subhadrā, and Sudarśana cakra as his *śakti*. From this peculiar iconic presentation one may gather the idea that this form of Vaiṣṇavism is a form of polytheism. Perhaps in no other Hindu temple such a triumvirate of brothers and sister is worshipped. So initially it may appear that the entire concept of *Śūnya Puruṣa* symbolised in the form of a monistic Godhead collapses miserably. But the Oriyā Vaiṣṇavas do not face any problem here as they present the four-fold iconic representation as the manifestation of the same principle. Sāralā Dāsa, the fifteenth-century *santha* poet describes the triumvirate as the three dimensions of the creative power of the *Brahman*, viz., the power of creation, sustenance and the cause of the cosmic process. On the other hand, Acyutānanda presents the four-fold God — Jagannātha, Balabhadra, Subhadrā and Sudarśana as the symbolic representations of the creator, His creative power, elements of creation and the first evolute of the *Śūnya Puruṣa*, respectively. The Oriyā *santha*s could not have discarded the four-fold representation of the deity, as this was already a popular cult of Orissa. Even Śrī Caitanya, who had identified Kṛṣṇa with Jagannātha, worshipped Him in this four-fold form. So this factor does not pose a challenge to the non-dualisic position adhered by the Pañcasakhā and the subsequent *santha*s. The God in His four-fold form and the *Śūnya Puruṣa* as the highest Reality continue to be one and identical. Acyutānanda, therefore, tries to assimilate this contradictory element by highlighting the unity in multiplicity. In his famous poem entitled *Śūnya Puruṣa* he says that a true *yogī* can visualise the highest Reality in His four dimensions (*caturdhā mūrti*) when his mind is raised to the level of the *sahasrāra* (the highest state of the meditative mind). The *yogī* in this state realizes that this four-fold form is nothing but the formless and taintless Reality.[47] Again the wooden form of Jagannātha in the temple is called *apuruṣa*, signifying "something impersonal." So Jagannātha is not a personal God in the ordinary sense of the term. Thus, the non-dualistic tenor of the *santha* philosophy is neither disturbed by the presence of the idol in the temple of Jagannātha, nor by the peculiarities of the iconic representation of the idols.

So far we have been analysing the intricate nuances of the concept of *Śūnya Puruṣa*. It is obvious that this metaphysical principle is so atypical that the theory cannot be put into the framework of any particular system of philosophical tradition of classical age. Though the stamp of Tāntric Vajrayāna is unmistakeably clear, yet it is not a Hinduised version of Vajrayāna metaphysics. There are traces of Upaniṣadic non-dualism too. Again the idea is not also a replica of the Upaniṣadic version of the *Brahman*. There are certain other nuances of the concept that may convince us that the theory of *Śūnya Puruṣa* is novel. I shall like to discuss other important dimensions of this concept in the next chapter.

---

47. *caturdhā rūpe bije nirākāra, padma phuṭiba keśara bhitara.*
nirākāra rūpa tāhāku maṇi nirlepa nirākāra yehu puṇi
— *Śūnya Saṁhitā* IX

7

Śūnya Puruṣa, Saṁsāra and Jīva

THE concept of *Śūnya Puruṣa* of the *santha*s of Orissa is uncharacteristic as a metaphysical theory. Here a pure absolutistic metaphysics mingles effortlessly with the religious conception of a Godhead. But this position is not altogether new to the Indian tradition. I have already pointed out in the introductory chapter of this book that the tradition has never maintained a clear-cut distinction between philosophy and religion. The same Reality can be viewed as *Brahman* from the metaphysical angle and again as *Īśvara* or *Bhagavān* from a religious angle.[1] However, all said and done certain valid doubts may still linger in our mind. We may agree with the Vajrayānīs as well as the Orissan *santha*s that the *śūnya* may be taken as the highest Reality as well as the object of devotion. But how the ineffable, non-describable and attributeless principle of *śūnya* could be related to the *saṁsāra* (phenomenal world)? Is the phenomenal world, including the individual souls an apparent manifestation of the *Śūnya Puruṣa* or is it the real manifestation. Interestingly, the Oriyā *santha*s view *Śūnya Puruṣa* as the potential womb of the phenomenal world. So the universe consisting of the conscious and material objects is taken to be the real manifestation of the highest Being. But such a viewpoint may seem paradoxical, for there is a conceptual gap between the *nirguṇatva* of the highest Reality and its manifestation as the plurality of names and forms. I

---

1. *brahmeti paramāteti bhagavāna iti śabdyate.*
   — *Śrīmad Bhāgavatam* I.2.2

intend to examine, in this chapter, how this paradox can be sorted out as far as the *Santha* tradition is concerned.

Śūnya Puruṣa as the Potential Womb of the Saṁsāra

If we take Śaṅkara's Advaitavāda as the model of a rigorous non-dualistic metaphysics then we have to take recourse to some other principle like *māyā* to explain the phenomenal world. *Māyā*, according to Śaṅkara, is the inherent potency of the one and ineffable *Brahman* that acts as the medium of projection of this world of plurality on the non-dual ground of the *Brahman*. Surprisingly, the Oriyā *santhas* do not accept this position. For them the world is the real manifestation. This will be evident from the following verses of Balarāma Dāsa:

> In those days my form was *śūnya*
> This way million years went by
> In my womb the universe was born
> This was the manifestation of the *Brahman*.[2]

He expresses this same idea in a different way when he says:

> I existed as the *Parama Brahma* and
> *śūnya* (before the creation)
> I existed as the *Bindu Brahman* in the
> Eternal space
>
> x x x
>
> I myself is *nirguṇa Brahman*
> But I desired to create the universe
> Out of myself.[3]

---

2. *se kāḷe mora śūnya rūpa, emanta galā koṭi kalpa.*
brahmāṇḍa mora garbhe hoi, rakhile brahmarūpa hoi.
— Balarāma Dāsa, *Virāṭa-Gītā*

3. *jei dine kehi nāhiṅ śūnya e samasta*
muhiṅ parama brahma muṭi, śūnyamaya hoi
bindu brahmarūpe ākāśe thili rahi.
— Balarāma Dāsa, *Premabhakti Gītā*, I.128-29

Again, Acyutānanda has to say the following words about nature of the *Śūnya Puruṣa* as the potential womb:

> Right from the insect to the highest form of being; from the inanimate to the animate — all these are in His womb. All the forms and creations in this world are due to him . . . creation, existence and delusion, all these three states contained within his body. The world arises as well as dissolves here.[4]

If this universe is the real manifestation of the *Śūnya Puruṣa*, as indicated by the above verses then obviously a paradox arises. How could an indeterminate, non-qualitative and absolutely non-dual principle manifest itself as plurality of forms and names? Either we accept that the Reality is *saguṇa* (qualitative), hence the manifestation as real (*pariṇāma*); or else, we view the highest Reality as *nirguṇa* (non-qualitative) and the manifestation as *mithyā* or apparent (*vivarta*). In any case indeterminateness and actuality of the phenomenal world (*saṁsāra*) may not go together. However, we can look for a third alternative provided by the Yogācāra theory of *abhūtaparikalpa* and its subsequent development in the notion of Vajrasattva. This may provide us some clue for resolving the contradictions involved in the case of handling of the notion of *Śūnya Puruṣa* as the potential womb of the phenomenal world. The word *abhūtaparikalpa* literally means — that which is devoid of all misconceptions or false mental constructions, i.e., the substratum where there is the *mere possibility of subjectivity and objectivity* "but in which the duality has no reality."[5] In simpler terms, it implies that though the empirical world is creation of false mental constructions, yet it is not

---

4. *kītuṅ brahma jāye jive ajīve achidra hoi achi sabu garbhe,*
jagata bhitare jetiki racanā, tahiṅki sabu upalamya sinā
. . . utupati stithi praḷaya tini abori achi e deha gheni.
ehāra tahuṅ jagata prakāśa tahuṅ upuji tahiṅ hue nāśa.
— Acyutānanda, *Śabda Brahma Saṁhitā*, 8-12

5. Dasgupta, *Tāntric Buddhism*, p. 22.

absolutely chimeral, because the highest Reality holds the possibility of subjective-objective distinction. Therefore, it can be taken to be the potential womb of all creations. The concept of creation is impossible without assuming the distinction between the subject and the object. According to S.B. Dasgupta, the Vajrayāna conception of Vajrasattva is an offshoot of the Yogācārī theory of *abhūtaparikalpa*.[6] So we find Anaṅgavajra, a *siddha* of the Vajrayānic order professing that the existence (*bhāva*), though originating due to false mental constructions (*kalpanā*), should not be taken as absolutely unreal. In his opinion it is better to take the world as real than to think everything as unreal. Unless it is conceived so, the very idea of *nirvāṇa* will lose its significance.[7] This is what is meant when Anaṅgavajra describes the highest Reality as *śūnyatā garbha* (womb).[8] Like the Vajrayānic notion of *śūnyatāgarbha*, these *santhas* too, present *Śūnya Puruṣa/Brahman* as the potential womb of the cosmos. *Śūnya Puruṣa*, thus, is not an abstract concept. It is the real ground of the *saṁsāra* (phenomenal world).

In case of the Orissan *santhas* a similar explanation is sought in overcoming the paradox involved in accommodating *śūnya* within the scheme of the phenomenal actuality. So we find Balarāma Dāsa raising the question: why the *śūnya Brahman* desired creation? And the answer seems to be characteristically Vajrayānic. Balarāma as well as Acyutānanda say that the unmanifest *Śūnya Puruṣa* manifests itself because He wants every human to realise the real truth and *nirvāṇa*. Therefore,

---

6. Dasgupta, pp. 22-28.

7. *nirvati jvalito dīpo nivṛtaḥ kaṁ gatiṁ vrajet.*
   — *Prajñopāya Viniścaya Siddhi* I.1

   See also verse I.10, qtd. in Dasgupta, p. 36.

8. *namaste śūnyatāgarbha sarvasaṁkalpa varjitaḥ,*
   sarvajña jñānasaṁdohā jñānamūrti namoḥstute.

   Prajñopāya Viniścaya Siddhi. II.39 in *Two Vajrayāni Works*, ed. B. Bhattacharyya, p. 12.

there is a metaphysical necessity to admit the reality of the phenomenal world. For the Pañcasakhās as well as the *santha*s of the subsequent period, the world of names and forms is not an illusion or *māyā.* To explain the validity of their position they argue that there is no contradiction involved in conceiving that the form can emerge out of formless. This will be clear from the following lines of Acyutānanda:

> All these forms are the creations
> Of the formless
> All manifestation of forms will
> Ultimately realize in the formless.
> Thus one ought to be able to look at the two as one.
> Only by looking at the seemingly opposite
> With an attitude of equanimity,
> Can one realise the whole range of truth.[9]

Once the Highest Reality is accepted as the real and the potential ground of the phenomenal existence, it automatically follows that it is immanent too. Vajrayāna has spoken explicitly about this immanence, Orissan *santha*s also highlight this aspect of the *Śūnya Puruṣa/Brahman.* Let us see how this idea of immanence finds expression in the words of these *santha*-poets.

Highlighting the aspect of immanence Yaśovanta Dāsa narrates:

> He has no definite place to reside
> So he is inside of created beings.
> He belongs to no caste, so he takes
> Food from every home (irrespective of caste).[10]

---

9. *arūparu rūpa prakāśa heva,*
rūpa jaiṇa arūpare miśiva.
rūpa arūpaku sama karithivu
samatā rūpare savu pāiṅbu.
— Acyutānanda, *Tattvabodhinī*

10. *sthāna nāhi sarva ghate basai,*
jāti nāhi sarva ghare bhuñjai.
— Yaśovanta Dāsa, *Ātmā Parace Gītā*

Divākara Dāsa, a *Santha* of the seventeenth century tries to show both the transcendence and the immanence of the Reality in the following way:

> The *Brahman* is manifested
> In the four realms of existence
> (Animate, inanimate, acquatic beings and flying beings)
> I myself is the *Brahman,*
> I pervade in all the spheres
> As, I am the master of all.[11]

Once a philosophical system admits the reality of the phenomenal world there seems to be a compulsion on its part to explain the process of evolution. Therefore, the *santhas* of Orissa also take a lot of interest in cosmogony. It is the natural outcome of their philosophical stance. However, in their case the task is daunting, as they have taken the ineffable *śūnya* as the highest Reality. Following their metaphysical position most of them take resort to the view that before the creation there was nothing but *śūnya*. I take here the famous lines of Balarāma Dāsa as a point for illustration.

> When the world was not existent,
> There were no sun nor moon,
> Neither day nor night.
> Neither land nor water
> Neither the earth nor the inconstant wind.
> Nor were there sky and stars in it.
> Then there were no Gods, no demon, no human beings.
> Then there was no world, no ocean, no force, no fire.
> Then there was no Brahmā, Viṣṇu or Hara.
> Then my form was *śūnya*.
> Thus the crore of *kalpas* passed.
> Then did I assume the form of *Brahman,*

---

11. *cāri khāni dehe brahma prakāśe, sabu brahma jāka mohara aṁśe.*
muhi vyāpī achi sakala theiṅ, mo binu karatā jagate nāhiṅ.
— Divākara Dāsa, *Parace Gītā* XIII

With the universe in my womb.
Then there were none, O, Arjuna,
I existed in the form of *mahāśūnya*.[12]

These lines are likely to remind us of the similar expressions found in the famous Nāsadīyasūkta of the *Ṛgveda*. Some of the *santhas* almost agree with this *sūkta*, but in most cases these *santhas* adopt a totally different line of thought. While in the Nāsadīyasūkta the primeval fecundity is referred to as the source of creation, in case of these *santhas* it is the *auṁ*, the *śabda Brahman* manifesting itself as the phenomenal world of names and forms. I shall discuss the varied interpretations available on this issue in detail in a separate chapter.

Śūnya Puruṣa and Jīvātman

Regarding the question of the relationship between *jīva* (individual self) and the *Brahman* the Oṛiyā *santhas* strictly adhere to their non-dualistic stand. Thus, *jīva* and *Brahman* are viewed as one and identical. This theory can be placed in sharp contrast to the general Vaiṣṇavite position. The Vaiṣṇava ontological position is primarily dualistic. Rāmānuja, one of the greatest exponents of Vaiṣṇavism, despite his monistic attitude could not think of an unalloyed identity between *jivātman* and *paramātman*. He rather argues that the individual soul cannot lose its identity, for such a loss of identity would be tantamount to the destruction of the soul. Rāmānuja, it seems, was bound by a metaphysical compulsion to accommodate the *bhakti* theory. So he argues that if the *jīva*'s individuality is lost then who will indulge in devotion. The subsequent Vedāntin Vaiṣṇavas were more vociferous about the continuation of individuality of the *jīva* even in the state of highest self-realisation. They claim that liberated soul only attains the nature of God, never identity with the God.[13] We

12. Balarāma Dāsa, *Virāṭa-Gītā* III.

13. *nāpi nirastā vidayasya svarūpaikya sambhavaḥ.*
— Rāmānuja, *Śrībhāṣya* 1.1.1.

can gather some general ideas of the nature of *jīva-Brahman* relation from Rāmānuja's scheme of five possible states of liberation. They are:

(1) *Sālokya* — In this stage the *jīva* attains the world of *Brahman.*

(2) *Sāraṣti* — In this stage the *jīva* enjoys the affluence of *Brahman.*

(3) *Sāmīpya* — In this stage the *jīva* attains nearness to *Brahman.*

(4) *Sārūpya* — It is the stage when the *jīva* attains the nature of *Brahman.* It implies that the *jīva* attains some of the divine qualities of the highest Reality.

(5) *Sāyujya* — This is the one in which the *jīva* identifies itself with the *Brahman.* But it is not to be confused with a relationship of identity between the two. There is (as if) a longing from both the sides. But the identity of the two is not mingled. The *jīva* does not lose its individual identity. Rāmānuja quotes from *Chāndogya, Taittirīya* and *Muṇḍaka,* and *Gītā* in support of his thesis.[14]

To vindicate their position on the duality between the *jīva* and *Brahman,* the Vedāntins like Madhva even go to the extent of reinterpreting the famous *mahāvākya* — *tat tvam asi* (that thou art), as implying *atat tvam asi* (you are not that). He argues that *jīva* is just a part of the empirical world so how can it be identical with Viṣṇu? This metaphysical position is in right consonance with the philosophy of *bhakti.* If *bhakti* stands for the intense love of God then the *jīvātmān*'s highest objective is to serve the *paramātman* or *Īśvara.* This would be conceptually

14. *Chāndogya* 8.1.6.
Taittirīya 2.1.1.
Muṇḍaka 3.1.3.
Gītā 14.2.

impossible if the two are identified. So whether the relation between the individual soul and the *Īśvara* is seen as that of the relationship of a servant (*dāsyatā*), a friend (*sakhyatā*), or a passionately attached beloved (*prema*) to the Lord, the distinctness between the two cannot be overlooked. This is why the Vaiṣṇavite sects subscribe to metaphysical dualism.

Interestingly, the Orissan Vaiṣṇavas, while adhering to the ideal of *bhakti,* prefer to deviate from the general Vaiṣṇavite stand. Unlike the Vedāntin Vaiṣṇavas, they believe in the total identity of *jīvātman* and *paramātman*. In their parlance there is no duality between *jīva* and *parama*. At first sight, this theory of identity appears very similar to the Advaitic position. But a deeper look at the theory of the Orissan *santha*s reveals the originality of their approach. Śaṅkara's *jīva-Brahman* identity theory is primarily centred on his conception of *jñāna* as the mode of self-realization. *Bhakti* has no place in his metaphysical scheme. But unlike the Advaita Vedāntins the Bauddha Vaiṣṇavas of Orissa place *jīva-parama* identity in the background of a *bhakti* theory. So their task and approach are different. In their attempt to put this theory of identity in a larger Vaiṣṇavite *bhakti* scheme they often use two important Vaiṣṇavite personas, viz., Rādhā and Kṛṣṇa, as symbolizing *jīvātman* and *paramātman*. However, for these philosophers they are not distinct entities but are like "two cotyledons of the same seed."[15] I shall discuss this interesting theory later.

The most important conceptual presupposition that makes the *santha* theory of *jīva-Brahman/Parama* identity drastically distinct from the Advaita position is their adherence to the *piṇḍa-Brahmāṇḍa* identity theory propagated by the Buddhist Sahajayāna and subsequently developed by the Nāth cult. The proclaimed identity between *jīva* and *parama* is used by these *santha*s as a step to facilitate the view that there could be no distinction between the *piṇḍa* (the gross individual body) and

15. *eka vīja beni phāla jugala aṅgare.*
— Acyutānanda, *Śūnya Saṁhitā* X

Brahmāṇḍa (the cosmic body). So they hold that the supreme consciousness is very much there in the human body itself; and realisable in this body alone. So the *jivātman* and *paramātman* are not distinct. Both of them can be realised in the same body. This novel idea is also reflected in the ritualistic practices of Jagannātha cult, too. The famous Jagannāthologist G.C. Tripathi while enunciating the daily rituals followed in Jagannātha worship points out that, "it is highly interesting that in the philosophical framework of the *pūjā* of Jagannātha we find the existence of both the types of consciousness — individual and cosmic (*jīvātman* and *paramātman*), side by side in the human body — one residing in the heart and the other in the head."[16] I shall discuss in detail the intricate nuances associated with the *piṇḍa-Brahmāṇḍa* identity theory in a separate chapter.

Now coming back to our discussion on the concept of *Śūnya Puruṣa* we note that the Orissan *santhas*, following the principle of *Piṇḍa-Brahmāṇḍa* identity, do not hesitate to identify the *Śūnya Puruṣa* (in this context, *paramātman*) with the individual soul. So there is nothing incongruous about Acyutānanda's depiction of the *Śūnya Puruṣa* as the soul, entrapped within the body. The following verse composed by this philosopher not only clothes the theory in beautiful imagery but says a lot more about the Pañcasakhā's conception of the human body.

> With goodness, peace, mercy and forgiveness as his companion
> *Śūnya Puruṣa* passes his days as a prisoner.
> Eleven sense faculties surround him.
> Lust, passion, delusion and anger act as the watchman.
> Twelve soldiers guard his fort.
> Twenty-five causes, five mental faculties,
> Six mystic circles of the body and the fifty letters,

16. "The Daily Pūjā ceremony of the Jagannātha," by G.C. Tripathi *The Cult of Jagannātha and the Regional Tradition of Orissa*, p. 303.

Seventy-two arteries and veins, all of them guard him
From all sides.
Look at his prowess, though a pure abstraction,
He enjoys all the powers of a king,
Yet not affected by the features of the phenomenal body.[17]

The identification of *ātman* and *Brahman* is not a novel concept but rarely we come across such a description of the embodied universal consciousness, which stands for the *paramātman* and in the ultimate sense, the *Śūnya Puruṣa*. Similar view is expressed by another eminent *Santha*, Caitanya Dāsa. He says that the *ātman* and *Brahman* are within our body as if chained by the bond of physical existence. Once the *ātman* leaves this body it can have eternal rest in the *śūnya*.[18]

The All-Pervasive Śūnya

Once we scan through the literature of the Orissan *santhas*, more and more dimensions of the concept of *śūnya* come to the forefront. Not only they conceive *Śūnya Puruṣa* as the individual soul, almost like the Mahāyāna Buddhists, they see the imprint of *śūnya* everywhere. They of course do so with some amount of justification. As *śūnya puruṣa* is conceived as the real ground of all that exists with names and forms, the Oriyā *santhas* see *śūnyatā* in everything. Not only is the Reality of the nature of *śūnyatā*, but also the phenomenal world of

---

17. *śūnya puruṣa paḍichi beḍhāre, sata śānti dayā kṣamā pākhare.*
yekādasa indri beḍhi achanti, kāma krodha moha dvārī jaganti.
dvādaśa daḷei gaḍanāyaka, paciśa prakṛuti pañcamaṅaka.
chaḍa cakrare pacāśa akṣara, bāstari nāḍi gaḍa pāśara.
gaḍa cāri pāśe emāne dvārī, śūnya puruṣaku thānti ābori.
śūnya puruṣara eteka teja, sukha baibhoga karai rājya.
śūnya puruṣa alage rahichi, śūnya pūre rahi līlā karuchi.
— *Śūnya Saṁhitā* IX

18. *se ātma brahmaku jagichi, bāndhī hoila praye achi.*
piṇḍaru chāḍi gale prāṇa, se ghaṭa haba mahāśūnya.
śūnya puruṣa saṅge jiba, khojile āu na pāiba.
— Caitanya Dāsa, *Nirguṇa Mahātmya* XVI

names and forms is stated to be of the same nature. This idea is very clearly presented in the following words by Jagannātha Dāsa,

> *Oṁkāra* is *parama śūnya,* all our activities too are *śūnya,*
> All our prayers and meditations are *śūnya,* all fancies and forms are *śūnya.*[19]

Elucidating this verse in prose he says,

> All the basic symbols of *Yoga* that are used for meditation on *Śūnya Puruṣa* like, *bindu, jyoti, dharma* and *oṁkāra,* are nothing but *śūnya.* Fifty-four letters, all *yantra* and *mantra, tattva* and *jñāna,* too, are *śūnya.* Even the celestial entities, such as the sun and the moon are nothing but *śūnya;* also the empirical world including the animate and inanimate beings are in *śūnya.*[20]

It is no wonder that the *mantra* for the worship is called *śūnya-mantra* and the figure (*yantra*) on which the worshipper concentrates is called *śūnya-yantra* by these *santha*-philosophers. This entire idea of conceiving the modes of worship as well as the object of worship as *śūnya* appears curious but it is not something unusual. One is likely to be reminded here of the cryptic lines from *Prajñā Pāramitā Sūtra,* "Form is *śūnyatā* and *śūnyatā* is form." But the following lines from the Vajrayāna text *Advayavajra Saṁgraha,* is closest to Jagannātha Dāsa's account:

> God who is worshipped, the worshipper who worships, the materials which are offered in worship and the *mantras* of worship are nothing but *śūnya.*[21]

---

19. *oṁkāra parama śūnya śūnya sarvamayo karma,*
śūnya śūnya japa dhyānam sarva śūnya matibhramam.

Jagannātha Dāsa, *Tulā Bhiṇā* 3.12.1. Qtd. in B. Mohanty, *Oṛiya Sāhityara Itihāsa,* vol. I., Cuttack: Friends Publishers, 1977, p. 278.

20. *Tulā Bhiṇā,* commentary on verse 3.12.1. Qtd. in Mohanty, p. 278.

21. *Advaya Vajra Saṁgraha,* p. 81, qtd. in N.K. Sahoo, *Buddhism in Orissa,* p. 132.

Thus, in this respect the Orissan *santha* literature definitely echoes Śūnyavāda rather than the Upaniṣadic Advaitavāda. The similar tenor is reflected in the following lines of Acyutānanda:

> O *vīra* look at *śūnya*
> By placing yourself in *śūnya*
> And meditate on *mahāśūnya*
> *Śūnya* itself is the form,
> Ground of all discriminating knowledge.
> Look at the whole world from the pedestal of *śūnya;*
> You will find everything manifested in the *śūnya*
> Everything arises out of *śūnya* and
> Everything flourishes in *śūnya Brahman.*[22]

When both the Reality as well as its manifestations, are regarded as *śūnya* it is natural on the part of the Orissan *santhas* to conceive *Śūnya Brahman* as the *Pūrṇa Brahman.*

This idea perhaps inspires Acyutānanda to say:

> It (*Śūnya Puruṣa*) is like air which fills everything. He as *nirguṇa parama Īśvara* has no shape, no form, but is omnipresent in the universe as the indestructible *pūrṇa Brahman.*[23]

In the verse quoted above the poet-philosopher most significantly transforms *śūnya* into *pūrṇa*. Here, *pūrṇatva* (self-

---

22. *śūnyara ākāra vīra śūnyara vicāra,*
śūnye thāi dekha vīra e sacarācara.
dekha e sacarācara śūnyare prakāśa,
śūnyu ude hoicanti śūnyare vilāsa.

Acyutānanda, *Śūnya Saṁhitā Causaṭhī Ṭīkā* pp. 55-57 (unpublished manuscript) MSS. O.l./617 Utkal University Library.

23. *nāhiñtā ākāra vikāra,*
nirguṇa parama īśvara.
khelanti sarvabhūte vyāpī,
akṣaya pūrṇa brahma rūpī.
— Acyutānanda, *Brahma Śaṅkuḷi* VIII

completeness) itself implies *śūnyatā* as *śūnya* now stands for the all-encompassing nature of the *Śūnya Puruṣa*. *Śūnya Brahman/Puruṣa* is regarded as the *Pūrṇa Brahman* because he is so self-complete that no description is good enough to pinpoint his powers and attributes.

Layers of Śūnya

The multiple and sometimes hierarchial presentation of *śūnya* can be said to be another important fall-out of the Buddhistic orientation of the Orissan *santha*s. Pañcasakhā as well as the subsequent *santha*s often talk of three, sometimes four and sometimes even seventy-two layers of *śūnya*. As such this classification of *śūnya* does not seem to add any new dimension to their theory of *Śūnya Puruṣa*, but may be connected with their theory of yogic *sādhanā*. Most probably they were following a tradition already set by the *siddha*s of the Vajrayāna and Sahajayāna. Nāgārjunapāda, the famous Buddhist tāntric (who had consequential influence on Orissa culture), in his treatise *Pañcakarma*, offers a hierachical scheme of *śūnya*, viz., *śūnya, atiśūnya, mahāśūnya* and *sarvaśūnya*.[24] According to him, the first stage, viz., *śūnya* stands for light (*āloka*). It represents knowledge (*prajñā*). But in this stage the mind is said to be associated with certain impurities. The second stage is *atiśūnya*. This stage is said to represent the manifestation of light (*ālokabhāsa*). In the third stage, i.e., *mahāśūnya*, there is the intuition of light (*ālokopalabdhi*). These are the three stages of *śūnya* that are relevant when the *citta* (mind) is at work. The fourth stage is the stage of the realization of the perfect *śūnyatā* (*sarvaśūnya*). This is self illuminant (*jyoti*). It represents perfect *śūnyatā* as it is, without the impurities of the mind; this is without change and any ascription of existence and non-existence. It is without duality. Interestingly, the Oriyā *santha*s

24. *śūnyañca atiśūnyañca mahaśūnyaṁ trīyakam*
caturthaṁ sarvaśūnyañ ca phala-hetu-prabhedataḥ.

Qtd. in Dasgupta, p. 43 fn. Also pp. 43-46.

also follow this trend of classifying *śūnya*. Acuytānanda talks of three grades of *śūnya*, viz., *śūnya*, *mahāśūnya* and *jyoti*, whereas, Yaśovanta talks of four, viz., *śūnya*, *jyotirśūnya*, *mahaśūnya* and *cetanā*.[25] In this context the experience of the highest level of *śūnya* as self-luminous light (*jyoti*) is of particular interest. Here the influence of the Buddhist *siddha*s seems to be more pronounced. So we find Jagannātha Dāsa describing *Brahman* as *śūnya jyoti*[26] whereas Acyutānanda Dāsa describes the intuitive experience of this effulgent light as the experience of the God Himself.[27] Interestingly, *Siddhasiddhānta Paddhati*, a work of the Nātha cult (which was considerably influenced by Tāntric Buddhism) also projects the *saccidānanda Brahman* as the *jyoti*, i.e., *svajyoti satyamekam jayati tava padam saccidānandamūrte*.[28] Thus, though the Bauddha Vaiṣṇavas of Orissa often talk of Jagannātha as the symbolical representation of *Śūnya Puruṣa*, the final experience of self-realisation comes, not from worshipping him as an idol but through the yogic *sādhanā* and the direct experience of the *Śūnya Puruṣa* as the *jyoti*. This divine experience is thus achievable with the phenomenal body here and now. This also makes it evident that the Oriyā Vaiṣṇavas believed in the *jīvanmukti*, and not the *videha mukti* like other Vaiṣṇava philosophers.

---

25. (a) *śūnyam śūnyaṁ mahāśūnyaṁ śūnya maddhye nirañjanaṁ,*
nirañjanāmaddhye tajjyoti, tajjyoti bhagavāna svayaṁ.

Acyutānanda, *Śūnya Saṁhitā Causaṭhī Ṭīkā.*

In this work he even talks thirteen types of *śūnya*.

(b) *śūnya pare jyoti jāṇa, tāpre mahāśūnya puṇa,*
se śūnya upare cetanā, cetanā maddhey mora ṭhaña.

Yaśovanta Dāsa, *Premabhakti Brahma Gītā*, p. 56.

26. Jagannātha Dāsa, *Tulā Bhiṇā.*

27. *tat jyoti bhagavāna svayam.* — Acyutānanda.

28. *na brahmā viṣṇu rudrou na surapatisur ānaiva pṛthvī na cāpo,*
naivāgnirnāpi vayurnaca gaganatalaṁ nodiśo naiva kālaḥ.
novedā naiva yajña naca raviśaśinou no diśo daiva kālaḥ,
svajyotiḥ satyamekaṁ jayati tava padaṁ saccidānandamūrte.
— *Siddhasiddhānta Paddhati*, qtd. in K. Kara, p. 196.

8

Jñānamiśra Bhakti

In my discussion on *Śūnya Puruṣa*, I have already indicated that the Orissan Vaiṣṇavas were monists but not exactly monotheists. Their conception of God as a personal deity, in a sense, is different from other forms of monotheism. *Śūnya Puruṣa* as an ineffable Reality appears as personal God in a devotee's devotion only, but He continues to be formless. Once the highest Reality is conceived as of the nature of *śūnya* and as an indescribable principle rather than an entity embodied in a form, there is bound to be a difference in the implications of the term *bhakti*. In case of non-dualists like Śaṅkara, we also find that the term *bhakti* is used with an altogether different connotation. It is self-knowledge; a form of investigation into one's own being (*sva svarupānusandhāna*). The emotional dimension of the concept is, thus, overlooked. This, to some extent, justifies why the Bauddha Vaiṣṇavas, and especially Pañcasakhās, could not have accepted *bhakti* in the sense the Vaiṣṇava theology presents it, i.e., an intense and passionate attachment towards a personal God. We have also noted that the Orissan *santha* philosophers laid a great stress on *nirākāra mantra* and *nirguṇa upāsanā*. Therefore, the role of emotion is underplayed and instead the importance is attached to self-knowledge and *yoga*. As a consequence we come across a novel theory of *bhakti* that is a juxtaposition of *bhakti* and *jñāna* both. To make the theory distinct from other popular forms of *bhakti* theory like, *śuddha bhakti*, *parā bhakti*, *prema bhakti*, etc., later interpreters give it a new name, i.e., *jñānamiśra bhakti* (*bhakti* accentuated by *jñāna*). This is a theory that is Vaiṣṇavite in letter but non-Vaiṣṇavite in spirit. So before I explicate the *bhakti* concept of the Orissan *santha*s I deem it proper to examine in brief two models of *bhakti* espoused by two important sects of Vaiṣṇavism, viz., the Vaiṣṇava Vedānta propagated by the southern *acārya*s like Rāmānuja, Vallabha, Madhva and Nimbārka; and Gauḍīya Vaiṣṇavism of Śrī Caitanya. Such comparative analysis will help us to assess to what extent the new theory of *Jñānamiśra bhakti* is indigenous. I prefer to confine my discussion to these two sects because they had great amount of impact on Orissan culture.

I

The Concept of Bhakti : Some Clarifications

Bhakti is a very common term, used frequently in different contexts. But as a mode of self-realization or *mukti*, the concept is grossly misrepresented and most often is projected as something very opposed to intuitive and contemplative mode of self-realization. It is used in a narrow sense implying an emotion/emotional state (*bhāva*). Besides, the concept is thought to be inoperative without the notion of a personal God. Naturally, unconditional faith in God and pining for the grace of God take the centre stage in the analysis of *bhakti*. Therefore, many modern scholars seem to resist any attempt to explore the possibility of an alternative explication of the term. Here I take G.C. Pande's following lines as a case in point. In the proceedings of a seminar, entitled *Bhakti*, published as late as 2001 he observes:

> Religion is possible without belief in a personal god. There may be a religion without belief in a personal god, but it cannot be called atheism. It is also theism: it is religion. But bhakti without faith, without belief in a personal god is not possible.[1]

1. Dayakrishna *et al.* (ed.), *Bhakti: A Contemporary Discussion*, New Delhi: Indian Council of Philosophical Research, 2000, p. 47.

It is clear that Pande tries to draw a line between religion and *bhakti*. We whole-heartedly admit that the two concepts are distinct. So when he talks of a religion without a God perhaps he has in mind the original Buddhism as a religion that did not subscribe to the notion of a personal God. But he seems to forget that if religion is possible without a personal God so also is *bhakti*. There are many *bhakti* sects that do not reconcile with the conception of a personal deity. I can cite the case of at least one such *bhakti* school, viz., the Mahimā *dharma* of Orissa. Even the *nirguṇa panthī santhas* of north India like Kabīr and Dādū, in the true sense of the term, never believed in a personal God. Did not Kabīr make it clear that when he talks of Rāma he is not specifically referring to a personal God, viz., Rāma, the incarnation of Lord Viṣṇu?[2] He is just a symbol here for the highest Reality. Yet Kabīr preached the importance of *bhakti* as a path of self-realization. So I strongly feel that we are likely to do injustice to many such *santhas* and sects of India if we confine meaning of the term *bhakti* just to signify faith or belief in a personal God. While analysing the theory of *Jñānamiśra bhakti* of the Orissan *santhas* I would like to prove that the faith in a personal God is not at all a basic to *bhakti* theory.

In this context I also intend to clear another misconception about the scope of the theory of *bhakti*. Most often we are made to understand that *bhakti* is primarily a Brāhmaṇical concept. But this is far from the real picture. *Bhakti* also plays an important role in Buddhism, too. With the develpoment of Mahāyāna Buddhism the existence of the historical Buddha took a back seat; and the theory of *trikāyā-dharma, nirmāṇa* and *saṁbhogakāyās* came into prominence. The *Avatāṁsaka-Sūtra* extolling the trancendental virtues of the Buddha states that

2. *nā jasarathadhari auvatarī avā, nā laṅkākā rāva saṅtāvā.*

Qtd. in Krishna Sharma, *Bhakti and the Bhakti Movement: A New Perspective,* New Delhi: Munshiram Manoharlal Publishers Pvt. Ltd., 1987, p. 167.

the Tathāgata is all-pervading in the *dharma-dhātu* (the universe) and the *Buddhakāyā* is visible everywhere in ten directions.[3] Thus, during the course of its development Mahāyāna Buddhism adopted a sort of theistic stance. The develpoment of the ideas of *bodhisattva* and *bodhicitta* were made popular through Pāramitā literature. The idea of *bhakti* seemed to have a deeper impact on later Buddhism. In this connection the views expressed by R.C. Majumdar and A.S. Altekar in their work *A New History of the Indian People* is worth quoting. The authors observe:

> Atheism was replaced by the gospel of a divine helper of men, and the apprehensions created by the doctrine of *anātma* (non-existence of soul) were practically all removed by the doctrine of *dharmakāyā*, through which an individual could get eternal existence. *Nirvāṇa* was not the tranquilization of human aspirations, but the fulfilment of human life; one can live in the whirlpool of life and death and yet be above it as *bodhisattvas* do. . . . The latter are always ready and present to save the genuine devotees, and can also transfer to them their good *karma* to secure their salvation. What mattered was not *jñāna* so much as genuine *bhakti*. . . .[4]

Similarly, Kern observes,

> Mahāyānism lay a great stress on devotion, in this respect as in many others harmonising with the current feeling in India which led to the growing importance to *bhakti*. It is by the feeling of fervent devotion combined with the preaching of active compassion that the creed had enlisted the support of sympathy of numerous millions of people and has become

---

3. *Avataṁsa Sūtra*, ed. Trien Bundle, I.36 ff. qtd. in Paritosh Das, *Sahajīyā Cult of Bengal and Pañcasakhā Cult of Orissa*, Calcutta: Firma KLM, 1988, p. 52.

4. R.C. Majumdar and A.S. Altekar, *A New History of Indian People*, vol. VI., qtd. in Paritosh Das, *op. cit.*, pp. 52-53.

> a factor in the history of mankind, of much greater importance than orthodox Buddhism.[5]

Thus, in course of its development Buddhism lost much of its critical rigour and turned into a form of theism by accommodating the idea of *bodhisattva* that ultimately led to the ascription of divinity to Buddha. This transformation was so great that in later phases a *stūpa* was identified with the divine Buddha.

Two Alternative Models of Vaiṣṇavism

I have stated earlier how the Jagannātha cult turned into a full-fledged Vaiṣṇava cult with the advent of Vedāntin Vaiṣṇavism of the southern *ācārya*s like Rāmānujācārya, Madhvācārya, Vallabhācārya and others; and at a later stage with the presence of Śrī Caitanya at Purī. Therefore, any analysis of the *bhakti* theory of the Orissan Vaiṣṇavism will be incomplete without comparing notes with these two important sects of Vaiṣṇavism. It is well known that the Vaiṣṇava *ācārya*s of south India introduced the element of *bhakti* in their interpretation of the philosophy of Vedānta. But as the interpreters of Vedānta they could not dismiss the claim of *jñāna* altogether. At the same time, with the advent of each new sect of Vedāntin Vaiṣṇavism *jñāna* as path of liberation was gradually giving way to *bhakti*. The concept of *bhakti* also assumed more romantic connotation in the process. Though Rāmānuja was not absolutely opposed to the idea of emotional attachment to the God, for, he also defines *bhakti* as love,[6] he does not find any opposition between *jñāna* and *bhakti*. *Bhakti* for Rāmānuja is constant contemplation of God (*druvansmṛti*). But by the time Nimbārka came to the scene with his new interpretation of Vedānta, *bhakti* had assumed a complete

---

5. Qtd. in Paritosh Das, *op. cit.*, p. 124.

6. *snehapūrvaṁ anudhyānaṁ bhakti.*
— *Śrībhaṣya* with *Śruta Prakāśikā* 1.4

romantic tenor. *Bhakti* no longer stood for the contemplative love, but love with a sweeter tinge that could only be experienced by a lover and his beloved. To validate this new dimension of *bhakti* female characters like Rādhā or *gopīs* were introduced. Yet these Vedāntin *ācāryas* did not have as much freedom as the Gauḍīya Vaiṣṇavas enjoyed in interpreting *bhakti* in terms of pure emotion. Being *ācāryas* they were expected to follow the path suggested by the *Prasthāna Trayī*, i.e., Upaniṣads, *Gītā* and *Brahma-Sūtra*. So despite the superiority accorded to *bhakti* it could not be projected as completely antithetical to *jñāna*.

Śrī Caitanya never offered a formal exposition of his metaphysical stand. Whatever he preached or believed can be gleaned through a series of biographies and also through the works of his disciples — Jīva and Rūpa Goswāmīs. These two Goswāmīs were largely responsible for giving a formal shape to the metaphysics of the neo-Vaiṣṇavism of Caitanya. The biographies of Caitanya record his affiliation towards a dualistic interpretation of *jīva-Brahman* relationship and his absolute resistance to the Advaitic theory of Śaṅkara. Accordingly, he also dismissed Śaṅkara's theory about the superiority of *jñāna* over *bhakti* as a path leading to *mukti*. For Caitanya, *bhakti* is always superior to *jñāna*. Along with this, Śaṅkara's definition of *bhakti* in terms of looking into one's own self is discounted. *Bhakti* now stands for a mental state (*bhāva*) of intense emotional attachment towards the object of love, viz., Kṛṣṇa. Vallabhācārya had already introduced the idea of *bhakti* as *prema* (love), but it was Nimbārka who brought to the limelight the sweeter dimension (*mādhurya pradhāna*) of devotional love for God. These two concepts were amalgamated to form the very basis of the Gauḍīya concept of *prema bhakti*. Unlike the Vedāntin Vaiṣṇavas, the Caitanites had *Bhāgavata Purāṇa* as their source of inspiration. So they had more freedom to develop a theory in which the concept of love could find a full expression. To vindicate their stand on the sweeter aspect of love the Gauḍīya Vaiṣṇavism incorporated a shift in the very idea of Viṣṇu as the Lord Supreme. The very impression of Viṣṇu as the wisest philosopher and a royal warrior God was relegated to the background; instead the focus turned towards Kṛṣṇa's childhood depicted in *Bhāgavata Purāṇa*. He is delineated here as a playful adolescent boy of Vṛndāvana. Caitanya wanted his followers to believe that this young Kṛṣṇa of Vṛndāvana is the *Parama Īśvara* (the Lord supreme). He is the personal God not in the usual sense but a personal God in human incarnation. So it now becomes easier for Gauḍīya Vaiṣṇavas to describe *bhakti* as the participation of a devotee in the divine play of Kṛṣṇa. Moreover, it is believed that his abode, Vṛndāvana, is a real place where the Lord is said to have spent his childhood in dalliance with Rādhā, his beloved. So *bhakti* is now interpreted in terms of *prema* (love) for Kṛṣṇa and the paradigmatic models of *prema* are Rādhā or her associates (*gopī*s) pining for union with Kṛṣṇa. Thus, the emotion of *śṛṅgāra* (erotic love) overtakes the concept of the contemplative dimension of the *bhakti*. It is no wonder that Jīva Goswāmī and Rūpa Goswāmī, the chief architects of Gauḍīya Vaiṣṇavism, make a scathing criticism of the concept of *jñāna mārga* (self-knowledge as a means of liberation). This is obvious from Rūpa Goswāmī's presentation of the hierarchical scheme of the devotees in his work *Bhakti Rasāmṛta Sindhu*. Here he puts the followers of the path of *jñāna* and *yoga* in the lowest wrung of *bhakta*s on the ground that this path is devoid of any trace of emotion. Therefore, *jñāna* is considered to be an obstacle in the path of the joy of Kṛṣṇa *bhakti*.[7] Besides, to facilitate a real emotional bond between the devotee and the God (*parama Īśvara*) the Gauḍīya Vaiṣṇavas stress the importance of the concept, "myness" (*mamatva*). Without this feeling of "myness" the devotee cannot partake in the divine sport of Kṛṣṇa nor

---

7. *Bhaktirasāmṛtasindhu* II.5.21.

can he experience the sweetness of his love for Kṛṣṇa.[8] With this theory, the dualism between the *jīva* and *parama* is firmly established.

The history of Orissa records the impact of these two models of Vaiṣṇavism on Orissan culture mostly through the royal patronage accorded to them. Despite such influences how the Oriyā Vaiṣṇavas of sixteenth century steered clear of the basic traits of these two very important strands of Vaiṣṇavism is a matter to be probed. It may be argued that the dominance of Vedāntin Vaiṣṇava theory on Orissan culture might not have extended beyond twelfth and thirteenth century. Therefore, the Oriyā *santha*s might not have faced any obstacle in developing an indigenous *bhakti* theory of their own. But on this ground we cannot dismiss the importance of *bhakti* theory championed by Śrī Caitanya, who was a contemporary of Pañcasakhās, the five great Vaiṣṇava *santha*s of Orissa. What is more perplexing about their distinct stand on *bhakti* is their professed allegiance to Śrī Caitanya. These five *santha*s seemed to be overenthusiastic in eulogizing him. Even they delineated Caitanya as the incarnation of Jagannātha himself.

It seems that despite the strong presence of Vaiṣṇavism from twelfth century onwards, and despite the royal support it received, the people of Orissa were not very favourably inclined towards a conception of *bhakti* centred on emotional love (*anurakti, prema* and *kṛṣṇa-rati*), be it conjugal or adulterous. The culture somehow maintained a sort of ambivalent attitude towards any form of "love" and especially towards adulterous love (*parakīya prīti*). This is reflected in the delineation of Kṛṣṇa in the Oriyā *Mahābhārata* of Sāralā Dāsa. He makes a scathing criticism of the romantic and immoral dimension of Kṛṣṇa's character while narrating the scene of Kṛṣṇa's death. The funeral pyre refused to engulf

8. *Bhaktirasāmṛtasindhu* II.5.9.

Kṛṣṇa's body (which, according to the Indian tradition is a ominous sign) because all his life he was involved in extra-marital affairs. Similarly, the famous *Gīta Govinda* of the Vaiṣṇava poet Jayadeva did not receive the accolade it deserved, because it dealt with the adulterous love of Kṛṣṇa and Rādhā. This same trait is found in the position of idols in Jagannātha temple. In the *sanctum sanctorum* Jagannātha (who has been identified with Viṣṇu himself), is not placed with his wife, as is the practice in all the Viṣṇu temples, but with his sister, Subhadrā. A small metallic idol of Lakṣmī placed in the *sanctum* is obviously a later addition and was most probably due to the influence of Rāmānujācārya. A separate temple for Lakṣmī was built in the later phase within the temple compound. But in this temple too she is worshipped without her consort. Similarly we do not find any idol of Rādhā in the main temple despite the popularity of Caitanite Vaiṣṇavism in Orissa. A very small temple dedicated to Sākṣīgopāla (a form of Viṣṇu) with Rādhā within the compound of the main temple cannot be said to be of very early origin. Thus a Viṣṇu without a consort may speak volumes about the unusual trend of Vaiṣṇava *bhakti*. This continues to be an inexplicable phenomenon of Vaiṣṇavism based on Jagannātha *dharma*.

II

Jñāna and Bhakti : The New Perspective

Now coming back to our original discussion on the theory of *jñānamiśra bhakti* we find that there is but very little commonality between other predominant forms of Vaiṣṇavism and the Orissan Vaiṣṇavism. Of cource, there are stray references to *prema bhakti* in the works of Balarāma Dāsa and Yaśovanta Dāsa, two important members of the group of the five *santhas*. Balarāma Dāsa defines *prema bhakti* as tasting the divine love of Kṛṣṇa by imaginatively placing oneself as Rādhā. He even claims that this form of *bhakti* is the best. Yaśovanta also reiterates this view occasionally.[9] From such infrequent references it will not be wise on our part to jump to the conclusion that at least these two *santha*s of Orissa were bent upon following the path of *prema bhakti*. On the other hand, both these *santha*s staunchly stuck to their non-dualistic stand and were never tired of emphasizing the identity between the *jīvātman* and *paramātman*. I have already made it clear that *prema bhakti* theory is conceptually linked to dualism therefore this theory cannot be conceptually accommodated within the scheme of a metaphysics based on non-qualitativeness and ineffability of the non-dual highest principle. On this issue there is irreconciliable difference between both the forms of Vaiṣṇavism. The Gauḍīya Vaiṣṇavas could not accept the idea of worship of a formless God as propounded by the Orissan Vaiṣṇavas. This is one of the reasons why the Orissan Vaiṣṇavas draw flak from the Gauḍīya Vaiṣṇavas. This will be clear from the following lines from the *Caitanya Caritāmṛta*: "God is the embodiment of six divine qualities and bliss. How can you call Him formless?"[10]

We have sufficient grounds to justify that the Pañcasakhā, though self-acclaimed followers of Śrī Caitanya, never could accept *bhakti* in terms of *prema*. It may appear that there was some other compulsion on their part to eulogize *prema bhakti*

---

9. *ātmāku stīrī veśa kari, śrīrādhā aṅge vihari.*
kṛṣṇa āsvāda rasa dei, ehāku premabhakti kahi.
— Balarāma Dāsa, *Vedāntasāra Gupta-Gītā* XXIV

Also

premabhakti thāru bhakti nāhiṅ,
prema nikaṭe thae muhiṅ.
— Yaśovanta Dāsa, *Premabhakti Gītā* III

10. *saṛaiśvarya purnānanda vigraha jāhār,*
hena bhagavān tumi kaha nirākār.

Qtd. in K.C. Mishra, *Oṛiyā Sāhityare Dharamadhārā*, Bhubaneswar: Orissa Textbook Bureau, 1997, p. 94.

as a means of self-realization. May be they did not want to invite the royal wrath, as the then King of Orissa was an ardent follower of Śrī Caitanya, for, we come across such anecdotes of royal persecution at least in the works of Acyutānanda and Balarāma Dāsa. But *Santha* Dvārakā Dāsa, a follower of the Pañcasakhā tradition perhaps did not have any such compulsion. So he is more explicit and articulate in declaring that their *bhakti* theory has nothing to do with the theory of emotional relation between Rādhā/*gopīs* with that of Kṛṣṇa or the inherent dualism between the *jīva* and the *parama*. This will be evident from the following lines of this *santha*:

> Those who worship me in dual form
> Are doomed to be born and reborn in this *saṁsāra*.
> They say, assume the form of a woman,
> To enjoy the erotic sport of Kṛṣṇa.
> But there is not even an iota of difference between Rādhā and me.
> Why should she be my beloved and why should I enjoy her love?[11]

This is obvious now that the very idea of *jñānamiśra bhakti* is conceptually independent of other Vaiṣṇavite forms of *bhakti*. Let us now turn attention to the way the Orissan Vaiṣṇavas delineate the concept of *bhakti*. According to these thinkers *bhakti* and *jñāna* should not be seen as antithetical; rather *bhakti* and *jñāna* are complementary. In Acyutānanda's words,

> by penetrating *jñāna* one gets *bhakti*,
> and by penetrating *bhakti* one gets *jñāna*.[12]

---

11. *jugaḷa bhābe je bhajai, aneka janma se labhai.*
bolanti hebu stri aṅga, karibu rati krīrā saṅga.
rādhāra mora tilemātre, bheda je nāhi kadā jñate.
se stīrī hebe keuṅthai, mu tāṅku labhibi kimpāiṅ?
— Dvārakā Dāsa, *Trayodaśa Skandha Bhāgavata* VII

12. *jñāna bhedile bhakti pāi, bhakti bhedile jñāna pai.*
— Acyutānanda, *Guru Bhakti-Gītā* III.50

Acyutānanda further uses the metaphor of two wings of a flying bird to explain the complementality of both the ideas. But if we probe deeper into their theory it becomes clear that *jñāna* is given a priority over devotion. Here *jñāna* means self-knowledge (*ātmajñāna*), not the scriptural knowledge, i.e., *vidyā*.[13] Acyutānanda in his work *Brahma Śāṅkuḷī* declares in the context of a dialogue between sage Vaśiṣṭha and the crow named "Bhuṣaṇda," "I tell you Vaśiṣṭha, *ātmajñāna* is the best of all the means available."[14] Interestingly the crow is depicted here as the teacher because even if animal, it is a realised soul. So it is supposed to know the best. With this emphasis on *ātmajñāna*, *bhakti* is redefined as "that experience which emerges from the knowledge of non-duality between *jīva* and *Īśvara*." In other words, it is a form of devotion towards the ultimate reality or may be towards God, in which case the bliss of devotion is realisable once the identity between the *jīvātman* and the *paramātman* is experienced. For this, the most important step is "knowing one's own self." To speak in the language of these *santhas*, *bhakti* signifies "seeing *ātman* in *ātman*." I have already hinted that any theory rooted in non-dualism cannot subscribe to a theory of pure emotional love without indulging in contradiction. So the Pañcasakhā as well as the subsequent *santhas* of Orissa do not emphasise the role of emotion, specifically the emotion of erotic love, in their theory of *bhakti*. Even, Santha Jagannātha Dāsa, while transcreating *Śrīmad Bhāgavatam* tries his best to accommodate his own version of *bhakti* by bringing about a broader synthesis between Kr̥ṣṇa-*bhakti* as enunciated in the original Sanskrit work and the *jñāna bhakti* of the Orissan tradition. He says,

> All those who deliberate on the highest truth offer varied interpretation of the same principle. Some call it *Brahman*, while others call it *paramārtha*, and there are still others

13. Acyutānanda, *Śabda Saṁhitā*, I.

14. *tote kahuchi vaśiṣṭha sabuhi ātmajñāna śreṣṭha.*
— Acyutānanda, *Brahma Śānkuḷi* I

> who call it *Bhagavān*. But those devoted to Kṛṣṇa see *ātman* in *ātman*.[15]

Summerising their stand on the issue, Dvārakā Dāsa says,

> There are innumerable paths suggested by different persons. Men fail to realise that there is but one *Brahman*. All these paths are of no avail without realising the *Brahman* in *ātman*.[16]

It may be a difficult path, but one has a scope to go step by step. As long as one cannot achieve this power one may worship varied incarnations of God, like Rāma and Kṛṣṇa. One has to strive for this knowledge. So Acyutānanda makes the following insightful remark:

> True knowledge of the *mahāśūnya* (the highest being) may not be accessible to celestial beings and *siddhas*. You need not look up to them for guidance. This knowledge is within your heart. You have to find it there and realise it.[17]

Again,

> *Brahma-jñāna* and *jñāna-Brahman* are never far from you, it is inseparably present withing your heart.[18]

---

15. *tattva bicāra jñāna jete, jñānī kahanti e jagate.*
kehu kahanti brahmatattva, kehu vā kahe paramārtha.
kehu kahanti bhagavāna nirmala parama je jñāna

x x x

karanti kṛṣṇa thāre bhakti ātmāre ātmāku dekhanti.
— Jagannātha Dāsa, *Bhāgavata* (Oriyā) I.1

16. *emante mārga bhinna bhinna kari bhajanti mūḍha jana.*
eka brahma boli na jāṇi aneka mārge bhaje prāṇī.
— Dvārakā Dāsa, *Trayodaśa Skanda Bhāgavata* VII

17. *to hṛda madhey achhi jñāna,*
tu tote khoji kara sthāna.
— Acyutānanda, *Brahma Śāṅkuḷi* I

18. *brahmajñāna jñāna brahma e nuhai dūra,*
gupata rahichi hṛudamandire tohara.
— Acyutānanda, *Jñānapradīpa Gītā* VI

In this context a valid question may be raised. In fact, Caitanya Dāsa, a contemporary of Pañcasakhā, himself raises this question. "If the Lord Viṣṇu pervades the whole *saṁsāra* and resides in all beings then why should not a man get *mokṣa* (liberation) spontaneously without any aid or effort?" In other words, if *Brahma-jñāna* is very much present within us then what is the need for us to follow the path of either *jñāna* or *bhakti*? To this quizzical issue he has a succinct answer —

> Fire is inherently present within dry fuel but it does not automatically produce fire. One has to make certain efforts to produce it. Similarly *Brahma-jñāna* is inherently present within human beings but one has to make sincere efforts to experience it.[19]

Elaborating this idea further Dvārakā Dāsa says,

> You are unnecessarily wasting your time in searching for *mukti* by different rites and rituals without an inkling of the knowledge that he (God) is very much within you and outside you.[20]

These statements may sound more or less Advaitic and also Upaniṣadic. But neither in the Upaniṣads nor in Advaita Vedānta self-realisation is considered to be a part of *bhakti* or mode of worship. However, the influence of *Śrīmad Bhagavad Gītā* seems to be palpable here. This is evident from the following stanza mouthed by its protagonist, Lord Kṛṣṇa —

---

19. *prāṇīṅka dehe kari sthiti, kimpāiṅ na die mokṣa gati?*

x x x

kāṭha bhitare agni thāiṅ, kāṭhaku na pāre dahai.
manthile kari bāhu bala, takṣaṇe jaḷe anaḷa.
sehi prakāre deva hari, agni svarūpe bhūte puri.
jñāna manthana kale nitye, prakāśa honti pañcabhūte.
— Caitanya Dāsa, *Nirguṇa Mahātmya*, pp. 12-13.

20. *jāhāku ete bhābe dhāyi, bhitare bāhāre ṭi sehi.*
— Dvārakā Dāsa, *Trayodaśa Skanda Bhāgavata* I

> Four kinds of virtuous men worship me, O Arjuna! — the distressed, the seeker, the seeker of knowledge and the wise (*jñānī*). Of them, the wise men, ever steadfast, with devotion to the One is dearest to me.[21]

Interestingly, in another stanza of the same treatise Lord Kṛṣṇa states that, since the path of *jñāna* is arduous, it is better to follow the path of pure *bhakti*. "Greater is their trouble whose minds are set on the unmanifested (*avyakta*); for the goal of unmanifested is very difficult for the embodied to reach."[22] Though the general spirit of *Gītā* is non-dualistic yet it also admits the difficulties involved in devotion to a formless impersonal God. In fact, in the *Gītā*, no strict definition of the object of devotion is given. It may be indescribable, formless and impersonal, Supreme Being or else a God who is personal in nature. So monotheism, and even polytheism, is given a chance, for, it is also stated that whichever God in whichever way is worshipped does not make much difference to the quality of devotion. The treatise being quite open-ended in nature accommodates multiple versions of *bhakti* within its framework. Therefore, pell-mell quotation from the *Gītā* will not justify the fact that *jñānamiśra bhakti* of the Orissan *santha*s is entirely inspired by this treatise. However, the concept of *yoga* as presented in the *Gītā* seems to bear a close affinity to the concept of *jñānamiśra bhakti* of the Oriyā Vaiṣṇavas. Though the term *yoga* has more than one dimension in the *Gītā*, the term ultimately refers to the bonding of *jivātman* and *paramātman*. That is why *Gītā* again and again emphasises the feeling of oneness with the cosmic whole. Here, I quote two such verses.

> He whose self is harmonised by *yoga* sees the self abiding in all beings and all beings in the self, everywhere he sees the same.[23]

21. *Śrīmad Bhagavad-Gītā* XII.16.
22. *Śrīmad Bhagavad-Gītā* XII.5.
23. *Śrīmad Bhagavad-Gītā* VI.29.

Again,

> O Arjuna! he who sees with equality everything in the image of oneself, in pleasure or in pain, is a true *yogī*.[24]

This predominantly Upaniṣadic theory had great impact on Indian philosophical traditions of both Brāhmaṇical and non-Brāhmaṇical origin. So it will be of some interest to examine how this central concept is developed in Tāntric versions of both Buddhism and Hinduism.

Yoga and Bhakti

Undoubtedly, the concept of *yoga* signifying an inherent bond between the self and the cosmic consciousness occupies a key position in subsequent philosophical movements of the medieval period. Though the theoretical core of this relation of identity was kept intact, the outward structure was changed beyond recognition under the influence of Tantra, (both Hindu and Buddhist). So *yoga* came to be viewed as a practical method, and sometimes an esoteric method of self-realisation. The meaning of the term *yoga* was extended not only to cover the practical dimension developed by Patañjali's system, but also the esoteric practices adopted by the Buddhist and Hindu Tantras and the Nātha cult. The Vajrayānīs named it *svādhi daivata yoga*, the Sahajayānīs called it *sahaja yoga* and the Nātha cult called it *haṭha yoga* and the Orissan Vaiṣṇavas following the Nāthas referred to it as *ghaṭa yoga* (the *yoga* of the body) also as *nisvātī yoga*. The concept of *yoga* cannot be said to be exclusively Brāhmaṇical in its denotation. Certain elements of *yoga* are almost common to Tāntric Buddhism, Śāktism and Śaivism, including Nāthism. All of them insist on the *kāyā sādhanā* (the culture of body), depicting holy places in different parts of the body. This became almost a common feature of the literature of all these sects. Most of these systems presented

24. *Śrīmad Bhagavad-Gītā* VI.32

yoga as a theory of devotion based on self-knowledge. This will become clear if we look into the theories of devotion and *yoga* of the above-mentioned sects.

It is believed that Asaṅga, the propounder of Yogācāra Buddhism, was responsible for introducing the elements of *yoga* into Buddhism. The system is called Yogācāra because it emphasises on the importance of *yoga* for the realisation of pure knowledge (*bodhi*). Asaṅga suggests that one can come out of the cocoon of the empirical ego by embracing the universal soul (*mahātman*). Seeing the right path and grasping the true meaning of *śūnyatā*, the enlightened person transcends the individual existence, realise the pure soul (*śuddhātman*) and becomes one with it. This is the pure existence of Buddha and is called *paramātman*. So Asaṅga says the goal is to become one, through *bodhi*, with the *dharmakāyā* of Buddha's body of existence. Thus, the merging of the empirical ego in the *paramātman* is the goal of a seeker. Vajrayāna made it more esoteric in nature and believed that through secret yogic practices the highest truth can be realised. Accordingly the Vajrayānīs, almost in the Upaniṣadic tenor claim that a *sādhaka*, who realises Vajrasattvahood, himself becomes the Vajrasattva. In other words, Vajrasattvahood can be realised through conceiving all created things as the self.[25] Adding further dimension to this theory Indrabhūti states that all human beings are potential *bodhicittas*. The term *bodhicitta*, in this case, stands for a mind bent upon attaining perfect enlightenment with a view to helping all beings to be liberated from the cycle of birth and death. A *bodhicitta* strives towards realisation of the self as god (*devatā*) and the process is called *svādhidaivata yoga*. It is a state in which a man realises his own self in all things, everywhere, in all aspects, by all means, and for all times, and realises the universalised self as the universal

---

25. *Bodhicittam idaṁ vajraṁ sarva-buddhatvam ātmanaḥ.*
— *Jñānasiddhi* XV

Qtd. in Dasgupta, *Introduction to Tāntric Buddhism*, p. 83.

perfectly realised one.[26] But later on other elements of Tantra like *mudrā*, *mantra* and *yantra* (drawing of mystical figures) assumed greater importance in Vajrayāna. So there arose another group of *yogis* within this group of Tāntric Buddhists who seceded away from the original group and stressed that the yogic method is the only method of self-realisation. This new branch of Tāntric Buddhism assumed a new name, viz., Sahajayāna. The word *sahaja* literally means that which arises with the birth of a being (*saha jāyate iti sahajaḥ*). It is that which all the beings possess by virtue of his own existence, and thus the quintessence of all *dharmas*. Like the Upaniṣads and Vajrayāna, this new school of Tāntric Buddhism believes that the *sahaja* nature is beyond the categories of thought and can be accessible only by intuitive experience. *Hevajra Tantra*, the famous text of this sect states that *sahaja* can neither be explained by any man nor can be expressed by speech.[27] Almost in the Upaniṣadic way that states: "when everything becomes the self who will see Him and by what means? And who will know him by what means?"[28] *Guhyasiddhi*, another text of this order says that it is a truth to be realised through personal intuition, it is never expressible by tongue.[29] This intuitive experience was later on renamed as *sahaja sādhanā* or *sahaja yoga*. The *sahaja* is also described as the self; and the world is the transformation of that self.[30]

---

26. *sarvatra sarvataḥ sarvaṁ sarvathā sarvadā svayam,*
sarva-buddhamayaṁ siddhaṁ svamātmānaṁ prapaśyati.

— *Jñāna Siddhi* XV.52. Qtd. in Dasgupta, *Introduction to Tāntric Buddhism*, p. 83.

27. Qtd. in S.B. Dasgupta, *Obscure Religious Cults*, p. 78.

28. *yasya tvasya sarvam ātmaiva 'bhūt tat kena kam paśyet, kam vijñānāt.*
— *Bṛhadāraṇyaka Upaniṣad* IV.1.5.1

29. *sva-saṁvedyaṁ tu tat tattvamvaktuṁ nā 'syaḥ-pāryate.*
Qtd. in *Obscure Religious Cults*, p. 79.

30. *Hevajra Tantra*, qtd. in *Obscure Religious Cults*, p. 85.

Thus, we find that in all these branches of Tāntric Buddhism the concept of *yoga* (with its new connotation) plays a central role in the process of self-realisation. All of them insist that the truth can be never found outside but it is to be intuited within. It is debatable to which extent these schools of Tāntric Buddhism inspired the *jñānamiśra bhakti* of the Orissan *santhas*. But sometimes the scale weighs in favour of such a hypothesis as we come across similar expressions in the writings of the Oriyā *santhas*. I cannot help citing some such famous lines from their works. Śiśu Ananta Dāsa, for example, proclaims, "can there be a God outside mind?" Dvārakā Dāsa, however, voices the same thought more explicitly when he says, "ignorant people worship gods and goddesses made of wood or stone without realising that I am nothing but the self." More facts about the interface between Sahajayāna and Orissan Vaiṣṇavism shall be made evident as we shift our focus on other important theories of the Orissan *santhas*. But for the time being I shall concentrate on their conception of *yoga*.

The Pañcasakhās and other *santhas* of this cult strongly believe that *yoga* is a part of *bhakti*. The essence of their *bhakti* theory is summarised in the following lines of Balarāma Dāsa:

> *bhakti* arises out of self-contemplation,
> and from *bhakti* emerges *yoga*.[31]

It is clear from the above lines that *yoga* is an integral part of *Jñānamiśra bhakti*. Obviously these *santhas* were not using the term *yoga* in the sense it is presented in the *Gītā*. For them *yoga* is a practical process through which the oneness of the individual self with the cosmic self is realised. The method of *yoga* suggested by Orissan Vaiṣṇavism is rather a combination of Tantra and Yoga. They apply these principles to explicate the intricacies associated with self-realisation.

---

31. *ātmā cintile bhakti hue,*
bhaktiru yoga udaye.
— Balarāma Dāsa, *Vedāntasāra Gupta-Gītā*, verse pp. 69-70.

Theory of Navadhā Bhakti : A New Scheme

The theory of *bhakti* understood in terms of Yoga and Tantra allows the Vaiṣṇavas of Orissa to develop a theory of nine-fold *bhakti*, more popularly known as *Navadhā bhakti*, that may appear very queer and, sometimes, quite antagonistic to the Vaiṣṇavite scheme of *Navadhā bhakti*. *Bhāgavata Purāṇa*[32] while articulating the steps to *bhakti* presents the theory of the famous *navadhā* (nine-fold) *bhakti*. The steps are as follows: *śravaṇa* (listening to the glories of God), *kīrtana* (chanting His name), *viṣṇu smaraṇa* (constant remembrance of Viṣṇu), *padasevana* (his service), *arcanā* (worshipping Him as an idol), *vandanā* (paying homage), *dāsya* (servitude to God), *sakhya* (treating him like a friend) and *ātmanivedana* (totally surrendering oneself to God). This nine-fold *bhakti* occupies an important place in the Vaiṣṇava theory of *bhakti*. However, the Orissan Vaiṣṇavas change the entire pattern of *Navadhā bhakti* and offer a new scheme of this nine-fold step to *bhakti*. These steps are as follows — *yantra, mantra, tantra, chāyā, jyoti, abāda, haja, samādhi* and *rasaguṇa*.[33] Not only do they alter the scheme but claim that *he who has the knowledge of these steps he alone is a Vaiṣṇava*. This is obvious that these philosophers are not following the well-settled tradition of the Vaiṣṇavas. The entire scheme of *navadhā bhakti* seems to be motivated more by tantro-yogic theory of *nisvatī yoga* rather than pure Vaiṣṇavism. Interestingly, there seems to be close similarity with the methods suggested by the *Śāradātilakatantra*, a Tāntric treatise centred on Viṣṇu worship. *Bhakti* is now associated with Tantra. In case of these Vaiṣṇavas, the first step to *bhakti* is chanting of God's name (*mantra*) followed by concentration on the mystical figures (*yantra*). *Tantra* is the next step that leads to inner concentration. When the mind attains

32. *Bhāgavata Purāṇa* VII.5.23.

33. *yantram mantram tantram caiva chāyā jyotrbāda,*
haja samādhi rasguṇam ca yo jānāti sa vaiṣṇava.
— Acyutānanda, *Gurubhakti Gītā* II

concentration through the preceding stages the *sādhaka* experiences the shadow light or *chāyā* (something like the *alokabhāsa* of Nāgārjunapāda). Gradually the *sādhaka* will have the vision of the light (*jyoti*). The next step is *abāda* that signifies diffused light. Mind thus concentrated on the experience of light is totally withdrawn from the senses, mental discriminations, and the objective and subjective limitations. This is the state of *samādhi*. This stage leads to the experience of *haja* or *sahaja*. This is the phase in which a *sādhaka* experiences the identification of his individual consciousness with the cosmic consciousness. Finally, there is the experience of the bliss, called *rasaguṇa*. This stage is comparable to the *mahāsukha* of the Vajrayāna. These nine steps to *bhakti* or more specifically, the *Brahman*-realisation is viewed by these *santhas* as a form of gradual progressive experience from the confusion to pure light. These stages are named *ūrma* (the desert) *dhūmra* (smoky confusion), *jyoti* (light) and *jvālā* (the final experience of effulgent light). The description of these stages of yogic experience seems to be very close to the Tāntric Buddhism. In *Guhyasamāja Tantra* there is a mention of five stages of self-realisation — they are *maricīkā* (desert), *dhūmra* (smoke), *khadyota* (twinkling light), *dīpajvālā* (illuminated light of the lamp) and *gagana* (the expansion like the sky).[34] As far as Vaiṣṇavism is concerned, such a scheme of *bhakti* not only seems strange but appears to go against the very spirit of Vaiṣṇvism.

I have tried to explore every nuance of the *Jñānamiśra bhakti* of the Vaiṣṇavas of Orissa. From our discussion it is clear that the theory is a kind of *bhakti* theory that does not have many parallels. It is a synthesis of both *āstika* and *nāstika* elements. Sometimes, it echos the Advaitic theory of *jñāna mārga* so

34. *prathamaṁ maricīkākāraṁ dhūmrākāraṁ dvitīyakam,*
tṛtiyaṁ khadyotākāraṁ caturthaṁ dīpavat Jvālām,
pañcamaṁ sadālokaṁ nirabraṁ gagana sannibham.

— *Guhyasamāja Tantra*, Ch. XVIII qtd in B. Mohanty, *Oṛiya Sāhityara Itihāsa*, vol. I, p. 98.

perfectly that one may mistake it to be a Vedāntin in letter and spirit; but the other moments we find it to be most un-Advaitic. This spirit of synthesis makes this theory innovative in its own right.

9

The Piṇḍa-Brahmāṇḍa Tattva

THE idea that the body is the microcosmic representation of the macrocosmic universe, that is otherwise known as *piṇḍa-brahmāṇḍa tattva* is one of the key theories of the Vaiṣṇavas of Orissa. The idea though repugnant to the traditional forms of Vaiṣṇavism, was not entirely unknown to the *nirguṇa panthī* Vaiṣṇavas of north India. But what makes Orissan Vaiṣṇavism distinct from the other santhic theories in this respect is the emphasis these philosophers attach to the divinity of the gross body. This is otherwise known as *kāyā sādhanā*. Both these theories can be said to have their genesis in the famous religio-philosophical movement known as Nātha *dharma*. This cult was one of the important ascetic movements of the medieval period, active in the northern part of the country during eleventh to fifteenth centuries CE. This cult had a huge role in shaping up the *nirguṇa panthī* philosophy voiced by such great *santhas* as Kabīr, Dādū, Razzab and many others. There were certain elements of novelty in Nātha philosophy so its impact ultimately could be felt in other parts of India as well as in Orissa. Like other parts of India, Nātha cult had its share of popularity in Orissa too. However, in the Oriyā versions of Nātha literature like *Śiśu Veda* and *Gorakha Saṁhitā*, the influence of Tāntric Buddhism is more pronounced. This is evident from the frequent reference to the word *śūnya* in the context of the highest Reality. While the Nātha cult is the fountain spring of the *nirguṇa*-based literature of the north Indian *bhakti* movement, in case of Orissa its influence is prominently displayed in the theories of *kāyā sādhanā* and *haṭha yoga* (also called *ghaṭa yoga*).

I

The Nātha Cult

The Nātha cult rose into prominence during the ninth century. The history and legends of the Nātha cult recognise Gorakṣanātha as the founder of the sect. Sometimes, Matsyendranātha or Mīnanātha, his preceptor, is also taken to be one of the earliest *yogī*s of this cult. Interestingly, both Gorakṣanātha and Matsyendranātha also figure prominently in the list of eighty-four *siddha*s of the Sahajayāna. This may give rise to a lot of confusion about the genesis of this new religious movement. Such anomaly at least indicates that there must have been some historical link between the Nātha cult and Tāntric Buddhism. It is probable that Gorakṣanātha and Matsyendranātha deviated from the path of Sahajayāna due to the preponderance of sexo-yogic practices amongst the Tāntric Buddhists. Gorakṣanātha wanted to purge the system of perverted interpretation of yogic *sādhanā*. So Nāthism is more puritanical and ethico-centric in nature.

As far as the metaphysics of the Nātha cult is concerned, we do not come across anything novel or striking. The shadow of Mahāyānic and Advaitic interpretation of the Reality as the One unique and ineffable principle looms large here. Again, the Reality is described almost in the similar fashion as *nirañjana* (taintless), *śūnya* (void), *anādi* (beginningless), and *nirguṇa* (non-qualifiable). But positively speaking, the highest Reality is seen as *parā Brahman*. As the all-pervading, self-existent, eternal and absolute Reality, it is also depicted as pure consciousness, pure-existence and pure-bliss, i.e., *sat-cit-ānanda Brahman*. It is also of the nature of *parā-saṁvit* (transcendent consciousness). Interestingly, the Reality Supreme is also identified as *Ādinātha* or *Śiva*.[1] As the *Ādinātha* (Primal lord),

1. A.K. Banerjee, *Philosophy of Gorakṣanātha*, Gorakhpur, Mahant Digvijai Nātha Trust, 1961, p. 47.

He is not just an abstract principle but also the object of devotion. From this, it is easier to jump to the conclusion that Nātha *dharma* is a form of Śaivism, and therefore purely an *āstika* system of thought. But our discussions about the Vajrayānic notion of Vajrasattva in earlier chapters may make it clear that this new theory of *parā Brahman* or *Ādinātha* is conceptually not very distant from the Śiva of the Hindu Tantra and the Vajrasattva of the Buddhist Tantras and the *Śūnya Puruṣa* of Orissan Vaiṣṇavism. The theory, in fact, is an amalgamation of *āstika* and *nāstika* elements very much like the Tāntric versions of Buddhism.

What interests us in the context of this book is the Nātha conception of *yoga* as a mode of self-realisation. Again, in this case, one may note uncanny similarities between the Tāntric Buddhism and the Nātha cult. Like the Buddhists, they too hold that the Reality can never be approached by sensuous or mental experiences. The sole means of final realisation is super-sensuous, super-mental direct experience in the state of *samādhi*. This is the state in which the empirical consciousness is completely transformed into purified unconditioned perfect consciousness, and the ultimate Reality is directly experienced not only as an object of experience but also as the experience itself. So, the consciousness of the self is taken as the highest medium to understand the ultimate Reality, as well as, His manifestation; and here comes the importance of the method called *yoga*. So the Nātha philosophers explain the highest state of self-realisation in the following way: "it is the state in which an enlightened *yogī* fails to identify the Reality as *sat* or *asat*, *śūnya* or *pūrṇa*, *dvaita* or *advaita*, because it is beyond all categories."[2] Thus, their conception of *yoga* neither pertains to the view of unity nor to that of duality; and, therefore, they name their metaphysical position as Dvaitādvaita-Vilakṣaṇa-vāda or Pakṣapāta Vinirmuktavāda. Though the idea of *yoga*, as the ultimate mode of self-realisation, is not a very original

2. *Philosophy of Gorakṣanātha*, 54ff.

concept these thinkers use the idea of *yoga* to formulate two fascinating concepts, viz., *piṇḍa-brahmāṇḍa* identity theory; and the theory of *kāyā sādhanā*. As my primary intention here is to assess the impact of the Nātha theory on the formulation of the metaphysical perspective of the Oriyā *santha*s I would like to come straight to those concepts that have something to do with the *santha* philosophy of Orissa. Therefore, I pick up three important Nātha concepts, viz., *kāyā sādhanā, haṭha yoga* and *piṇḍa-brahmāṇḍa tattva,* for further discussion.

II

Kāyā Sādhanā

The Nātha cult enjoyed immense popularity in Orissa. Kiāri Maṭha of Kendrapara district, Bhāratī Maṭha situated at Bhubaneswar and many such *maṭha*s situated at different corners of Orissa still bear evidences of the predominance of this cult at certain points of Orissan history. The followers of this Nātha cult are still there in Orissa and are referred as the *yogī*s. Their poems and songs are very popular among the common masses of Orissa. Though most of the scholastic works on Nātha cult are absolutely silent about its presence and influence on Orissa, its impact on Orissan culture cannot be simply wished away. Quite a good number of works of this cult, believed to have been composed between thirteenth and fourteenth centuries in archaic Oriyā, are worth noting. Most important among them are — *Śiśu Veda, Amara Kośa Gītā, Rudra Sudhānidhi, Gorakha Saṁhitā* and *Gorakha Hadipā Saṁvāda*. These works offer a glimpse of the theories and practices of the Nātha *sampradāya* (community) in Orissa. But the most authentic proof of its profound influence can be gathered from the literature of fifteenth and sixteenth century. In Sāralā Dāsa's *Mahābhārata,* a fifteenth-century Oriyā work, one comes across references to Gorakṣanātha and Matsyendranātha on more than one occasion. Other Nātha *guru*s of this order like Mallikānātha and Lohī Dāsa are also referred to in the *Śūnya Saṁhitā* of

Acyutānanda. We can infer from such repeated allusion to the Nātha *gurus* that this sect was a very important part of the cultural milieu of Orissa. This religio-philosophical tradition was popularly known as Yogānti or Yogāṅtaka *vidyā* in this land. I have indicated earlier, the Orissan *santhas* owe the theories of *kāyā sādhanā* (worship of the body) and *piṇḍa-brahmāṇḍa tattva* (the body as a microcosm of the universe) to the Yogāṅtaka metaphysics. Both the theories, in turn, are rooted in a form of yogic method called *haṭha yoga* popularised by the Nātha cult. The Orissan *santhas* call it *ghaṭa yoga* (*ghaṭa* implying the body).

Yoga literally means "union," i.e., spiritual union of the individual soul with the universal soul, as is used in the Advaita Vedānta and the *Gītā*. According to Patañjali, on the other hand, *yoga* does not mean union but the spiritual effort to attain perfection through the control of the body, senses, mind, and through right discrimination between *puruṣa* and *prakṛti*. It is the name of a practical path that culminates in *viveka-jñāna*, which, in turn, leads to liberation. The Nātha philosophers do not exactly follow the footprints of Patañjali in their interpretation of *yoga*, though they are in general agreement with Patañjali's methods. It rather is a synthesis of the Upaniṣadic and Sahajayānī conception of *yoga*. They seem to draw inspiration from the Upaniṣads when they elucidate *yoga* in terms of *praṇava* or *oṁkāra sādhanā*. At the same time they put a lot of emphasis on *sahaja sādhanā* and *sahaja samādhi* emphasised by Sahajayāna Buddhists. This is one of the important reasons why the Nātha cult is said to have its roots in Sahajayāna. In fact, the three basic ideas of the Nātha cult, viz., *yoga*, *kāyā sādhanā* and the identification of the body with the universal self are not entirely unknown to the Buddhist Tāntrics. This is evident from their explication of *yoga* in terms of oneness of the individual consciousness and the cosmic consciousness. The very idea of *sahaja samādhi*, that finds a prominent place in the Nātha practice, is the brainchild of the Sahajīyā Buddhists. So it is not surprising that, very much like the Sahajayāna Buddhists, Nātha Panthīs also conceive *sahaja samādhi* in terms of a state of mental equilibrium in which the *yogī* transcends all conceptual and perceptual discriminations to become one with the whole universe. In the language of the Sahajayāna *siddha*, in such a state a *yogī* "himself is the goddess, the god, the disciple, the meditator and the object meditated upon."[3] This is the very goal Nātha *yogīs* aspire to achieve by what they call as *haṭha yoga*. This is an elaborate method of practical *sādhanā*. However, one must not overreach in claiming that the Nātha cult is nothing more than a Hinduised version of Tāntric Buddhism. It has a very rich philosophy of its own and the cult very smoothly amalgamates the principles of Advaita, Tantra and Yoga to churn out a new method of self-realisation.

One of the corollaries of the Nātha conception of *haṭha yoga* is the theory of *kāyā* or *piṇḍa*. Though in our ancient tradition the gross body is identified with *annamaya Brahman*,[4] in the Purāṇic and the later phases of its development body came to be considered as profane. So a lot of emphasis was laid on purifying the body by ritual bathing and the torture of the body of various dimensions. Nātha cult raises its voice against such fruitless practices. As a corollary to the control of the mind through *yoga* the culture of the body is highlighted. This is known as the *kāyā sādhanā*. *Kāyā sādhanā* for them is one of the indispensable accessories for yogic realisation. Thus, the body itself is regarded as the seat of divinity. In other words, body (*piṇḍa*) is the medium of experience of the cosmic self (*brahmāṇḍa*). However, a little probe shows that this is not an independent philosophical presupposition of the Nātha Panthīs. This bold theory has its genesis in the theory of Sahajayāna branch of Tāntric Buddhism. Sahajayāna, in many

---

3. S.B. Dasgupta, *Obscure Religious Cults*, Calcutta: Firma. KLM, 1969, p. 196.
4. *annaṁ brahmeti vyajānāt.*
   — *Taittirīya Upaniṣad* III.2.1

respects, was a reactionary movement against some of the practices of the Vajrayānīs. This branch of Tāntric Buddhism initially projected the ineffable Vajrasattva as the only God. But later on the system included innumerable gods and goddesses within its pantheon and included meaningless rituals within its fold. Sahajayāna voiced its protest against such polytheism and idolatry. Laxmīnkarī, one of the eminent *siddhas* of Sahajayāna (she incidentally was the sister of Indrabhūti, the king of Orissa) therefore proclaimed:

> No suffering, no fasting, no rites, no bathing, no purification, nor other rules of the society are necessary nor do you need to bow down before the images of gods, which are constructed out of wood, stone or mud but you should with concentration offer worship to your own body where all gods reside.[5]

Similarly, Saraha Pā, another *siddha*, who is said to have spent a considerable time in Orissa and learnt Mantrayāna here, puts this theory in a simpler form — "scholars explain many scriptures, but fail to know that Buddha resides in the body."[6] Saraha says, "Someone bodiless is hiding in the body — he who knows him there (in the body) is liberated."[7] The emphasis on the practical aspect of *yoga* along with an uncompromising spirit of revolt against all formalities and orthodoxy in religion has resulted in laying greater stress on the human body (*piṇḍa*)

---

5. *na nastakalpanāṁ kuryāt nopavaso na ca kriyām.*
   snānam śaucaṁ na caivātra gramadharma vivarjanam.
   na cāpi vandayeddevān kaṣṭha pāṣāṇa mṛṇmāyān.
   pūjāmasyeva kāyasya kuryānnityaṁ samāhitaḥ.

   Qtd. in B. Bhattacaryya, *An Introduction to Buddhist Esoterism*, Delhi: Motilal Banarsidass, 1989, p. 77.

6. *panditasra sasralasatya bakhāṇaiṅ,*
   dehaiṅ buddha vasantasgā jagaiṅ.

   Dohā Koṣa of Saraha Pada, qtd. in N.K. Sahu, *Buddhism in Orissa*, Bhubaneswar: Utkal University, 1958, p. 139.

7. *Dohā Koṣa of Saraha*, qtd. in Dasgupta, *Obscure Religious Cults*, p. 90.

as a microcosm of the universe (*brahmāṇḍa*). This feature predominates in all forms of Tantra in general, but the Sahajīya Buddhists lay their whole stress on the theory that body is the epitome of the whole universe. In *Hevajra* Tantra, a text of this order, we come across many insightful accounts of this unique theory. Here I cite one of them for illustration. When the Lord (*Bhagavān*) was asked by a *bodhisattva* whether there was any necessity at all of this physical world and the physical body, everything being in reality nothing but pure void, He replied that without the body there is no possibility of the realisation of the great bliss and here lies the importance of the body.[8] We also find that a similar view is voiced by Kālacakrayāna, another branch of Tāntric Buddhism. *Śrī Kālacakrayāna*, one of the treatises of this school, states that without the body there can be no perfection, nor can supreme bliss be realised in this life without the body. If perfection (*siddhi*) of the body can be attained all kinds of perfection in the three worlds are very easily obtained. The Nātha cult takes up these foundational concepts and develops an elaborate system of *yoga* based on the Tantra and Yoga.

Whatever may be the source of the Nātha conception of *kāyā sādhanā*, it is obvious that the Orissan *santha*s were profoundly influenced by the Nātha cult. The theory of *kāyā sādhanā* plays a very significant role in Orissan Vaiṣṇavism. The literature of these *santha*s clearly reveals that they conceived *kāyā sādhanā* as a means of yogic realisation. Therefore, we find that by sixteenth century Oriyā *santha*s have become very vocal about the idea that self-realisation or *mukti* can fructify if the *piṇḍa* (gross body) is preserved and perfected. In Nātha terminology this is called *siddha deha*. The idea of the immortality of the *siddha deha* also exerted considerable influence on Orissan Vaiṣṇavism. So we find Orissan Vaiṣṇavas, specially, Acyutānanda, repeatedly emphasising the importance of the body. Sometimes, Acyutānanda's arguments for the preservation of a healthy

8. *Hevajra Tantra,* qtd. in *Obscure Religious Cults,* p. 89.

body are so radical that he may remind us of Cārvāka. He, for example, says:

> O, mind, why are you deluded by the *māyā* and think that truth can be achieved by torturing the body? You must know that you are here in this world because of this body. By torturing your body you lose the chance of attaining *mahāsukha*.[9]

Here, of course, *mahāsukha* (bliss) does not signify the sensual pleasures of the body as stressed by Cārvāka. Its connotation is almost equivalent to the Vajrayānic notion of the bliss that comes through the self-realisation. Again Acyutānanda points out, "the knowledge, riches and youth — all that a man aspires for can be there if the body is preserved, but if the body itself is destroyed, then of what use are these things! Once your body is gone you are declared dead. So is it not better that we think in terms of immortalising the body itself?"[10] Thus, with all this emphasis on the preservation and perfection of the body the ground is prepared for the *sādhanā* of the body. So Acyutānanda again specifies:

> Within your body there is infinite space,
> The cosmos itself is within your body.
> The person who has not penetrated
> (understood the secret power of the body) the body,
> His wisdom is of no avail.

---

9. *āpaṇā bhala tu na bujhilu āpe,*
bhulilo māyā moha paritāpe.
jaun deha dhari saṁsāre achu,
jāṇi jāṇi kimpā tāhāku lechuṅ.
ehāku lecchi kāhiṅ kisa pāu,
eḍe mahāsukha upekṣi jāu.
— Acyutānanda, *Śabda Brahman Saṁhitā* II. 1-4

10. *deha ante jīva jahiṅki galā,*
se kathā jāṇile na boli malā.
etaka mātra vicārare thauṅ,
e deha jemante nāśa na jāuṅ.
— *Śabda Brahman Saṁhitā* I.93-94

> Those who do not see me in their body
> How can they know me?[11]

Summarising their position on *kāyā sādhanā*, Śiśu Ananta, another *santha* of the Pañcasakhā group says — "all these theories about *Brahman* and *śūnya* can be demonstrated and realised in your body. You must realise that God (myself) is within your body, as both are one and non-different."[12]

Ghaṭa Yoga

The Nātha concepts of *haṭha yoga* and *kāyā sādhanā* are collateral theories. But in order to highlight the close link between these two concepts the Oriyā *santha*s rename their system of *yoga* as *ghaṭa* (body) *yoga* or the *yoga* of the body. One comes across a lot of discussion on this theory in their writings. Therefore, it is necessary to describe in brief the concept and the process of *ghaṭa yoga*. This *yoga* aims to realise the *nirākāra* (formless) Reality by transmuting the gross physical body into the subtle and superconscious one. So following the procedure prescribed for *haṭha yoga* the Orissan *santha*s accept the theory of the six plexuses (*ṣaḍa cakra*) of which the highest is *sahasrāra* (the thousand-petal lotus). They also adopt the idea of three mystic nerves or *nāḍī*s, i.e., *iḍā*, *piṅgalā* and *suṣumnā*, from earlier Tantra and Yoga practices. Here are some of the salient features of the *haṭha/ghaṭa yoga*. The Orissan *santha*s believe that there are seventy-two thousand nerves in the body. Only three out of them are very important and are located in the spinal column. *Iḍā* on the left, *piṅgalā* on the right and *suṣumnā* in the

---

11. *deha bhitareṭi aśeṣa pūra*
deha bhitareṭi sacarācara
deha jeun loka bhediṇa nāhiṅ
tāhāra jñānaku jñāna na kahi
dehare jebe mote na dekhilā se loka kemante mote pāilā.
— Acyutānanda Dāsa, *Caurāsī Yantra*

12. *ye brahma śūnyara vicāra tora dehe hetukara*
tora dehe dekhā mote tuhi sakala ehi sinā hoi
— Śiśu Ananta, *Hetu Udaya Bhāgavata* III

middle, all running parallel to one another. These three nerves meet inside the forehead between the two eyes. This juncture is known as *trikūṭa*. Above the *trikūṭa* there is a small slit known as the *brahmarandhra* leading to the region of *śūnya* or *Aḷekha* and the valve of the slit is as delicate as the skin of the sesame seed (*tila chopā*). The *sādhaka* is to raise the vital wind upward through *suṣumnā* and keep it in the *trikūṭa* and then open the gate of *brahmarandhra* to concentrate upon the *Brahman*. The vital energy conceived in the nature of the coiled snake called *kuṇḍalinī* is taken to be moving downwards in case of ordinary human beings who live in worldly indulgences. In yogic *sādhanā* the path of *kuṇḍalinī* is reversed and directed upwards. This is known as *olaṭa sādhanā* or *ujāṇi* implying a process of reversal from the *pravṛtti* to *nivṛtti*. The upward journey of the *kuṇḍalinī* towards the highest *cakra* (*sahasrāra*) is the march of the finite towards the infinite. Adding their own interpretation of this traditional theory of Tantra the Orissan Vaiṣṇavas sometimes view the *sahasrāra cakra* as the spot of eternal union of *jīva* and *parama* or else as the place of eternal dalliance of Rādhā-Kṛṣṇa; sometimes the plexus is also depicted as the seat of Jagannātha and *Śūnya Puruṣa*. The Orissan Vaiṣṇavas believe that the *brahma cakra* or *sahasrāra* is as luminous as the rays of thousand suns and is a spot of effulgent light (*jyoti*). In a rare spirit of universalism they even say that the *sahasrāra cakra*, "though the seat of *śūnya*, can also be directly experienced as the abode of gods depending on one's own religious affiliation: for the Śaivas it is the abode of Śiva, for the Śāktas of the Devī and for the Vaiṣṇavas the seat of Viṣṇu."[13] As far as it is a matter of realisation of the ultimate

---

13. *e śūnyasthānaku śivabhakta jeuṅmane,*
śivasthāna boli ehā bhābithānti mane.
vaiṣṇavagaṇa ehāṅku parama puruṣa,
viṣṇuṅka sthāna boli karanti prakāśe.
śāktamāne mahāsaktidhārī deviṅkara,
bāsasthāna boli ehā karanti pracāra.
je jāhāra iṣṭdeva brahmarūpa jñāne,
ehi sthāna nirdeśa je karuthānti mane.
— Acyutānanda, *Chayāliśa Paṭaḷa*, XXV

Truth in the *sahasrāra cakra,* such discriminations hold no meaning.

As these *santha*s follow the tradition of *haṭha yoga* to its minutest detail large portions of their literature are replete with religious symbolism and technical details. As my basic intention is to concentrate on philosophical dimensions of the system I need not spend time in going into the details of their religious symbolism.

One of the important upshots of the yogic method of self-realisation is the denunciation of all that is associated with religious formalities. The Nātha cult is most vocal about its antipathy towards external formalities as a mode of devotion (*bhakti*). That was why the *siddha yogī*s of this cult had castigated rituals and formalities so sanctimoniously upheld by Brāhmaṇism. This same spirit of anti-idolatry is prominently displayed in the writings of the Orissan Vaiṣṇavas too. They very assiduously connect the concept of *ghaṭa yoga* with the idea of *jñānamiśra* (*bhakti* accentuated by knowledge). So rituals and formalities associated with the Brāhmaṇical form of worship appeared meaningless in their scheme of God-realization. According to these *santha*s the yogic knowledge of the discovery of the non-identity between the *jīva* and *parama* is the sole method available for a true *bhakta*. This gives them enough ground to discard all that is passed in the name of propitiating numerous gods and goddesses. Similar voices of protest were heard from different corners of India during that phase of Indian history. But in the case of the Oriyā Vaiṣṇavas, the concept of *ghaṭa yoga* is used as an instrument of fighting polytheism and ritualistic practices. With this concept at their disposal they become more vociferous in their attack against the popular versions of the ways of God. Let us have a look at some illustrations to have a first hand knowledge of their attitude. Acyutānanda says,

> A person who has mastered the art of *ghaṭa yoga* has no need of all that is contained in the Vedas and Śāstras. For

such a person the idols we worship are nothing more than just the pieces of stone.[14]

Dvārakā Dāsa expresses similar sentiments when he says:

They worship others neglecting me
And know not that I am *ātman*
Making idols of wood, stone and metal
Happy in their ignorance.[15]

Does not the remark remind us of the Sahajiyā Siddha Lakṣmīṅkarī's famous observations about the so-called religious practices?

Piṇḍa-Brahmāṇḍa Tattva

Once the potential power of the gross physical body is recognised as divine in nature, the natural outcome is a conceptual non-discrimination between *piṇḍa* (the body) and *brahamāṇḍa* (cosmic soul) identity. A major work of the Nātha cult, entitled *Siddha Siddhānta Paddhati* states: "whatever is in the *brahmāṇḍa* is in the *piṇḍa* too."[16] In the "Tṛtīyopadeśa" section of this treatise we find a detailed comparison of different limbs of the body with different elements of the universe. Interestingly, the universe (*brahmāṇḍa*) here also

---

14. *e ghaṭa yoge jebā jāṇe,*
se veda śāstra hiṅ na gaṇe.
śiḷāku na kare śocanā,
bolaiṅ ye pathara sinā.
— Acyutānanda, *Brahma Saṅkuḷi* VI. 21-22

15. *mote chāḍi āna diaṅ pūjanti,*
mu ātmā boli se na cinhanti.
dāru citrapaṭa śiḷā dhāture,
pratimā kari pūjanti sukhare.
— Dvārakā Dāsa, *Pareca Gītā* X

16. *brahmāṇḍavarti yat kiñcit tat piṇḍehayarsta sarvathā.*
Siddha Siddhānta Paddhati 3.2, qtd. in N. Pradhan, *Prācina Oṛiyā Sāhityare Nirguṇadhāra*, p. 304.

includes infinite number of gods and goddesses.[17] The Oriyā *santhas* follow this idea in letter and spirit. (In the chapter dealing with *Jīvātman-Paramātman* relationship I have briefly mentioned about the theory of *piṇḍa-brahmāṇḍa* identity.) While talking of the identity between the *jīvātman* and *paramātman*, these philosophers have stressed the need for recognising the presence of divinity within the individual self. Here, the immanence of the highest Reality is presented from another angle. In this case body becomes the medium of self-realisation; and the cosmic divinity is experienced in the body through yogic *sādhanā*. So *piṇḍa* is conceived as the microcosm and the *brahmāṇḍa* as the macrocosm. In other words, the individual being (*piṇḍa*) is considered to be the microcosmic form of the macrocosm (*brahmāṇḍa*, the cosmic being). Acyutānanda clarifying the notion of such identity says:

> The *piṇḍa* is small and the *brahmāṇḍa* is huge. But this wonderful experience of merging the huge in one's small *piṇḍa/jīva* could be possible by expanding the limits of one's mind.[18]

But it was Santha Balarāma Dāsa who took up this idea and developed it into a full-fledged theory in his famous works *Gupta-Gītā* and *Virāṭa-Gītā*. Here I quote a few lines from these works for illustration:

> Whatever is in the *brahmāṇḍa*
> is in your *piṇḍa*.

---

17. *Triyātriṁśat koti devatā vāhuloma kupeṣu vasanti.* Qtd. in Pradhan, p. 305.

18. *piṇḍa kṣudra brahmāṇḍa aṭai bruhata,*
bruhata brahmāṇḍa sattā piṇḍe birājita.
bhāva vicārare anubhāva badhaile,
ajaṇā janā hoiba sthuḷa sukṣma tule.
— Acyutānanda, *Chayāliśa Paṭaḷa* XXIX

> I express this *tattva* to you.
> *Piṇḍa* and *brahmāṇḍa* are identical.[19]

These lines echo the famous statement of *Siddha Siddānta Paddhati*. But this great *santha* tries to explicate this central idea in manifold ways. Sometimes he attempts to project the human body (*piṇḍa*) as the replica of the *virāṭa puruṣa* of the Veda and the *Viśvarūpa* of the *Gītā*. Again he goes on to compare the *piṇḍa* with the temple of Jagannātha itself.

> What is known as the grand temple
> (Jagannātha temple)
> Is nothing but your body.[20]

In this specific canto he goes to the extent of comparing different limbs of human body with different parts of the Jagannātha temple. If we go deep into the very modes of Jagannātha worship one finds the relevance of Balarāma Dāsa's comparison.

In this context I would like to deviate a little to throw some light on an interesting aspect of the ritual of the Jagannātha worship of the temple. In the Jagannātha temple a secret worship is conducted four times a day. This is known as *dhūpa*. During this ritual, the worshipper first of all dissolves his mundane body in meditation in order to create a new ritualistic pure divine body. It is endowed with character and nature of the deity. Thus, in the process of worship the worshipper and deity become one and indivisible entity. The body of the *arcaka* (worshipper) becomes the seat of the divine.

---

19. *brahmāṇḍe jete bidhimata,*
piṇḍare achanti samasta.
piṇḍa brahmāṇḍa ekāmata,
to āge kahideli tattva.
— Balarāma Dāsa, *Virāṭa Gītā* IV

20. *bada deuḷa boli jāhā,*
niścaya se tohar kāyā.
— Balarāma Dāsa, *Viraṭa Gītā* IV

Thus, his body is the God and also the temple. This very ritual is, no doubt, inspired by the Nātha conception of *piṇḍa-brahmāṇḍa* identity. In this context the Vajrayānic conception of *ahaṁkāra*[21] is specifically of some interest. According to this theory, there is but no distinction between the worshipper and the deity worshipped. So *ahaṁkāra* theory suggests that instead of worshipping an external object, the self or the mind of the worshipper himself should be worshipped. In the Vajrayānic parlance, the *bodhicitta* is identical with the Vajrasattva himself. One may not be very sure of the exact source of the Nātha theory about *piṇḍa-brahmāṇḍa* identity. But this theory played a crucial role in Orissan as well as *nirguṇa panthī* philosophy of the medieval age.

21. B. Bhattacaryya, *An Introduction to Buddhist Esoterism*, p. 100.

10

Sṛṣṭi Tattva

THE theory of creation is an important aspect of philosophical speculation in India. The mysterious universe with all its assorted manifestations in the form of astral, living and non-living entities has made the philosophers curious about the why and how of creation of the universe. This curiosity is reflected in the famous Nāsadīya Sūkta of *Ṛgveda*, one of the earliest records of Indian wisdom. The *sūkta* very brilliantly expresses the primal inquest of the man in the following words.

> Then there was neither Aught nor Naught,
> No air or sky beyond.
> What covered all? Where rested all?
> In watery gulf profound?
> Nor death was there nor deathlessness,
> Nor change of night and day.
> That one breathed calmly self-sustained,
> Naught else beyond it lay.
> Gloom hid in gloom existed first-
> One sea, elevating view.
> That one, a void in chaos wrapt,
> By inward fervour grew.
>
> x x x
>
> Whence sprang this world and whether
> Framed by hand divine or no-
> Its Lord in heaven alone can tell,
> If even he can show.[1]

---

1. Nāsadīya Sūkta, *Ṛgveda*. X, p. 129.
   J. Muir's tr., qtd. in *The Cultural Heritage of India*, vol. I. pp. 167-68.

This *sūkta* may be said to be the beginning of the metaphysical quest about the nature of the Reality that found expression in the Upaniṣadic conception of *Brahman* — the Reality that transcends all conceptualisation and predication. While discussing the theory of *Śūnya Puruṣa* I have stated that the Oriyā *santhas* swear by the absolutism of Advaita as well as Śūnyavāda variety. So there is no wonder that their inquiries about the genesis of the empirical world reflect the tone and tenor of the Nāsadīya Sūkta. All these *santhas* echo the same idea while describing the unmanifest state of the manifested. Here I quote one of such stanzas that may give us a glimpse of their way of thinking on the issue.

> Then there were no circumference, neither water nor fire nor energy,
> Neither wind, nor sky nor night, neither moon nor the sun,
> Neither angels, nor Brahmā, neither men, nor demons nor celestial beings.
> Then there were no earth, nor the fifty-six scores of animals.
> Neither gods nor goddesses, nor the stars.
> What then existed? Please tell me O! The killer of Tripura.[2]

The answer to this query is obviously, *śūnya*.

> In those days my shape was *śūnya*.
> This way million years went by.
> In my womb the universe was born.
> This was the manifestation of *Brahman*.[3]

But the question that arises is — how the *śūnya* manifested itself. The inquisitiveness about the process of transformation

---

2. *jebe na thilā e maṇḍaḷa, na thilā āpa teja jaḷa.*
pavana gagana rajanī, na thile candra sūrya beni.
na thile brahmā sura nara, gandharva rākṣasa kinnara.
chapana koṭi jīva jantu na thilā saṁsārara hetu.
na thile devā devi māne, na thile śūnye tārā gaṇe.
tebe ke thile tripurāri, mote kahiba nisṭhā kari.
— Balarāma Dāsa, *Amarakoṣa Gītā* I

3. *sekāḷe śūnya mora rūpa, emante galā koṭi kalpa.*
brahmāṇḍa mora garbhe hoi, rakhile brahma rūpa hoi.
— Balarāma Dāsa, *Brahmāṇḍa Bhūgoḷa* II

of the formless (*arūpa*) to the form (*rūpa*), the one into the many, needed some basis. The question regarding the manifestation from this state of absolute nothingness has also bothered the seers and philosophers of yore. A look into our philosophical tradition reveals that varied explanations are offered regarding this interesting question. If we look at the way the *santhas* of Orissa deal with this issue we notice that they have relied on more than one philosophical explanation offered by our ancient tradition. Sometimes, even the same philosopher offers theories that are at variance with one another. Still it will be of some interest to explore their ways of thinking.

Śiśu Ananta, one of the members of the Pañcasakhā group prefers to go along with the Nāsādiya Sūkta by describing the beginning in terms of the creative energy (*reta*) of the highest being. Nāsādiya Sūkta had hinted about the desire (*kāma*) and the creative energy (*reta*) of the highest Being as the primary components of the process of creation.[4] But the most popular explanation comes from the Sāṁkhya School of thought. This is one of the earliest philosophical schools to provide a systematic account of creation through the concepts of *prakṛti* and *puruṣa*. *Puruṣa* stands for the principles of pure consciousness and the self, whereas *prakṛti* stands for change and materiality. These two concepts are brought together to explain the elements of life, consciousness, matter and change. Interestingly, *puruṣa* is most often depicted as the male and *prakṛti* as the female principle. The theory seems to have wide appeal for the later religio-philosophical movements. So the speculation of such a pair of concepts became the standard feature of theory of creation. For the Tantra it is Śiva and Śakti, for the Vajrayāna Buddhists it is *prajñā* and *upāya* and also *ādi Buddha* and *ādi prajñā*; for the Nāthists it is *nāda* and *bindu*.

---

4. *kāmastadāgre samavartatatādhi manaso retaḥ prathamaṁ yadāsīt.*
— *Ṛg* X 129

We have noted earlier that the Orissan Vaiṣṇavas believed that the phenomenal world is not illusory but real. So the Sāṁkhya theory of cosmogony may seem to suit their position best. A survey of their literature reveals that most often these thinkers seem to follow the trodden path of elucidating the idea of creation in terms of male and female principles. So along with the *Śūnya Puruṣa*, who is unanimously accepted as the material cause of the universe, they introduced a second concept standing for the female force. It is variously called as *yogamāyā*, *prakṛti* and *ardhamātra*. But in certain cases their description has the shades of Tāntric Buddhism. K.C. Mishra, the well-known scholar on Jagannātha cult and Orissan culture, holds this view.[5] The Tāntric Buddhists explain creation in terms of *ādi Buddha* and *ādi prajñā*. In the case of the Pañcasakhā the female principle corresponding to the idea of *prajñā* is called *ādi śakti* or *yogamāyā*. This principle is conceived to be immanent in the *Śūnya Puruṣa*. Mishra further points out that according to Tāntric Buddhism, Buddha first came out of *ādi prajñā* and then uniting with her created the empirical world.[6] This idea is also echoed in the Śaiva theories. They too offer a theory in which *ādi Śakti* is considered first as the mother, and then as the wife of Śiva. But in case of these *santha*s the union between the mother and son appears to be repugnant and so discarded. Therefore, they offer a slightly different account of the process of creation in which the supremacy and the uniqueness of the *Śūnya Brahman* is not disturbed. They hold that the *Śūnya Puruṣa/Brahman* desirous of creation generated from his body five elements — *ūmra, dhūmra, jyoti, jvālā* and *bindu*. No sooner they fell into the sea of causation, the *yogamāyā* emerged. *Kālarūpa* (the eternal time) who was in deep slumber also was reawakened and was united with *yogamāyā*; and thus the process of creation was initiated. This theory provided by Yaśovanta Dāsa in his *Premabhakti Brahma Gītā* is interesting in

---

5. K.C. Mishra, *The Cult of Jagannātha*, p. 161.
6. *Tantratattva*, part I chapter on *Śakti tattva*, qtd. in K.C. Mishra, *The Cult of Jagannātha*, p. 161.

the sense that it also conceives *yogamāyā* as eternal space and *kālarūpa* as eternal time. So he talks of the union of space and time[7] as the ground of creation. But the account seems to come in the way of the general trend of the monistic theory championed by the Orissan *santhas*. Śaṅkara while expounding his non-dualistic stand got rid of this anomalous situation by explaining the world in terms of appearance caused by *māyā*. But at the theoretical level the Oriyā Vaiṣṇavas are not in a position to adopt Śaṅkara's strategy. They have already accepted a realistic stance. For them the empirical world is the real manifestation of the *Śūnya Puruṣa*. It is obvious that these *santhas* are not logicians or dialecticians. So most often their imaginations fly high. Yet in certain cases they were aware of the paradox involved in explaining the creation in terms of male and female principles. So Acyutānanda makes it clear that though he talks of "male and female, in reality there is no specific male or female principle."[8] Accepting the primal realities couched in specific genders would have gone against the formlessness of the *Śūnya Puruṣa/Brahman*.

Śūnya Puruṣa as Śabda Brahman

I have stated earlier that the Orissan *santhas* offer varied accounts of the theory of creation. Some of them are very fascinating. I intend to throw some light on two such interesting accounts. One of the most interesting theories that seem to be metaphysically coherent with the theory of *Śūnya Puruṣa* is crystallized in the idea of creation from the *Śabda Brahman* and *praṇava* (*auṁ*). Both Balarāma Dāsa and Acyutānada Dāsa depict that creation is rooted in *Śabda Brahman* and *praṇava*. As these two philosophers were explicitly bothered about explaining the issue of transformation of the nameless to name and the formless to the form, this particular

7. *Tantratattva*, qtd. in Mishra, p. 161.

8. *stiri puruṣa dui rūpa tāra,*
nuhai stiri se nuhai aṇḍira.
— Acyutānanda, *Tattvabodhinī* VI

metaphysical position stands to their advantage. Acyutānanda in his *Jñānapradīpa Gītā* offers a lucid exposition of this theory. He explains:

> In the beginning there was name and it is the name (word) that created the form, that was already implicit there. Unless you know the name how can you know the form of an object? Again, if there is no form of what use is the name? So all the objects in the world have their identity as they have both, the name and the form.[9]

Again he says,

> In fact, I (*Brahman*) do not have a name, I manifest myself from the formless to form with the help of name (words).[10]

This type of novel interpretation of the empirical world in terms of words and names has very few parallels in the theories of cosmogony. In this respect, their theory comes closest to the theory propounded by Bhartṛhari, the fifth-century grammarian philosopher. His concept of *Śabda Brahman* as well as his theory of creation in terms of *śabda-tattva* is very fascinating. Bhartṛhari crystallized the ideas projected in the Vāk Sūkta of the *Ṛgveda* and the Upaniṣads[11] into a full-fledged metaphysical absolutism with his theory of *Śabda Brahman*. Bhartṛhari begins his *magnum opus*, *Vākyapadīya* with the following lines:

---

9. *agahu je nāma thilā rūpaku gaḍhilā,*
rūpara bhitare nāma puri prakāśilā.
nāmaku cinhile sinā rūpaku jāṇiba,
rūpa na thile nāma kāhiṅ bhaṇāiba.
nāmarūpa dharī rūpa udaya jagate.

Qtd. in C.R. Das, *Oṛiyā Santha* (*bhakti*) *Sāhitya*, p. 409.

10. *prakruta mora nāma nahiṅ, arūpa brahma muṅ bolāi.*
arupu rūpavanta hoi nāma svarūpe kheluthaiṅ.
— Acyutānanda, *Chyālisa paṭala*

11. *vāk vāi brahman.*
— *Bṛhadāraṇyaka Upaniṣad* IV.1.2.

anādi nidhanam brahma śabda tattva yadakṣaram,
vivartate artha bhāvena prakriyā jagato yataḥ.

The verse can be translated in the following way:

> The *Brahman* is without beginning and end, whose essence is the word (*śabda-tattva*), who is the cause of the manifested phonemes, who appears as objects, from whom the creation proceeds.[12]

This cryptic *kārikā* of Bhartṛhari shows that the world and its objects, as well as the phenomenal activities are there because we can ascribe names and words to them. If we take out the names the world is as good as non-existent. In his commentary on this verse Bhartṛhari further elaborates,

> Because in our cognitions, we identify objects with their words (*śabdopagrāhī*) and our cognitions are intertwined with words (*śabdopagrāhya*), they are essentially of the nature of the word (*śabda*).[13]

In this context the following lines of Balarāma Dāsa is equally noteworthy. He says, "There can be no entity without name. It is intertwined with name (*nāma je sarvathare grāhī*)."[14] These lines bear a sort of uncanny affinity to Bhartṛhari's theory of *śabda-tattva Brahman*. One cannot be sure how this theory of the ancient grammarian philosopher could find a place in the cosmogony of the Oriyā *santhas*. Though, Bhartṛhari can be termed as one of the first systematic Advaitin he did not find favour with the later Advaitins, including Śaṅkarācārya. However, it is well known that the Hindu Tantra Schools, especially Kashmir Śaivism incorporated some of his

12. Bhartṛhari, *Vākyapadīya*. I.1.

    Here I follow the translation of K.A.S. Iyer in *The Vākyapadīya of Bhartṛhari*, Chapter, I, Poona: Deccan College, 1965.

13. Iyer, 1.

14. *nāma na thiba thāba nāhiṅ,*
    nāma je sarvathare grāhī.
    — Balarāma Dāsa, *Virāṭa Gītā* I

interesting ideas into their philosophy. It may be conjectured that the influence of Bhartṛhari's *Śabdatattva-Vāda* reached Orissa through another Tāntric work of Kashmiri origin, viz., *Śāradā Tilaka Tantra*. The treatise was written by Lakṣmaṇa Deśika of Kashmir, towards the end of tenth or the beginning of eleventh century. This work has exerted immense influence on the religio-philosophical views of the people of east India, especially of Bengal and Orissa, as is proved by the copies of manuscripts available in the households of Orissa. The theory of creation from *Śabda Brahman* is very elaborately discussed in *Śāradā Tilaka Tantra*. In fact, the very first verse of this work almost echoes Bhartṛhari's views. It states that *mahah*, the inexpressible ultimate Reality creates the universe from the *śabda*. The treatise says, "by the fifty letters of the alphabet which are constantly emanating from the *mahah*, is the universe of moving and motionless objects, of sound and meaning thereof, pervaded."[15] This line can be compared to the following lines of Acyutānanda:

> Hari (the Reality) contains fifty letters of alphabet and twelve *matras* within its unmanifest form. Thus, the manifested universe is pervaded by letters, though he transcends the series of alphabets.[16]

We also note that these *santhas* of Orissa copiously use the concept, *praṇava* or *auṁ* in their theory of creation.

> *Śūnya* arises out of *mahāśūnya*,
> From this arises *praṇava* (*auṁ*).[17]

---

15. Arthur Avalon (tr. & ed.), *Introduction, Śāradā Tilaka Tantram*, Delhi: Motilal Banarsidass, 1982, IX.

16. *dvādaśa mātrā pañcāśa akṣara,*
japa hari guṇa ethi bhitara.
akṣara bhitare jagata lekhā,
akṣara bāhāre se rūpa ekā.
— Acyutānanda, *Śabdabrahma Saṁhitā* I.15-17

17. *śūnyaru mahāśūnya jāta,*
tahiṅru praṇava saṁbhūta.
— Jagannātha Dāsa, *Tuḷā Bhiṇā*

Balarāma Dāsa makes this idea more explicit in the following lines:

> Thus, there was *mahāśūnya*, from that *śūnya* emerged *praṇava*,
> *Praṇava* is *auṁ* as well as one lettered *(ekākṣara)*.
> From the *auṁ* arose the phonemes and from this the Vedas.[18]

Sometimes these *santhas* conceive that the creation is a gradual progression from *auṁ* (*ekākṣara*) to *nāma* (words) and from *nāma* to *rūpa* (form). However, there is nothing to be surprised about such an explanation. Upaniṣads often talk of *praṇava* or *auṁ* as the seed of all creations. Such lines as *omiti etad akṣaraṁ sarvam,*[19] reflect the importance attached to this mysterious syllable. We also find that the Mahāyānī Buddhists use this concept and renames it as *evāṁkara*. But Bhartṛhari offers a very interesting interpretation of the term. Following the Upaniṣadic seers he identifies *Śabda Brahman* with *praṇava* or *auṁ* (that is otherwise called as *ekākṣara* (one-lettered) by the Oriyā *santhas*). Bhartṛhari adds a further dimension to this seminal term *auṁ* (also *praṇava*). He conceives it as the melting ground of all contradictory principles that may arise due to the differences of names and forms. So in his commentary on *Vākyapadīya* I.9, he says,

> It is one and it is not one, it is both and it is not both. Those who are for action speak of diversity (*viṣama*) and those who are for knowledge see unity (*sama*).[20]

One can compare these words with the following lines of Acyutānanda,

> that which is nameable is also non-nameable, that which is *rūpa* can also be *arūpa* . . . that which is without letter can

18. *emante mahaśūnya helā, se śūnya praṇava hoilā.*
praṇava oṁkāraku kahi, ekākṣara ṭi se aṭai.
oṁkāru nāma helā jāta, tahiṅru praṇava saṁbhuta.
— Balarāma Dāsa, *Brahmāṇḍa Bhūgola* III

19. *Māṇḍukya Upaniṣad* I.

20. Bhartṛhari, *Vākyapadīya,* Commentary on I.IX.

> become series of words. That which is indestructible *Brahman* can also be seen as the destructible world.[21]

We know that Bhartṛhari's theory of *śabda-tattva Brahman* and *vāk* were later on accepted by Tantra as well as by some later Upaniṣads like *Maitrī Upaniṣad*. But Bhartṛharian way of exploring the worldly process (*jagato prakriyā*) in terms of the principle of speech (*śabda-tattva*) is very strikingly reflected in the cosmogony of the Orissan *santhas*. Whatever may be the source of this theory, their explication of the empirical world in terms of names and letters is very different from other theories of cosmogony.

In this context another remarkable digression in the interpretation of the word *aum̐* may be noted. The word *aum̐*, though a single syllable, can also be seen as a combination of three letters, viz., *a-u-m̐*. As this word is taken as a sacred symbol, most often these three letters are interpreted as signifying different aspects of the same principle. Gauḍapāda in his *Māṇḍukya Kārikā* explicates these three letters symbolizing three states of human mind, viz., *jāgṛta*, *svapna* and *suṣupti*. The last stage *turīya* is the transcendental state of *aum̐*, i.e., the whole syllable. Similarly the Hindu Tantra while absorbing Bhartṛhari's analysis of the progression of one *śabda-tattva* into multifold human speech in terms of *vaikharī, madhyamā, paśyantī* and *para*, reinterprets that *a-u-m̐* stand for the first three stages of the expression of the syllable. Only the *parā vāk* is identified with the *praṇava*. Oriyā *santhas* also follow the tradition and believe that the Jagannātha triad symbolises three letters of the syllable *aum̐*. But when it comes to the theory of creation they present *aum̐* as symbolising three *guṇas* of Sāṁkhya, viz., *sattva, rajas* and *tamas*. They state that out of *aum̐* emerge three

---

21. *anāma se sthānare thilā, eṭhāre nāma je hoilā.*
sethāre arūpa bolāi, ethāre rūpa prakāśai.

x x x

anākṣara thilā tahiṅ, ethāre akṣara bolāi,
se avināśī brahma ate, ethi vināśre prakate.

— Acyutānanda, *Chayālisa Paṭala*. III

*guṇa*s and from these, the gods, as well as the empirical world, are created. Here the Sāṁkhya dualism is transformed suitably to fit into their non-dualistic framework.

The Idea of Pañca-Viṣṇu

Another interesting account of cosmogony comes from Caitanya Dāsa. In his work *Viṣṇugarbha Purāṇa* he seems to put the idea of *pañcadhyānī* Buddhas of the Tāntric Buddhism in a strikingly Vaiṣṇavite setting. In Tāntric Buddhism, one comes across the theory of five *tathāgata*s or *dhyānī* Buddhas, apart from the original God-head, viz., Vajrasattva. Corresponding to the five *skandha*s there are five *dhyānī* Buddhas who preside over these *skandha*s. They are — Akṣobhya, Ratnasambhava, Amitābha, Vairocana and Amoghasiddhi. The Oriyā *santha* following their footsteps introduces the notion of six Viṣṇus, one of which is the primeval *Nirākāra Śūnya Puruṣa/Aḷekha Puruṣa,* while the other five are considered to be the representatives of this original Viṣṇu. Caitanya Dāsa's delineation of *Nirākāra Aḷekha Puruṣa* is very similar to the idea of Vajrasattva, as He too is characterized as formless and indescribable *śūnya*. The five Viṣṇus emanating from the *Aḷekha Puruṣa* (Viṣṇu) do undoubtedly resemble the five *dhyānī* Buddhas. Even one can note a close similarity between the *pañcadhyānī* Buddhas and the *pañca* Viṣṇu in matter of minor details. Like the *pañcadhyānī* Buddhas, these five Viṣṇus are placed in five *maṇḍala*s. The tradition about the position of the *pañcadhyānī* Buddhas in the *maṇḍala*s is also akin to *pañca* Viṣṇu in the *śūnya-maṇḍala.*[22] Interestingly, even the colour scheme found in the Buddhist pantheon is not missed and like the five *tathāgata*s the six Viṣṇus, (five representing subsidiary forms of Viṣṇu and one, the original Viṣṇu), are represented by six different colours, viz., white, yellow,

---

22. *urdhe vairocanasyāpi pūrve akṣobhyamityapi,*
dakṣine ratnasambhavaṁ amitābham pascime'pi,
uttare 'moghasiddhisca iti pañcatathāgatam.
— *Svaymbhū Purāṇa* XXXVI.12.370

Qud. from *The Cult of Jagannātha* by K.C. Mishra, p. 162.

saffron, red, blue and green. Moreover, as the five *tathāgata*s are said to have their respective *bodhisattva*s, similarly, the five Viṣṇus are stated to have their own Brahmās, who are credited with the creation of eighty-four worlds. Delineating the process of creation Caitanya Dāsa narrates that the five Viṣṇus emerging from the Primeval Viṣṇu, are always immersed in deep *yoga*; this results in the appearance of the trinity, viz., Brahmā, Viṣṇu and Maheśvara. From them the empirical world proceeds. However, the entire process of creation is due to the desire of the *Aḷekha Puruṣa* Viṣṇu. This account may seem more mythical than philosophical. But it clearly reveals the extent of influence the Tāntric forms of Buddhism exerted on the Vaiṣṇava tradition of Orissa.

Regarding the question — why the manifestation? The Orissan *santha*s offer a very interesting explanation. First reason they allude to is about God's desire to create a perfect world. This results in the cyclic process of creation and destruction, virtue and sin.[23] The second reason is ascribed to the *karuṇā* or *dayā* of the *Śūnya Puruṣa*. Both Acyutānanda and Balarāma Dāsa shared the view that *Śūnya Puruṣa* willed creation out of compassion. Here the Mahāyāna conception of *karuṇā* seems to have some influence on these thinkers. According to Buddhism, the Buddha is bound to the humanity by the bond of compassion. That is why the Buddha is born again and again till everybody is liberated. We find the reflection of this ideology in Acyutānanda's proclamation that the unmanifest *Śūnya Puruṣa* manifests himself because he wants every human being to realise the real truth.

23. *naṣṭa bhrama karma jebe saṁsāre nohantā,*
kāhā gheni brahma āu sruṣṭi sarajantā.
— Acyutānanda, *Kaivarta Gītā* 9

11

Mana

THE way the human mind works has always been a subject of fascination for the philosophers. There are elaborate discussions on different dimensions of mind in most of the philosophical systems of India. In Advaita and Upaniṣadic literature a distinction is made between *mana, buddhi, citta, ahaṁkāra* and *cetanā* or *citśakti*. Out of them *citśakti* is prioritised as it is held to be the power that transcends other dimensions of the mind. The other four are taken to be the basis of our conceptualised thought. But yoga, one of the ancient systems of thought deals elaborately with philosophical psychology. The dimension of mind highlighted in this system is *citta*. Patañjali emphasises that true yoga means controlling of the propensities of the *citta* (*yogascittavṛtti nirodha*). Here *citta* implies *mana, buddhi* and *ahaṁkāra*, all taken together. *Citta* is that which either indulges through *pravṛtti* or withdraws from the sensual world through *nivṛtti*. Therefore, in the philosophy of *yoga nivṛtti* or self-restraint is taken as a means of self-realization. I have stated earlier that Buddhism in later phases incorporated the principles of yoga into their philosophical fold. Naturally, Vajrayāna and Sahajayāna pay equal attention to *citta*. In the *santha* philosophy of Orissa, however, the concept highlighted is *mana*; they seldom use the word *citta*. Yet it is obvious that the word *mana* is used with the same significance as *citta*. So very much like yoga and Vajrayāna they emphasize that the empirical world, its manifestations, as well as all the activities of the human life are conrolled by the mind and its faculties. This theory of the Pañcasakhā as well as other philosophers of this period bears a great resemblance to the Vajrayānī notion of *citta*.

The Vajrayānī Buddhists draw their philosophical inspiration from both the Mādhyamika as well as Yogācāra. But as far as their philosophical psychology is concerned they follow the trend set up by Yogācāra. It is well known that this school of Buddhism regards the empirical world as the creation of our false mental constructions (*kalpanā*). The Vajrayānīs very effectively adopt this idea and envision that both the *saṁsāra* (the phenomenal world along with its transience) as well as *nirvāṇa* are due to our *citta* or mind. This is evident from Anaṅgavajra's definition of both these concepts. In his *Prajñopāya Viniścaya Siddhi* he defines *saṁsāra* and *nirvāṇa* in the following way:

> The holder of thundebolt (*vajra*) defines *saṁsāra* as the condition of the mind which is overwhelmed with darkness arising out of numerous false constructions, is as fleeting as the lightning in a storm, and is besmeared with dirt of attachment, etc., not easily removable. So the *saṁsāra* is due to the conditions of the mind (*saṁsāram hy cittam uvīca vajrī*).[1]

Again *nirvāṇa* too is a condition of the mind. So *nirvāṇa* is defined as "a condition of the mind, which is bright with purity, is free from all mental constructions and the dirt of attachment, etc., and which does not know, can not be known, and is eternal."[2]

---

1. *anantasaṁkalpa tamo 'bhibhūtaṁ,*
   prabhañjānomattcaḍiccañcalaṁ.
   rāgādīdurvārmalāvaliptaṁ,
   cittaṁ hi saṁsāram uvāca vajrī.

   Prajñopāya Viniścaya Siddhi, qtd. in B. Bhattacharyya, *An Introduction to Buddhist Esoterism*, p. 41.

2. *prabhāsvaraṁ kalpanayā vimuktaṁ,*
   grahīṇarāgādīmalapralepam.
   grāhyaṁ naca grāhakamagrasattvaṁ.
   tadeva nirvanvaraṁ jagād.

   — Qtd. in Bhattacharyya p. 41

We notice that the *santhas* of Orissa almost echo such ideas of *saṁsāra* and *mukti*. *Yoga*, both in its Buddhistic and Hindu version, plays an important role in the shaping up of Orissan *santha* philosophy. While examining the theory of the *jñānamiśra bhakti* of the Orissan Vaiṣṇavas, I have pointed out that these philosophers lay considerable emphasis on *yoga* as a method of self-realisation. So it is natural that they offer a special status to the concept of mind (*mana*). Most of the philosophers of this form of Vaiṣṇavism project mind as the cause of bondage and liberation, i.e., *saṁsāra* as well as *mukti*. This philosophy of mind is explicitly analysed in Śiśu Ananta's *Hetu Udaya Bhāgavata*. He writes:

> It is due to false mental constructions (*kalpanā*) we are in the bondage of *saṁsāra*. These false constructions hide from us the real nature of the truth. This mind when freed from all such conditions, knows the highest truth, for there is no God outside your mind.[3]

Similar ideas are reflected in the following lines of Acyutānanda,

> O, *Muni*, listen about the ways of the mind,
> For this alone can conquer the world.
> This mind itself is *Īśvara*, the king of
> The universe.
> All the sense-organs are nothing but
> Its obedient subjects.
>
> x x x
>
> Contemplation on this mind can give
> You all knowledge,

---

3. *manara kaḷpanāṭi kāḷa, bedhi rahichi bindusthaḷa.*
manati āpe āpe hoi, mana bāhāre diaṅ kahiṅ.
— Śiśu Ananta, *Hetu Udaya Bhāgavata*

For, as pure consciousness (*caitanya*) it is the
Guru of your self.

x x x

If you worship your mind, you can be
Oblivious of all other gods.
For this mind itself is *Śūnya Puruṣa*
As this mind itself manifests in every thing and being.[4]

Even Acyutānanda believes that it is our mind that decides what is virtue and what is vice. Interestingly enough we come across a similar view in *Jñāna Siddhi* of Indrabhūti. He says that all our actions are initiated by three elements — the body, mind and speech. But our body and speech cannot function without the mind. So it is our mind, which decides what is to be called virtue and what is to be considered as vice.[5]

Five Dimensions of Mind

The simple yet erudite *santhas* of Orissa were no psychologists. But the way they analyse the propensities of mind is really astounding. They conceive *mana* or mind as five-dimensional. So they frequently refer to *pañcamana*, i.e., five states of mind. One may argue that there is nothing very novel about such a theory. In Indian classical philosophy we come across excellent

4. *manara vicāra suṇa ho munī,*
eka mana pāre jagat jiṇi

x x x

manaṭi īśvara manaṭi rājā
manara sabu indriya prajā

x x x

mana cintile savuku pāiṅ,
caitanyati guru rūpare rahi.
— Acyutānanda, *Tattvabodhinī* VIII

5. *manaḥ śreṣṭha manojābatḥ,*
manasāhi prasannena bhāsate va karote vā.
— *Jñānasiddhi* IX. 6-7.

theories of philosophical psychology. *Māṇḍukya Upaniṣad* for example, offers us the theory of four stages of mind, viz., *jāgṛta* (wakeful state), *svapna* (dream state), *suṣupti* (deep sleep) and *turīya* (the state of total transcendence). We also come across similarly interesting account of the states of mind in the *Yogasūtra* of Patañjali. He too talks of the five modes or *vṛtti*s of the mind, viz., *pramāṇa* (valid knowledge), *viparyaya* (illusion), *vikalpa* (imagination), *nidrā* (sleep) and *smṛti* (recollection). But the Orissan *santha*s seem to provide an altogether distinct account of the five dimensions of mind. They call it *pañcamana*. These five dimensions of mind are — *mana, amana, vimana, kumana* and *sumana*. Acyutānanda in his work *Cabīsī Upadeśa* and *Jñānapradīpa Gītā* discusses in detail the dimensions of the five-pronged concept of mind. Similar reference is also found in Dvārakā Dāsa's *Chatīsa Gupta-Gītā*. *Mana* means that through which our sense-organs collect ideas about the empirical world that is presented in the form of sensations, pleasant or painful. It is regarded as fickle. *Amana*, on the other hand, implies that level of thought which is impenetrable by the mind with its ordinary faculties as well as with the limitations of conceptual categorizations. It is often described as *nirviśeṣa* (indeterminate) and *nirmoha* (non-attached). So it refers to the state of mind where there is no experience of categorial distinctions. *Vimana* implies that state of mind, when it withdraws itself from the temporary pleasures and experiences of the objects of the world. *Kumana* is the state of the mind tainted by desires and passions. Finally, *Sumana* refers to the state of mind inclined towards good and noble thought. These five dimensions of mind, taken together, control our experience, thought and actions. Thus, it is the *mana* (mind) that can lead us either to self-realisation or else to bondage. So the Orissan *santha*s again and again emphasize on the practice of turning the fickle and restless mind to the *amana*, the mind that is totally turned inwards to become absolutely free from the outward attachments. According to Acyutānanda,

> Once you transform your *mana* to *amana* you can be in a position to realise how ignorance covers everything. It is the ever-fickle *mana* that plays around *māyā* by creating all sorts of imaginative constructs, as this is the root of all illusions. But the moment this fickle and ever fleeting mind is made steady and freed from attachments (*nirmoha*) and determinations (*nirviśeṣa*) the *mana* is transformed into *amana*.[6]

One is not sure what is the source of this interesting theory of mind. However, if we take it for granted that the yoga theory of *citta* has some influence on santhic theory of *mana* then one may relate it to Vyāsa's theory of *cittabhūmi* or levels of attention. These five levels are identified as — *kṣipta, mūḍha, vikṣipta, ekāgra* and *niruddha*.[7] According to Vyāsa, *kṣipta* (distracted) level of the *citta* refers to the fickle and unstable nature of the *citta*. In this state the mind is directed towards the affairs of the external world. On the other hand, the infatuated mind or *mūḍha* state is fixed on non-righteous actions. It is a state in which mind is totally confused and unable to discriminate between the right and wrong. *Vikṣipta* (occasionally unsteady) mental state, though usually unsteady, is capable of being steady as it sometimes is directed towards pleasurable objects. These three states according to Vyāsa are unfit for yogic realisation. *Ekāgra* or one-pointed mind is withdrawn from the outward objects and is focused on the object of thought. There is complete introversion in this mono-eidetic stage. Finally, in the *niruddha* (restrained) level the mind withdraws from all mental functions and retains only the subconscious dispositions. In this state there is total suspension

---

6. *manaku amana jebe karipāru tuhi,*
   avidyā maddhya purichi taḷa kara tuhi
   cala cañcala kaḷpānadi kari kheḷuchi mana māyāku ābori.
   nirvikaḷpa nirmoha je sthiracitta hoi,
   mahānitya hele mana amana bolāi.
   — *Jñānapradīpa Gītā*, qtd. in C.R. Das, *Santha (bhakti) Sāhitya*, p. 430

7. *Yoga Bhāsya* I.i.

of all mental modes. This is the ultimate state of *yoga*. Thus, yogic perfection enjoins complete suppression of all mental modes and dispositions. However, this five-layered theory of *cittabhūmi* has a very slender resemblance with the theory of *pañcamana* espoused by the Orissan *santhas*, as the five-fold classification of the yoga system is more concerned with the grounds and levels of attention than the dimensions of the mind. So both the theories cannot be said to be identical. Only the states of *kṣipta* and *niruddha* may be compared to the states of *kumana* and *amana*, respectively. So we can conclude that this theory of *pañcamana* is indigenous and novel. Sometimes, however, the Orissan *santhas* advise to strike a balance among the five states of mind so that one can live a peaceful and harmonious life. Acyutānanda for example says, "harmonize *kumana, vimana* and *amana*; add *sumana* to these three then only you can obtain peace. The five-pronged mind (*pañcamana*) is very much within us as five gross elements (*pañcabhūta*)."[8] The last line of the verse seems very queer. It is not clear why five dimensions of mind are aligned to five gross elements. We find that Acyutānanda and other *santhas* very frequently associate *pañcamana* with *pañcabhūta*. The equation is very fascinating. The five gross elements — earth (*kṣiti*), water (*āp*), fire (*tej*), air (*mārut*) and ether (*vyoma*), are conceived to stand for *mana, sumana, kumana, vimana* and *amana*, respectively; thereby implying that these five dimensions of mind are but integral parts of our physical existence. They are universally potent in each living being. Though it is never made explicit why the five states of mind are aligned to five gross elements yet it is not very difficult to infer the reasons for such alignment. Earth is compared to *mana*, i.e., the mind with ordinary propensities because, it is mostly guided by the empirical world and the experiences arising out of the sense-object, contact. *Sumana*, the pure mind, is linked with the water because water

8. *kumana vimana saṅgate, amana kariba ekatve.*
sumana saṅge kari mela, śānti manaku kariba ṭhula.
e pañcamana pañcabhute, basiṇa achanti ekatve.
— *Brahmā Saṅkūḷi* X

is associated with purity. Fire stands for all-engulfing passion; therefore, it is compared with *kumana*, the mind engrossed in passion and desire. Air symbolises detachment as it blows indiscriminately over everything, ugly or beautiful. In this sense *vimana* is like the air. It is the non-attached mind. Finally, the *amana* is compared with the sky as in this state the mind becomes limitless and expansive like the sky.

The *santha*s of Orissa also talk of five kinds of *ātman* — *jñāna ātmā, dhyāna ātmā, tattva ātmā, jīva ātmā* and *parama ātmā*. However, it is very difficult to trace the philosophical implication of this five-fold conception of the self (*ātman*). Excepting *jivātman* and *paramātman*, it is very difficult to decipher the significance of the other three concepts. Unfortunately, these *santha* philosophers do not bother to elucidate these concepts though they frequently refer to this five-fold *ātman*. It seems they take this idea for granted. There must be some reason for such an attitude. May be this concept was so common during the period that they did not feel the necessity for explaining the idea. So it is very difficult to trace the origin of the idea of the five-fold concept of the *ātman*. The only theory that comes very close is Asaṅga's way of identifying *jīvātman, mahātman, suddhātman* and *paramātman*. Asaṅga, the proponent of Yogācārī Buddhism while delineating the stages of a man's journey from ignorance to knowledge, states that when an enlightened person realises the futility of all that exists and of the banefulness of the empirical ego (*jivātman*) he embraces the universal soul (*mahātman*). This leads to the clear grasping of the principles of *śūnyatā* and *nairātmya* and realisation of the pure soul (*śuddhātman*). This ultimately readies him to become one with the Buddha and attain the highest soul (*paramātman*). But it cannot be claimed conclusively that the *pañca ātmā* theory of the Buddhist Vaiṣṇavas of Orissa is directly inspired by the four-fold classification of Asaṅga. Whatever may be their source of inspiration it remains a fact that the *santha* philosophers had very fascinating theories about the nature of mind and self.

12

Śūdrabhāva

We have noted earlier that for the Bauddha Vaiṣṇavas of Orissa, *bhakti* is not mere surrender to God; nor just intense attachment to God. The essence of *bhakti* lies in realising *ātman* in *ātman*. This in turn, implies that *bhakti* stands for the realising the non-discrimination between the highest Being and the universe, with its four realms of existence. Thus, a true *bhakta* is one, who identifies himself with the universe; who suffers the pain of the suffering humanity and who seeks to ameliorate it. Here lies the basic difference between a *bhakta* (in the usual sense) and a *santha*. A *bhakta* can afford to be selfish and individualistic in seeking *mukti* for his ownself, but a *santha* cannot afford to be selfish. Realising *ātman* in *ātman* thus entails expanding oneself at the level of consciousness and tearing down the wall between oneself all. It is not running away from the world but looking at the world with compassion by sublimation of the ego. So they revolted against the social custom that segregated man from man. Here we come across an example of metaphysics serving as the basis of social reconstruction.

The *santha* philosophers of Orissa, like the other *santha*s of the medieval period, were no armchair speculators. They sincerely wanted to free the suffering humanity from the clutches of ignominy and humiliation. So they raised their voice against the social discrimination that had turned the lowly born into less than animals. These *santha*s were in need of a conceptual apparatus that could be used to register their protest against the caste-ridden social order. A scrutiny of their literature reveals the impact of two important concepts of Buddhism, viz., *karuṇā* and *samatā*. In the introductory chapter of this book, I have stated that the *santha* philosophy of India, as a whole, draws support from these two concepts. So I intend to examine in brief the implications of these two concepts and their significance in the context of the Vaiṣṇavism of Orissa.

One of the most important contributions of the Mahāyāna Buddhism is its altruistic interpretation of the concept of *nirvāṇa*. The Buddha had advised his followers to seek *nirvāṇa* for themselves. But for the Mahāyānīs personal liberation is not the goal, it is the liberation for the whole humanity. *Sūtrālaṅkāra* very succinctly puts this point in the following lines: "there is no *puṇya* if you feed yourself, but when you feed others, similarly, there is no greatness in personal liberation, it must be liberation for one and all."[1] This compassionate identification with the whole humanity lying in the vortex of misery and suffering is called *karuṇā*. The Mahāyānī ideal of *karuṇā* is encapsulated in the example of Avalokiteśvara, the compassionate one, who refused his personal *nirvāṇa*, until all worldly creatures could obtain freedom from suffering. The idea of *karuṇā* leads to the conception of *samatā*, i.e., equality between the enlightened one and other ordinary people. Nāgārjuna describes this ideal in the following way:

> The Buddha is like the sky (which has neither origination nor cessation), and all the beings are like him, therefore, they are of the same nature as the Buddha.[2]

These two ideals play an important role in the Pañcasakhā philosophy too. But before I discuss this, I must give a brief outline of the modifications made by the Vajrayāna school in the conception of *karuṇā* and *samatā*.

---

1. *yathā pūnyaṁ prasabate paresām bhojanaṁ dadāt,*
   na tu svayaṁ sa bhunajanaḥ tathā pūnya mahodayaḥ.
   — *Sūtrālaṁkāra* V.72

2. Nāgārjuna, *Mahāyāna Viṁśaka* II.

The Concept of Samatā

We come across the notion of *samatā* for the first time in the philosophy of the great Mahāyāna teacher Aśvaghoṣa. He describes the Reality as *tathatā* or "suchness." This word may be taken as the positive expression of the word *śūnyatā*. According to him, when a seeker realises the true nature of *tathatā* he becomes conscious of the absolute oneness of the universe. This realisation of "oneness with the universe" is called *samatā*. Vajrayāna, being a branch of Mahāyāna develops the idea of oneness with the universe or *samatā* in greater detail. Indrabhūti, the famous *siddha* of this order, *jñānasiddhi* categorically states that all these notions about pure and impure; *pāpa* and *puṇya* are but relative in nature.[3] What ultimately matters is sublimation of the ego and inculcating a sense of *samatā*, i.e., the knowledge that there is no distinction between the God and the universe.[4] According to Vajrayāna, the primal Buddha (Ādi Buddha) is believed to have generated five kinds of knowledge. One of them is *samatā jñāna*.[5] This type of knowledge signifies the wisdom that enables one to develop equal vision towards all. Sahajayāna Buddhism further modifies this ideal by introducing the concept of *samarasa*. Etymologically speaking, *sama* means "sameness"; and *rasa* belongs to its cycle (*cakra*). So *samarasa* means, the oneness of the nature of all that is there in the universe.[6] According to these Buddhists in the state of *samarasa* the mind is free of all discriminations. The famous *siddha* Sarhapā, therefore, writes,

---

3. *Jñānasiddhi* IX.34.

4. *yadi cittaṁ samaṁ yasya jñānaṁ tasyodayaṁ bhaved,*
anyathā nahi tatprāptiḥ kalpakotiśatairapi.
— *Jñānasiddhi* XX.4

Qtd. in C.R. Das, *Oṛisāra Mahimā Dharma*, Santiniketan: Odiya Gavesana Bibhaga, Visvabharati, 1952, p. 220.

5. Referred in F.D. Lessing and A. Wayman, *Introduction to Buddhist Tāntric Systems* Delhi: Motilal Banarsidass, 1978, p. 34.

6. Dasgupta, p. 125.

> Where the mind sets in, all bondage is torn off — there in a non-dual state everything becomes same, there is neither the śūdra nor the brāhmaṇa.[7]

Pañcasakhā admitted the importance of both *karuṇā* and *samatā*. They believed that the creation or manifestation of the world is due to the *karuṇā* of the *Śūnya Puruṣa*. For, without the creation of the world there would be no scope for self-realisation. Perhaps this is the reason why Jagannātha is conceived as Buddha-Jagannātha, who appears in the embodied form for the deliverance of the people from misery. However, the concept of *samatā* plays a greater role in Pañcasakhā philosophy. Their ardent desire to protest against the social discrimination perpetuated in the name of *varṇa dharma* finds necessary support from the ideal of equality. So the Buddhistic notion of *samatā* came in handy for such social remonstration. Pañcasakhā, especially Acyutānanda takes up this idea and makes this the justificatory ground for introducing the notion of *śūdrabhāva* and *śūdrabhakti*. He applied these two concepts to challenge the Brāhamaṇical supremacy. *Varṇa dharma* (class system) was introduced in ancient Indian tradition to envisage a social order based on *guṇa* (inherent nature) and *karma* (the role assigned by the society). But later on the concept of class was turned into caste that ultimately became the very tool of social oppression. In this scheme of caste system śūdras are regarded as the lowliest, as no specific duty is assigned to them in the society like the other three castes. Their only duty is to serve the three higher castes with a sense of humility. Acyutānanda transforms this disqualification into a great qualification by declaring that in the spiritual realm to

---

7. *javve mana atthamaṇa jāi taṇu tuṭṭai vandhana,*
   tavve samarasa sahaje vajjai nau sudda na vamahaṇa.
   — *Dohākośa* of Saraha, 46

   Qtd. in S.B. Dasgupta, p. 127.

be humble and low frees one from the sense of ego.[8] A real *bhakta* like a śūdra has no scope for displaying his ego. This sort of attitude is called *śūdrabhāva*. This, according to him, is a great quality that enables a seeker to serve mankind with the sublimation of his ego. A man who wants to realise the highest truth has to inculcate this feeling of humility and a sense of service. This only provides him with the right mental state so that he can work for the welfare of mankind and through this serve God. For Acyutānanda, service to mankind with the total sublimation of ego is the real service to God. *Bhakti* also stands for service; and egoless service is called the *śūdrabhakti*.

Acyutānanda's analysis of the concept of *śūdrabhakti* is quite novel. He offers an innovative theory of *bhakti* that elaborates on four stages through which a *bhakta* makes his journey. These stages are delineated in ascending order. Very creatively he uses the scheme of *varṇa* and reinterprets it in terms of the human propensities for God realisation. The first stage is equated with the propensity of a kṣatriya. At this stage a man aspiring to be a *bhakta* controls his meanness and destroys the negative elements of his character. At the second stage a *bhakta* becomes a tradesman, signifying the caste duties of a vaiśya. He has the name of the Lord as his capital. In the third stage a *bhakta* displays the propensities of a brāhmaṇa by following the path sanctioned by the Śāstras. In this stage a *bhakta* comes closer to the *Brahman* realisation. Once a *bhakta* knows the real essence of God he discards the last shreds of ego and becomes a servant at his feet. Here he shows the propensities of a śūdra. In the first three stages *bhakti* is confined to religious level. But in the last stage, i.e., the stage of *śūdrabhakti* a man is elevated to the spiritual level. He is described as a *Brahmadarśī*. Thus, through *śūdrabhakti* alone, a man finds fulfilment as a

---

8. *śūdra varṇare sevā prāpata hue,*
ahaṁkāra nāhi śūdrara dehe.
—Acyutānanda, *Varṇa Ṭīkā*

servant of God as well as the humanity. In terms of spiritual experience and fulfilment *śūdrabhakti* is the highest form of *bhakti* that can sustain itself without being entrapped by egoistic feeling in its onward journey.[9]

The Dream of a Casteless Society

With this new interpretation of *śūdrabhāva* at their disposal the *santhas* raised their voice against social injustice. They proudly declared themselves to be śūdras, though in fact, most of them belonged to higher castes. Obviously they became śūdra by choice. So these Vaiṣṇavas preferred to drop their hereditary surnames to be known only as *dāsa* or servant.[10] With a new connotation attached to the term "śūdra" they tried to inject a sense of dignity into the life of the people suffering from low esteem about themselves. The message of equality was very clear and explicit in Acyutānanda's work. So in his work he makes Kṛṣṇa say, "Well did you ask, O Arjuna! about the status of a scavenger. I tell you he is not distinct from me."[11] Balarāma Dāsa, however, is more bold and direct in his approach. This is evident from the anecdote described in Balarāma Dāsa's *Praṇava Gītā*. Here he narrates his personal experience of suffering humiliation at the hands of the priests as well as the king for taking part in the scriptural discourse being a non-brāhmaṇa. In the face of such humiliation he reminded the king that God is nobody's property. In his own words,

---

9. Refer C.R. Das, *A Glimpse into Oriya Literature*, Bhubaneswar: Orissa Sahitya Akademi, 1982, p. 83.

10. *nāhi mora vipra varṇe āśā,*
kṣatriya vaiśyare nāhi bharasā.
sāna hele mana saruā huai,
teṇu achyuta je śūdra varṇahi.
— *Varṇa Ṭīkā*

11. *hāḍi boli jāhā pucchilu arju a,*
mohari vyatirake se nuhai ti bhinna.
— Acyutānanda, *Kaivarta Gītā* IV

> Listen O protector, God is nobody's exclusive property (as a matter of birthright). God belongs to him who is pious and good, be he brāhmaṇa or *cāṇḍāla* by birth. On the merciful Jagannātha nobody has monopoly. The brāhmaṇas are only boasting when they say God is theirs. Vain men, they say so out of ignorance.[12]

Balarāma Dāsa was so much convinced about the ruinous effect of discriminations against the lower caste that he almost reformulated the description of the primeval *puruṣa* in the Puruṣa Sūkta of the *Ṛgveda*. In this Vedic hymn śūdra is shown to be emerging from the feet of the *puruṣa*. Unfortunately, this depiction has often been used as ground for placing the śūdra class in the lowest wrung of the social hierarchy. Balarāma Dāsa changes the order and envisions all the castes as representing sense-organs of the *Brahman*. He would rather say, vaiśya is the eye of the Lord; kṣatriya is his ear, brāhmaṇa his breath and śūdra his mouth.[13] As all these organs are placed on the face of the Lord, there is no scope for depicting the śūdras as lower in hierarchy. But the most popular work dealing with anti-casteism is *Lakṣmī Purāṇa*. Here Balarāma Dāsa makes an attempt to incorporate the theory of equality through a story relating to the misunderstanding between Jagannātha and his consort, Lakṣmī. His intention was to make the message of equality accessible to the womenfolk. Once Lakṣmī was so pleased with the devotion of a *cāṇḍāla* woman that she visited her home. This enraged Jagannātha as well as

---

12. *suṇa he nrupa gajapati, kāhāra nuhai śrīpati.*
bhakta janaṅkara se hari, vipra cāṇḍāla se ādi kari.
karuṇāmaya jagannātha, kāhāra nuhanti ekata.
vipra je bolānti āmbhara, garba karanti nrupavara.
— Balarāma Dāsa, *Praṇava Gītā*, 1.12-15. Qtd. in Vasu, p. 66

13. *vaiśya to nayana atai, kṣatriya śravaṇaku kahi.*
brāhmaṇa nāsāra pavana, śūdra je mukhare pramāṇa.
yemante cāri jāti kahi, jyoti madhyaru janma hoi.
— Balarāma Dāsa, *Gupta-Gītā* VI

Balabhadra, his elder brother. They enjoined that by visiting the unholy home of a lowborn woman she had desecrated herself; so had no place inside the temple. As Lakṣmī stands for wealth and prosperity, the moment she was driven out of the temple dismal days dawned upon the two brothers. They had to come out of the temple and beg from door to door for a morsel of food. Everyone turned them away as Lakṣmī had played her divine trick. At long last they reached the house that was coincidentally the abode of Lakṣmī. When they asked for food the attendants of the house informed that the house belonged to a *cāṇḍāla* lady. The brothers were so much famished by the pangs of hunger that they readily agreed to accept any food whatever it might be. After they savoured the food they could very well realize that it was no other than Lakṣmī who had so carefully cooked that food for them. So they beseeched her to return to the temple. She agreed, but not before eliciting a promise; "hereafter there would be no discrimination of caste and creed inside the temple. All people right from a brāhmaṇa to a scavenger should be treated equally."[14] Interestingly, in this story even the most revered Lord of the people of Orissa is made to learn the lesson of equality from his wife. So with this work he aims to dislodge two well-entrenched social stigmas, viz., śūdras and the people of lower caste have less right on God's grace; and women must not have the right of expressing their preferences. Interestingly, this purāṇa continues to be part of Oriya home. Women of Orissa, however sophisticated they may be, recite this purāṇa on the auspicious occasion of Lakṣmī *pūjā* on all Thursdays. In this purāṇa, Balarāma Dāsa also tries to trace the origin of the unusual practice of sharing the *prasāda* (edible offering) of Jagannātha without any discrimination of caste and creed inside the temple precincts.

---

14. *āji ṭhāru yethe jāti bheda na rahiba,*
hāḍiru brāhmaṇa jāyeṅ samāna hoiba.
— Balarāma Dāsa, *Lakṣmī Purāṇa,* verse, 534

The sincere attempt of these *santha*s to break through the caste and creed distinction was not taken very kindly by people belonging to the higher echelon of the society, especially the brāhmaṇas. So they disapproved of this new interpretation of social order. They, therefore, argued that these *santha*s were ignorant of Śāstras, therefore, they could come out with such funny interpretation of the sacrosanct *varṇa dharma*. But clarifying their stand Acyutānanda said, they indeed knew the Śāstra but as the servants at the feet of the Lord they could not think of discriminating between the high and the low. So it was better for them, that they be known as śūdra.[15]

The voice of protest raised by these *santha*s against the social discrimination might have been choked by the ever-predominant orthodox mindset of the powerful and the rich, but is it not enough that these *santha*s of Orissa dared to dream of a casteless society in which every human being could live with dignity?

---

15. *Avatāra Māḷikā*,

 Cited in C.R. Das, *Acyutānanda o Pañcasakhā Dharma*, Santiniketan: Odiya Gavesana Bibhaga, Visvabharati, 1951, p. 265.

Conclusion

In my introductory chapter I have claimed that philosophy in India is never the name of a specialized activity of conceptual analysis. Soteriology and practical concerns of life always formed the motivational core of what is usually referred to as *Darśana*. I also claimed that philosophy in India did not end with Navya-Nyāya. It continued with equal vigour. Only the medium of expression changed. The regional languages replaced Sanskrit. Unfortunately, our myopic vision about the supremacy of Sanskrit as the language of philosophical elites has largely been responsible for bundling off the philosophical treatises in regional languages as "literature." In case of the Orissan *santha*s the matter is still worse. Their affiliation to Jagannātha and the occasional allegiance to Śrī Caitanya created an impression that the philosophical ideas propagated by these *santha*s, were nothing more than an extension of love-soaked *bhakti* sect. The word Vaiṣṇavism came to mean only Caitanite form of Kṛṣṇa-*bhakti*. Thus, Vaiṣṇavism gathered more religious connotation than a metaphysical one. So I have tried my best to explore and analyse a philosophical system that at every step deviated from the philosophical presuppositions of Vaiṣṇavism of all possible forms. If Vaiṣṇavism means, singing paean to Viṣṇu or Kṛṣṇa or Rāma or Jagannātha, then these *santha*s of Orissa were definitely Vaiṣṇavas. But when it came to the expression of their philosophical ideas they were ready to adopt a non-Vaiṣṇavite stance. This is one of the reasons why it will be better if we use the appellation Bauddha Vaiṣṇavism rather than the popular designation Utkalīya Vaiṣṇavism or Oṛisī Vaiṣṇavism. Both the two words have regional implications. The argument often offered for such use is very simple. Since the Vaiṣṇavism propounded by Śrī Caitanya of Bengal is identified as Gauḍīya Vaiṣṇavism, on the same ground the Vaiṣṇavism adhered to by the Oriyā *santhas* should be called Utkalīya or Oṛisī Vaiṣṇavism. But this ascription has not helped to project the true essence of the philosophy that has very little in common with all other forms of Vaiṣṇavism, as far as the philosophical presuppositions are concerned.

How Vaiṣṇavite is Bauddha Vaiṣṇavism?

I have already offered a brief sketch of the history of the development of Vaiṣṇavism in the fifth chapter of this book that shows its gradual growth from *Pāñcarātra* literature to a form of philosophy centred on the concept of *bhakti*, specifically Kṛṣṇa-*bhakti*. To make the theory of *bhakti* tenable, Vaiṣṇavism had to be centred on two metaphysical presuppositions — (i) the object of *bhakti*, i.e., God has to have divine powers and qualities. In other words, there has to be a *saguṇa Īśvara*; and (ii) the conceptual gap between the devotee (*ātman*) and the object of devotion (*paramātman*) has to be maintained at any cost so that devotee must be assured that the God is always superior. In the later stages of its development Vaiṣṇavite theory of *bhakti* acquired an aesthetic undertone with the introduction of "love" as the cornerstone of this concept.

By the twelfth century Vaiṣṇavism was gathering momentum all over India. The rise of Sahajīya cult and its association with Vaiṣṇavism resulted in the inclusion of the female power as an essential part of its philosophy. Thus, there emerged the concept of Rādhā as the *śakti* of the *śaktimat parama Īśvara*, i.e., Kṛṣṇa. The very reason for offering this exalted status to Rādhā, is grounded on the conception of Rādhā as the paradigmatic model of love. *Bhakti* as love had to be associated with the highest degree of intensity. This intensity could not be reflected in conjugal love (*svakīya prīti*). Thus, the conception of adulterous love started to symbolise *bhakti*. Rādhā's love for Kṛṣṇa stood as the symbol of that intensity.

With this delineation of *bhakti* as love, the focus shifted from the love of the consort to the love of a mistress. It is assumed that the love of a mistress can be of highest intensity than the love of a consort. Thus, idea of *bhakti* as love was redefined in terms of the adulterous love (*parakīya prīti*) between Rādhā and Kṛṣṇa, so much so that the chanting of Kṛṣṇa was considered incomplete without uttering the name of Rādhā. In Gauḍīya Vaiṣṇavism, that overtook all other forms of Vaiṣṇavism by seventeenth century, the very idea of Rādhā came to symbolise the manifestation of God's blissful power (*hlādinī śakti*); and along with this the relation between *jīva* and *parama* were distanced.

Of course, the depiction of *bhakti* in terms of amorous love is not also new to Indian tradition. Tamil *āḷvār*s, perhaps, were the first group of *santha*s who had taken this emotional *bhakti* to the unprecedented heights. That is why most often it is believed that the *bhakti* theory has its origin in the south. Obviously, this belief has relevance so far as the significance of the term *bhakti* is confined to Kṛṣṇa-*bhakti* and the erotic mysticism associated with the concept. Most probably, after the *āḷvār*s we find the same passionate attitude saturated in the series of Purāṇas, culminating in the theory of *bhakti* of the *Bhāgavata Purāṇa*. *Bhāgavata Purāṇa* has already successfully established the intense love between *gopī*s (the cowherd maids of *gopa*) and Kṛṣṇa, as a settled devotional doctrine. The idea of utter self-abandonment or a passionately romantic love of the *gopī*s for their adolescent and playful lover Kṛṣṇa came to represent the soul's intense longing for the God. Yet it should be noted that the idea of Rādhā as the amorous partner of Kṛṣṇa was a later innovation. It is believed that the idea of Rādhā was for the first time introduced by Nimbārka. But the Rādhā as the role model of love found an important place in the Vaiṣṇavite conception with the composition of *Gīta-Govinda* by the famous poet Jayadeva. It is very difficult to ascertain whether its author was influenced by the philosophy of Nimbārka or the philosophy of the Sahajayāna. The impact of this work was so great that Narasiṁha Deva, who ruled Orissa between CE 1278 and 1306, introduced the recitation of the *Gīta-Govinda* in the liturgy of the Jagannātha temple of Purī. But it seems that the concept of erotic love depicted in *Gīta-Govinda*, had very little impact on the common people of the land. At the same time it could not be said the idea of *bhakti* as *prema* was totally unknown to the people of Orissa. For, we know from Caitanya's biography, that in course of his encounter with Vāsudeva Sārvabhauma, the famous Advaitin scholar of the land, he advised him to meet Rāy Rāmānanda (a royal employee of the king of Orissa), who championed the cause of *premabhakti*. The idea of Kṛṣṇa-*bhakti* as depicted in the *Bhāgavata Purāṇa* might have been popular in Orissa too. But deep emotionalism attached to the theory of Kṛṣṇa-*bhakti* and the amorous mysticism associated with it, was not very popular in this land.

When we come down to the writings of the Bauddha Vaiṣṇavas we find that they too talk of Rādhā and Kṛṣṇa following the Vaiṣṇava tradition. But from this we should not jump to a hasty conclusion that despite their non-dualistic stand they surreptitiously admit the *premabhakti* tradition. We must deal with two important issues before we come to a conclusion. First issue concerns a relatively minor question. It is about the cultural response to the interpretation of *bhakti* in terms of adulterous love. But the second issue is metaphysically significant. It is concerning the metaphysical symbolism ascribed to the dual concept, i.e., Rādhā and Kṛṣṇa.

The Orissan culture as such was opposed to the idea of interpretation of *bhakti* in terms of adulterous love, or for that matter any sort of erotic love. This is one of the reasons why despite being very close to certain Vajrayānic ideals the Orissan thinkers did not pay any attention to the concept of *Yuganaddha*, i.e., the concept of the Reality as a combination of male (*śūnyatā*) and female (*karuṇā*) principles. Exactly due to this puritanical attitude the Orissan culture was not enamoured of the Rādhā-Kṛṣṇa-*tattva*. This may be one of the reasons why up to CE 1740 not a single sculpture of Rādhā and Kṛṣṇa was found anywhere in Orissa. Besides, the centre of Vaiṣṇava cult in Orissa at that point of time was Jagannātha, not Kṛṣṇa. So we find that Sāralā Dāsa in his *Mahābhārata* makes Kṛṣṇa regret his amorous exploits. Caitanya Dāsa in his *Viṣṇugarbha Purāṇa* has presented Kṛṣṇa as a man with immoral traits. Such depiction in widely read works of these *santha*s would not have been possible unless the popular sentiment was in favour of such depiction. The idea of *parakīya* love, most probably, was an anathema to the culture. That is why Divākara Dāsa, a *santha* of seventeenth century, proclaimed:

> All these imaginations about Rādhā and Kṛṣṇa are the part of *bhakti* based on the model of adulterous love (*parakīya*). If Jagannātha is ever to be associated with Rādhā, then she is to be seen as His consort: and the image conjured is that of a conjugal love (*svakīya*).[1]

Beside this cultural abhorrence towards erotic mysticism in case of religion, there were important metaphysical constraints involved in accommodating the Vaiṣṇavite theory of *bhakti* in terms of passionate love. *Bhakti* for these *santha*s stands for devotion accentuated by *jñāna* or self-knowledge; and self-knowledge in turn implies the realisation of the identity between the *jīvātman* and *paramātman*. Therefore, Rādhā and Kṛṣṇa naturally symbolise individual soul and the universal soul. Obviously, the relationship is more of a metaphysical nature than emotional. We have already noted that the Oriyā *santha*s were unflinching non-dualists, and their emphasis was

---

1. *gopa rādhā kṛṣṇa bhāvanā,*
   se bhakti parakīya sādhanā.
   jagannātha rādhā sevanti,
   se bhāva svakīyābhimati.

   Divākara Dāsa, *Jagannātha Caritāmṛta*, qtd. in K.C. Mishra, *Oṛiyā Sāhityare Dharmadhārā*, Bhubaneswar: The Orissa State Bureau of Text Book Preparation and Production, 1997, p. 111.

all along on the principle of unity. They viewed the relation between *jīvātman* and *paramātman* as that of identity rather than difference. Therefore, they depicted Rādhā and Kṛṣṇa as the symbolic representations of *jīva* and *parama*, respectively. For them, Rādhā and Kṛṣṇa are two dimensions of the non-dual Reality. In the words of Śiśu Ananta, "Rādhā-Kṛṣṇa is a two-fold entity. One is *jīva* and the other is *parama*."[2] Acyutānanda also repeats the same idea in the following manner —

> Rādhā is the *jīvātman* that is why Hari is called the *paramātman*. Rādhā is the half and Kṛṣṇa is the other half of the same *ātman*.[3]

More appropriately speaking, "their dual bodies are like two cotyledons of the same seed."[4] Moreover, Kṛṣṇa and Rādhā are not conceived as male and female principles engaged in love dalliance. Acyutānanda makes it clear that,

> Though he is *puruṣa* He does not have a *liṅgam* (male organ), though Rādhā is a woman, she too does not have a *yoni* (female organ), yet they are engaged blissfully in *rasa* (love sport) day and night.[5]

---

2. *śrī rādhā kṛṣṇa beni jāṇa, jīva parama rūpa jāṇa.*
— Śiśu Ananta, *Hetu Udaya Bhāgavata.*
qtd. in K.C. Mishra, p. 99

3. *jīva ātmā rādhe boli parama murāri,*
eṇukari paramātmā bolabānti hari.
adhe rādhā adhe kṛṣṇa ardha ātmā eka,
ardha ardha yuga rūpa jāṇanti viveka.
— Acyutānanda, *Śūnya Saṁhitā* II

4. *eka vīja beni phāḷa jugaḷa aṅgare.*
— *Śūnya Saṁhitā* II

5. *puruṣa hoiṇa liṅga nāhi tāra,*
nārī hoi nāhi yoni.
ati harasare rāhāsa karanti,
nāhi divasa rajanī.
Qut. in *Oṛiyā Sāhityare Dharmadhārā* by K.C. Mishra, Bhubaneswar, Orissa Text Book Bureau, 1997, p. 93.

In their broad scheme of philosophical syncretism of Vaiṣṇavism there was enough place for a non-dualistic principle like *Śūnya Puruṣa* Jagannātha, as well as the dualistic principle of Rādhā and Kṛṣṇa. But ultimately this dualistic principle was fitted in their absolutistic and monistic framework. On the other hand, Gauḍīya Vaiṣṇavism might have agreed with this novel idea of identity between Rādhā and Kṛṣṇa, provided they were not seen as *jīva* and *parama*. For them, Rādhā as the *hlādinī śakti* of Kṛṣṇa under no circumstances could be identified with the *jīva*, the *taṭhastha śakti* of the *paramātman*.

Again, we note that the *santha*s of Orissa in consonance with their yogic interpretation of *bhakti* prefer to give a very interesting depiction of the holy places of Vaiṣṇavism. According to Gauḍīya Vaiṣṇavism, Gopa, Mathura and Vṛndāvana are accorded the status of holy, holier and holiest spots respectively. Vṛndāvana is considered to be holiest for this is the place where the eternal sport of Rādhā and Kṛṣṇa is going on. This sport is called *nitya rāsa*. Astonishingly, the Oriyā Vaiṣṇavas do talk of *rāsa*. But their depiction of *rāsa* (love dalliance) has altogether a different flavour. Acyutānanda following the Vaiṣṇava tradition composed some works on *rāsa*. His most popular work of this genre entitled *Nitya Rāhāsa,* provides a clear picture of his own version of this eternal love dalliance (*rāsa*). Here the entire thing is depicted in terms of yogic *sādhanā*. Acyutānanda's Vṛndāvana is *śūnya maṇḍala* where there is neither day nor night; where Rādhā and Kṛṣṇa are not entities, nor are they male or female, they are but two sides of the one and unique Reality. Obviously he is referring here to the yogic state of mind, not any specific place either on earth or heaven. So he refers to the place as the land where thousand-petalled lotus blooms. Obviously, Acyutānanda means by Vṛndāvana, the *sahasrāra cakra* of the yogic plexus. According to him, this is the place where Nitya Rādhā is lodged. He then goes one step further and places the supreme *puruṣa,* i.e., the Kṛṣṇa, above this plexus. He calls him *Anādi* Kṛṣṇa. Thus, he makes a distinction between Kṛṣṇa, the romantic hero (*Mānava* Kṛṣṇa) and eternal Kṛṣṇa (*Anādi* Kṛṣṇa), the supreme Reality. We come across similar descriptions in Balarāma Dāsa's *Vedāntasāra Gupta-Gītā.* He locates all the holy places of Vaiṣṇavas like, Gokula, Vṛndāvana, Mathurā in the *trikūṭa* (the middle point between the eye-brows), that is regarded as the vital point of the yogic *sādhanā.*[6] Such depictions are obviously influenced by the yogic interpretation of *bhakti.* The entire conception may appear very abhorrent to the Gauḍīya Vaiṣṇavas as they were opposed to this theory.

Now it is time to return to the original question: How Vaiṣṇavite is the Bauddha Vaiṣṇavism? To be very honest, this form of Vaiṣṇavism has virtually no doctrinal affinity with the major forms of Vaiṣṇavism. The very conception of Reality as the non-qualifiable (*nirguṇa*), indeterminate (*nirviśeṣa*) and ineffable *Śūnya Puruṣa* defies the basic principles of Vaiṣṇavism. Therefore, one can call it the most non-Vaiṣṇavite form of Vaiṣṇavism. Yet we cannot but label it as Vaiṣṇavism. Perhaps, the answer to such an intriguing issue may be sought from *santha* Divākara Dāsa's following declaration:

> Have respect for all the forms of Vaiṣṇavism, but never reconcile with your own stand. Treat other's views with love but be firm on your own stand.[7]

It now appears that the Vaiṣṇavas of Orissa wanted to have their own brand of Vaiṣṇavism however much non-Vaiṣṇavite it might appear to others.

---

6. *bhrulatā madhey jeuiṅ sthāna,*
sethāre debu caitana.
nitya madhyare vṛndāvana,
tathiṅ madhyre kalpa sṭāna.
— Balarāma Dāsa, *Vedānta Sāra Gupta-Gītā.*
Quoted from the same book, p. 110.

7. *sakaḷa vaiṣṇava pūjiba, āpaṇā sūtra na chāḍiva.*
samasta saṅge prīti heba, nija bhāvare dṛḍha thiba.
— Divākara Dāsa, *Jagannātha Caritāmṛta* I

Santha Philosophy and Orissa

I have started with the assumption that unless a philosophy is close to life it loses its appeal. We have already had acquaintance with a philosophical position that is based on the idea of a God as *śūnya*, who can be approached by *bhakti* alone. But it is no ordinary *bhakti*; it is a meditative mode that ultimately culminates in the union of the self with the *Brahman*. Here is a conception of God who cannot be appeased by external rites but by identification of the self with the universe; *piṇḍa* with the *brahmāṇḍa*. Thus, in every respect, Bauddha Vaiṣṇavism stood for a non-sectarian, rational and secular form of life. Naturally this new tradition directly challenged the orthodox tradition emphasising idol-worship, external rites and strict hierarchy of caste-creed distinction. What made this system work despite opposition from the powerful section of the society was its popular base. Unfortunately it could not hold on to its own with the resurgent Brāhmaṇical dominance in the post-Caitanya phase. The Indian mind is somehow so prone to *bhakti* in terms of appeasing God by external rites, that it always finds Brāhmaṇical conception of religion more appealing. Śaṅkara in his effort to revive Hinduism in terms of such non-sectarian principle had failed. Similar attempts made by the great *santha*s like Kabīr, Dādū also met with the same fate. People find it easier to look outside for a God than to look inside and make an effort to understand that there is but little distinction between the Highest Being and His creation. This is the fundamental reason why the orthodox conception of religion superseded the ideal of non-sectarianism, so dear to the *santha*-philosophers of Orissa.

Orissa, in the subsequent phases witnessed a renewed rigidity of caste system. The institution of Jagannātha that once stood for universal love, equality and non-sectarianism was turned into an emblem symbolising all the banes of orthodox Hinduism. By nineteenth century the religious and social scene took a worse turn. In late 1880s Hunter in his *A Statistical Account of Bengal* noted, "the temple of Jagannāth in which every creed obtained an asylum and in which every class and sect find its god now closes its gate to low caste population."[8] The introduction of the caste system demolished all the lofty ideals that Jagannātha stood for. The grand syncretism that formed the basis of Jagannātha cult was already overshadowed by typical Hindu orthodoxy.

> The close association with the royalty, coupled with the introduction of caste discrimination in the practices of the temple at Purī, made Jagannātha appear in the nineteenth century as an exclusive and distant Lord, a monopoly of Brāhmaṇas and rulers. He had moved far away from his initial devotees and had come to be identified with those who wielded power and authority.[9]

Even during the lifetime of the Pañcasakhās themselves, they had distanced themselves from the hub of orthodox activities at Purī and had taken shelter in remote and secluded places. This may be one of the reasons why subsequent *santhas* like Caitanya Dāsa and Arakṣita Dāsa shifted their emphasis to Viṣṇu instead of Jagannātha. Fortunately for Orissa, the spirit of social reactionism was not buried with time. During the last part of nineteenth century and early part of twentieth century, Mahimā *dharma,* a Hindu reactionary movement started gaining popularity. In every respect it was the continuation of the spirit of the land. This was the voice that rose from within the tradition. Mahimā *dharma* championed all the ideals that Bauddha Vaiṣṇavas stood for. But Jagannātha was no longer at the centre. As I have pointed out, during this phase of history Jagannātha no longer symbolised the hopes and aspirations of the common and downtrodden. They were, as if waiting for a spiritual order that could assure them dignity as human persons. So they became very enthusiastic

8. Qtd. in Ishita Bannerjee-Dube, "Mahimā Dharma," in *Jagannāth Revisited: Studying Society, Religion and State in Orissa,* ed. H. Kulke and B. Schnepel, New Delhi: Manohar, 2001, p. 161.

9. Qtd. in Ishita Bannerjee-Dube, p. 162.

about this new form of *dharma*. Surprisingly, Pañcasakhās had predicted in their later *Mālikā* literature that Jagannātha would leave the temple and reappear as an *Avadhūta* to preach the message of *śūnya dharma*. So the Mahimā cult immediately caught the imagination of the people oppressed and subjugated by the higher castes. In Mahimā *dharma* the concept of *Śūnya Puruṣa* or *Śūnya Brahman* was taken to its logical conclusion with the last relics of Vaiṣṇavism thrown out of the system.

I have already stated how Bauddha Vaiṣṇavism was most non-Vaiṣṇavite in spirit. I have also hinted at the fact that the Vaiṣṇava *santhas* of sixteenth century were constrained by the pressure of the time and clime. They had to compromise with certain amount of freedom of thought and expression. But by twentieth century, and specifically with the introduction of British rule, all such compulsions were removed. So Mahimā *dharma* could come out with a full-fledged *śūnya*-centric absolutism with no idol or deity to symbolise it. It truly became a Godless *bhakti* movement. Though Mahimā Svāmī, who appeared on the scene sometime in 1882, was the founder of the sect, it was *santha* Bhīma Bhoi who took the popularity of the *śūnya*-centric metaphysics to the height of its popularity. Bhīma Bhoi, a Kondha by birth, may be said to be the last representative of the santhic movement. Mahimā *dharma* is a major religio-philosophical movement and needs to be studied independently. But I just want to hint that Mahimā cult, as it was presented by the *santha* Bhīma Bhoi, stood for all the ideas that were so dear to the Bauddha Vaiṣṇavas of Orissa. The theories of *Śūnya Puruṣa*, *ātmajñāna*, *samatā* and *karuṇā* formed the foundational principles of this new system. But this powerful cult too was pushed to oblivion and is now confined to a minor section of the society.

At this stage one may very validly ask: Why such non-sectarian and secular philosophical trend based on the theory of *Śūnya Puruṣa* had to lose its appeal in the subsequent period, if Orissan culture had all along nurtured a spirit of religious syncretism? The answer lies partly with the attitude of the followers of these once-revolutionary cults; and partly with the mindset of the so-called educated people. After the death of these great spiritual leaders their followers became more interested in setting up establishments (*gaddī*s or *maṭha*s) and highlighting the esoteric and miraculous dimensions of these great masters. As a result these great *santha*s were made into some sort of mystics and *guru*s than philosophers. On the other hand, the introduction of the Western model of education helped the educated elites to reformulate their conceptual categories in terms of essential contradiction between reason and contemplation, philosophy and religion, objectivity of science and subjectivity of the major concerns of life. They were taught to believe that the first of the members of the cognates, i.e., reason, philosophy and objectivity of science are not only superior to the alternative cognates, but they should be the guiding principles of our life. The neo-elites believed that such ideal parameters of life could only be imbibed from the Western tradition. Naturally all that comes from our tradition is dismissed as outdated, non-rational and unscientific. As a result the average educated Indian loved to hate his own tradition.

Should we finally admit that all the efforts made by these great *santha*s to raise the concept of God above the sectarian concerns were in vain? A section of Orissan population might think so. But its impact is still very pronounced in the rural areas of Orissa. Still these simple people ecstatically sing, "He has no form nor limit. The *śūnya*-bodied has manifested in *śūnya*"[10] or "O! Crazy mind, allow the swan to play in your heart."[11] Here swan symbolises the presence of *jīva* and *parama* within the human form. This may be true that these semi-

---

10. *rūpa rekhā nāhi he śūnyadehī,*
śūnye ude hoi.
— A popular *bhajan* of Bhīma Bhoi

11. *bāi manahe haṁsaku kheḷā,*
haṁsa uḍigale buṛiba bheḷā.
— A popular *bhajan* of Acyutānanda

literate do not understand a large portion of the works of these *santhas* that essentially deal with the technical matters of *yoga* and *sādhanā*. Yet there is something in their writings that is embedded in the great tradition of Orissa, and also in the collective unconsciousness of the general rank of the people that it appeals to them instantaneously. It may be difficult for the modern people to understand the implications of such terms as *Śūnya Puruṣa, piṇḍa-brahmāṇḍa, olaṭa sādhanā*, etc., but the ordinary people of Orissa are still at home with such concepts. The attitude of secularism and large-heartedness in the matters of religion that comes through very transparently in the works of these *santhas* seem to have left a lasting impression on the heart and soul of these people. Therefore, Orissa continues to remain one of the states of India least affected by communal tension and religious fundamentalism.

Appendix I

Śūnya Puruṣa vis-à-vis the Dharma Ṭhākura of the Dharma cult of Bengal

In the preceding sections I have made an attempt to cover all the dimensions of the theory of *Śūnya Puruṣa*. In fact, this concept plays such a pivotal role in the Orissan *santha* metaphysics that all other theories appear to draw support from this concept. I have also tried to claim that the conception of God as *śūnya* is one of the most original contributions of Orissa to the history of ideas. Of course, one may come across some stray references to the term *śūnya* in *santha* literature as such. The famous *santha*, Kabīr for example uses the term *śūnya mahal*, *śūnya basti*, etc., with reference to the highest point of yogic *sādhanā*, viz., *sahasrāra cakra*. But *śūnya* never becomes the focal point of their metaphysics. Rather the term *nirguṇa* is more highlighted in the writings of the north Indian *santha*s like Kabīr, Dādū, Nānak and others. So it comes as a jolt when such eminent scholars as N.N. Vasu, H.P. Sastri and P. Mukherjee come up with the claim that the Orissan Santhic theory of *Śūnya Puruṣa* is just an extension of the Dharma cult that flourished in some interior parts of Bengal.[1] If this is the case then my entire effort to present the theory as indigenous product of the soil stands on a shaky ground. So there is certain amount of compulsion on my part to discuss at length the

1. N.N. Vasu, p. 10., P. Mukherjee, p. 19.

basic tenets of the *dharma* cult and examine the authenticity of the claim made by such eminent writers. Orissa and Bengal being geographically contiguous and culturally close to one another such a possibility cannot be overruled. So I shall scan in brief some important literatures of Dharma cult to assess how far this cult bears resemblance to the Orissan Vaiṣṇavism.

The *dharma* cult (which in no way is a part *santha* movement) is an obscure religious cult that flourished in the south-west region of Bengal. The Dharma cult owes its name to the deity central to this religion, viz., Dharma Ṭhākura. The religious history of Bengal records the popularity of the Tāntric form of Buddhism under the royal patronage of the Pāla dynasty sometime between twelfth and thirteenth century. So it is natural that the theory and the practices of the later Buddhism must have left its marks on this culture. At the same time it may appear somehow puzzling that the Dharma cult, believed to have been influenced by later Buddhism, had remained in the oblivion till the first part of the twentieth century. Unlike the Orissan Vaiṣṇavism the cult had virtually no influence on the mainland of Bengal; it was mostly confined to certain remote villages of Bengal. It goes to the credit of the two great scholars of Bengal, Mm. H.P. Sastri and N.N. Vasu who brought to the limelight the practices as well as the literature of this cult. N.N. Vasu published the most celebrated compendium of the Dharma cult under the title *Śūnya Purāṇa* ascribed to Rāmai Paṇḍit, who incidentally is believed to be the founder of the Dharma cult. The compilation was originally called the *Hākaṇḍa Purāṇa*. On the basis of some verses referring to the word *śūnya* and infrequent identification of Dharama Ṭhākura, the presiding deity of the cult, as the *śūnyadeva*, Vasu opts for the title *Śūnya Purāṇa*. But a thorough scrutiny of this Purāṇa is likely to betray the expectations of a reader. The work in no way presents a consistent metaphysical position. In this connection S.B. Dasgupta's observations about the nature of this work is noteworthy. He comments:

> As for the *Śūnya Purāṇa* which is ascribed to Rāmai Paṇḍit, there are sufficient reasons to believe that the text in its p blished form does not represent the contents of a single k composed at any particular point of time by any particular author. On the other hand, the text seems to be a collection of varied accounts of the *dharma* cult which grew during the thirteenth and the seventeenth centuries among the adherents of this cult. It will be observed that the same topics under the same headings have been introduced thrice or even four times within the text with slightly different readings. There is no order in the arrangements, — cosmological, liturgical, ceremonial and legendary accounts have been introduced here and there pell-mell.[2]

Dasgupta is of the opinion that the text might have been composed not earlier than sixteenth century.[3] Many celebrated Bengali scholars like Suniti Kumar Chattopadhyaya, Yogendra Ray and others also share this view.[4] Besides, there exists more than one version of this book that is likely to create a lot of confusion. So I have followed two versions included in the compendium entitled *Śūnya Purāṇa* edited by Bhaktimadhav Chattopadhyaya. This anthology includes N.N. Vasu's version as well as the version available in the Asiatic Society Archives.[5]

The other important text of this cult is *Dharma Pūjā Bidhāna.* The work, though ascribed to Rāmai Paṇḍit is of much later origin. It again is a compilation of verses composed in pseudo Sanskrit interspersed with Bengali verses, most likely compiled by somebody known as Raghunandana. In both, *Śūnya Purāṇa* and *Dharma Pūjā Vidhāna,* Dharma Ṭhākura, the primal deity of this cult, is often described as *nirañjana, nirākāra* and *śūnya*

---

2. S.B. Dasgupta, *Obscure Religious Cults,* Calcutta: Firma K.L.M., 1976, pp. 399-400.
3. *Obscure Religious Cults,* pp. 399-400.
4. Bhaktimadhav Chattopadhyaya, *Śūnyapurāṇa.* (Bengali), Calcutta: Firma K.L.M. Pvt. Ltd., 1977, p. 12.
5. *Śūnya Purāṇa,* Manuscript no. 5438, Asiatic Society Archives.

deva. *Śūnyatā* is conceived to be the quintessence of the Dharma Ṭhākura. Here one may be reminded of the similar identification of the *Śūnya Puruṣa* with Jagannātha. While scanning *Śūnya Purāṇa*, one may come accross certain passages that are apparently similar to the views of the Orissan *santhas*. Let us take for example the following lines in which Dharma Ṭhākura is being described as "beyond all positive and negative attributes. He is of the form of *śūnya* (*śūnya rūpam)* and the formless saviour of all."[6] Again, in the introductory chapter of the book that deals with the cosmogony it is stated that in the beginning the Lord was moving alone in the great *śūnya*, having the *śūnya* as his only support. The whole cosmos is nothing but the evolution from this state of *śūnya*. I quote some lines from this work that sounds almost like the theory of the Oriyā *santhas*.

> Then there was neither form, nor shape.
> No sun, nor moon,
> Neither earth, nor water nor ether
>
> x x x
>
> There were no gods for worship,
> The Lord existed in the *mahāśūnya*.[7]

However, such points of similarity does not lend any support to the conjecture that the entire Dharma cult is out and out *śūnya*-centric. In no way the work develops a theory of *śūnya*, and the reference to this concept is very infrequent. Besides, the work does not aim to present a metaphysical stand. Rather the Purāṇa elaborately deals with injunctions about certain rituals and obscure practices.

The other work, *Dharma Pūjā Bidhāna* seems to be a little more explicit as far as the use of the concept of *śūnya* is

---

6. *śūnya rūpam nirākāraṁ sahasra bighnanāśanaṁ,*
sarvaparaḥ parodevaḥtasmattaṁ varadobhava.
— *Atha Ṭīkā Pābana, Śūnya Purāṇa* 152.

7. *Śūnya Purāṇa, Sṛṣṭi pattana.*

concerned. Special reference may be made to the "Meditation on the *dharma*" that beautifully encapsulates the idea of an ineffable and indeterminate highest Reality —

> Let the Lord of the form of vacuity, who has neither end nor middle, nor beginning, neither hands nor legs, neither body nor voice, neither form nor any primordial shape, nor fear nor death, nor even birth, — who is accessible to *yogin*s in deep meditation, who permeates all sects (or who permeates all the petals of the lotuses within the body), who is bereft of all mental constructions, who is one, stainless, the giver of the boon of immortality, protect me."[8]

Dharma Ṭhakura is sometimes described as

> the absence of all, yet the abode of all. He is said to be incarnated in the world to relieve the beings of the three worlds from their bondages. He is the great *Brahman* of the beginningless luminous form. He is the knowledge and consciousness, pure and changeless, and is to be only known by the syllable *auṁ*. He transcends all qualities, the underlying reality not yet manifest in existence (*avyakta*). He has incarnated in the bank of Balluka seated on his favourite mount Ulluka.[9]

All these lines may support the hypothesis that the Dharma cult is an offshoot of the Tāntric Buddhism and, therefore, it subscribes to a *śūnya*-centric metaphysics. But the claim that this cult is philosophically inspired by Tāntric Buddhism seems to be ponderous. First and foremost there is no systematic delineation of the theory of the *śūnya* as the God. Such sporadic and infrequent reference to the concept of *śūnya* does not make a system of thought Buddhistic in its tone and tenor. In fact,

---

8. *oṁ yasyā 'ntaṁ nā 'di madhyaṁnaca kara caraṇaṁ nā 'sti kāyo ni dānaṁ nā 'kāraṁ-nā 'di rūpam nā ca bhaya maraṇaṁ nā 'sti janmaiva yasya. yogīndra dhyānagamyaṁ sakala dala gataṁ sarva saṅkalpa-hīnaṁ. tatraiko 'pi nirañjano maravaradaḥ, pātu mām śūnyamūrtiḥ.*
— *Dharama-pūjā-bidhāna*, p. 70. Qtd *Obscure*, p. 287.

9. *Obscure Religious Cults*, p. 288.

we notice a lot of confusion in the presentation of the religious faith of the Dharma cult. Sometimes the Dharma Ṭhākura is identified with the Vedic God of Dharma, i.e., Yama. Again He is identified with such Hindu Gods as Śiva, Viṣṇu and also the Sun God. The abode of Dharma wavers from Kailāsa to Vaikuṇṭha. Actually this book seems to contain *mantra*s and injunctions "regarding the worship not only of Dharma Ṭhākura but of almost all the gods and goddesses of the popular Hindu pantheon, of esetoric Buddhism as well as the purely local deities of indigenous origin."[10] Again, there is no direct reference to the Buddha as it happens in the case of the Orissan Vaiṣṇavism, wherein the Lord supreme is addressed as the Bauddha Jagannātha. Rather in this work whenever there is any reference to Buddha it is always in the context of Bauddha Jagannātha. Therefore, one cannot be sure whether the Dhārmic notion of the *śūnya* is entirely influenced by Buddhistic metaphysics. Besides, some eminent scholars like Dasgupta feel that the work properly belongs to seventeenth century or still a later date.[11] So the comparison between the Orissan *santha* literature (mostly composed during fifteenth to sixteenth century) and the litearture of the Dharma cult cannot be dragged beyond a certain limit.

In the background of this comparative survey of Dharma cult *vis-à-vis* Orissan Vaiṣṇavism let us examine Vasu's claim on this issue. In the "Introduction" of his book *The Modern Buddhism and its Followers in Orissa*, he remarks that

> the endeavours made by the Pāla Kings to improve the depraved religious tone of the country and more especially the personal influence of Rāmai Paṇḍit in this direction, were not confined within the limits of Mayurbhanj [a district of Orissa], but pervaded the whole of Orissa.[12]

10. *Ibid.*, p. 405.
11. *Ibid.*
12. Vasu, *Modern Buddhism*, p. 10.

Regarding this off-handish remark I want to make the following observations. First, if the Pāla kings made such sincere efforts to resurrect Buddhism in the country then how come the importance of the Dharma cult was so much relegated to the background that most of the people of Bengal were not even aware of the existence of this cult. Second, Rāmai Paṇḍit himself is a controversial figure and nobody is sure about the time he flourished and which portion and how much of the *Śūnya Purāṇa* is composed by him. Finally, there are certain evidences in the liturgical texts of the *Śūnya Purāṇa* that suggest just the reverse of what Vasu claims. In the literarture of the Dharma cult there are frequent references to "Lord Jagannātha worshipped near the sea shore." It becomes clear from such references that protagonists of the Dharma cult were already acquainted with the religio-cultural faiths and beliefs of the Jagannātha cult that finds its full expression in the works of the Oriyā *santhas*. I would like to bring into light some relevant passages from the *Śūnya Purāṇa*[13] that may help us in assessing the impact of Jagannātha cult on the Dharma cult. The introductory chapter of this text contains the following lines:

> In the ninth incarnation Hari dwelt on the sea-coast known by the name Jagannātha and distributed his grace to all to save the humanity and destroy the evil.[14]

Interestingly, in the same chapter we find that Lord Jagannātha is being identified with the Buddha. It is stated:

---

13. N.N. Vasu discovered a specific version of the manuscript of the Purāṇa of the *dharma* cult for the first time and published it under the title *Śūnya Purāṇa*. Since then all other versions of this Purāṇa are also known by that name. Many Bengali scholars are of the opinion that the Vasu's reading of the text is not perfect. So I shall now refer to another palm-leaf manuscript of this Purāṇa preserved in the Asiatic Society No. G. 5838, edited and published by Bhaktimadhav Chattopadhyaya. This version of the *Śūnya Purāṇa* is codified by Arjun Paṇḍit Karmakar, and written sometime in 1117 Bengal almanac.

14. *navama murtete hari jagannāth nām dhari jaladhir tīre kailā bas.*
— *Śūnya Purāṇa*, ed. Bhaktimadhav Chattopadhyaya 198

> Appearing as the Buddha on the sea-coast O Lord you looked at all with compassion.[15]

However, in the section entitled "Āgamer Ninnaya" Jagannātha is depicted as the tenth incarnation of Viṣṇu who is made up of *nīma* wood and has the hands of gold; and in this incarnation the Lord removes all discrimination between the Hindu and the Muslim.[16] This passage is particularly crucial in more than one sense. First, we find here a specific reference to the idol of Jagannātha as made up of *nīma* wood. It is well known that the idol at Purī temple is made of the *nīma* wood. Second, there is reference to the two golden hands of Jagannātha. I have stated earlier that the iconography of Jagannātha is very unusual in the sense that it does not resemble any created form either human or animal. It is without hands or legs or ears, etc. But on certain ceremonial occasions golden hands are fitted on his body. This shows that the author, whoever he may be, Rāmai Paṇḍit or any of the *gurus* of this cult, must have been very much acquainted with the rituals and practices of Jagannātha worship. The above-mentioned passages provide enough justifications for us to discard Vasu's claim that the Dharma cult had largely been responsible for the development of the *śūnya*-centric Vaiṣṇava cult of Orissa.

---

15. *jaladhir tīre sṭhān buddha rūpe bhagavān haiyā tumi kripāvalokan.*
— *Śūnya Purāṇa* 199

16. *daśama murute gosāiṅ balāle jagarnnāth nimer pitim gośaiṅ suvarner duti hāth*
hindu musalmān tethā ekachatra kariyā, apanā jānān prabhu āpani jāniā
— *Śūnya Purāṇa* 200

Appendix II

The Buddhist Archaelogical Heritage of Orissa

THE Buddhist heritage of Orissa has not only shaped the philosophical views of the *santha*s and the social life of the common mass, it has also left its indelible print on this soil through its rich architectural innovations and sculptural wealth. There are many places in Orissa where we come across beautifully laid-out Buddhist *vihāra*s, *stūpa*s and *caitya*s. Besides, the Vajrayāna range of sculptures found in Orissa, are unique for their novel conception, fine execution and sensitive presentation; very rarely noticed in other parts of India. These vestiges of remarkable sculptural art of both Mahāyānic and Vajrayānic pantheons stand as a mute witness to their powerful and glorious past. Such artistic heritage proves that Orissa had nurtured a number of Buddhist centres of learning, art and establishments at several places which flourished here up to the twelfth-thirteenth century CE. Unfortunately this opulent legacy has not received the attention it deserves. This may be one of the reasons why the scholars on Buddhism are either absolutely silent about the role of Orissa in promoting and nurturing later Buddhism or else prefer to vehemently oppose the claim. So, in this part of my work, I intend to set the record straight by providing a select list of such sites of Buddhistic heritage. My aim is not to provide a tourist guide but simply to put forth the claim that justice be meted out to both the history of Buddhism as well as the cultural heritage of Orissa, for architectural evidences are the most foolproof method of mapping out the past.

Dhauli

This is a village situated on the banks of river Dayā, not very far from the present capital of Orissa. The great Kaliṅga war that transformed Aśoka into a devout Buddhist and a great champion of peace had been fought here. As a testimony to this great transformation we have the major rock-edicts (XIII and two special edicts) of Aśoka at Dhauli. Close to the village are two short ranges of low hills. From the remains of the hill it can be assumed that once upon a time it was a great Buddhist centre.

Lalitgiri

Situated in the modern district of Jājpur, Lalitgiri is one of the earliest Buddhist complexes, most probably built during Gupta dynasty (first century CE). Lailtgiri lies majestically in the ruins singing the glory of a past heritage. The huge brick monastery, the remains of a *caitya* hall and a stone *stūpa* at the apex of a small rugged sandstone hill dominate the site. The complex includes one huge *Apsidal temple, caitya gṛha* and four monastic complexes. A museum built by the Archaeological Survey of India in the complex itself displays some fascinating and rare images of the Gods of the Buddhist pantheon. Life-sized images of *bodhisattva* Padmapāṇi, Vajrapāṇi, Padmapāṇi Avalokiteśvara and also Jambhala are preserved here. We also find two interesting statues of Vajra Tārā, one of them seated and the other in standing position in *tri-bahṅga* pose. Another rare image discovered from this site is that of Aparājitā Tārā. Interestingly, most of the sculptures contain short inscriptions on them. The treasures of Lalitgiri also include standing images of Buddha, dressed in flowing outer garment resembling the Graeco-Roman Toga. Similarly, the statue of Buddha seated on the coil of a seven-hooded serpent attracts the attention of those interested in Buddhist sculpture. The recent discovery of a casket containing sacred relics, probably of the Tathāgata himself, from the stone *stūpa* at the top of the hill further enhances the sacredness of the place. This also reminds one of the descriptions given by Hiuen Tsang, the Chinese pilgrim, about the *stūpa* that emitted brilliant light because of its sacredness.

Udayagiri

The hill of Udayagiri is situated not very far from Lalitgiri. This is the largest Buddhist complex found in Orissa. It is a sprawling brick monastery with a number of images of *Bodhisattva* and *dhyānī* Buddhas. Recent excavations reveal that the ancient name of the monastery was Madhavapura Mahāvihāra. At the base of the hill there is a rock-cut well and there are stone railings on the three sides of the well. These railings are decorated with the images of both Mahāyāna and Vajrayāna order. At the southern part of the terrace, at some distance, a temple of Mahākāla is situated. Now it is worshipped as a Hindu deity. The beautiful gateway of the temple is now placed at Patna museum. A little farther one finds the image of Jaṭāmukuṭa Lokeśvara. At the back of the image there is an urn containing the relics of Padma-sambhava, the son of Indrabhūti, the famous *siddha* of Vajrayāna and a king of Orissa. One can also find on the slopes of the hill the images of Maitreyanātha and Mañjuśrī. On the western side of the spur there is a gallery of figures carved out of the rock. One such figure is that of Kurukullā, the Goddess of the Vajrayāna order. The image of this Goddess is found nowhere excepting Orissa. From the debris of the complex a huge image of the Buddha made of bluish chlorite stone has been excavated.

Ratnagiri

The hill is separated from Udayagiri by the river Kimiria. This area has been identified by the experts as one of the ancient seats of Buddhist learning. Excavation at a lower level of the hill has unearthed the remains of two monasteries, a big *stūpa* and some Buddhist shrines. Besides, one can find the images of Heruka, Padmapāṇi Avalokiteśvara and Tārā. On the slopes of the hill there is a Mahākāla temple. On the precincts of the temple one can find the statues of Tārā and the Tāntric God Trailokya Vijaya. A very interesting feature of this site is the discovery of a large number of votive *stūpas*, lying scattered near the main *stūpa*. Such *stūpas* used to be gifted by pilgrims on fulfilment of their wishes. The heads of the Buddha at Ratnagiri are of special significance. The excavation carried out here reveal that Buddhism was nurtured here up to the twelfth century CE. Udayagiri, Lalitagiri and Ratnagiri form a triangle of Buddhist sites of importance in Orissa.

Lānguli Hills

A Buddhist settlement was discovered on this hill. It is located in Salipur of the modern Jājpur district of Orissa. Very recently, a Buddhist *stūpa* has been discovered in the north-west corner of this hill. The uniqueness of the *stūpa* is that it has a circumbulatory passage.

Solampur

This place is situated in the north-west of Jājpur district. A large number of Mahāyānī and Tāntric deities are found in the outskirts of the village. Among the images found here a special mention may be made of the well-sculpted statues of Avalokiteśvara, Tārā and Vajraśatru.

Ārāgarh

This place is located in Khurda, a place very close to Bhubaneswar. Excavations undertaken in the recent past unearthed the existence of a big Buddhist establishment here. With the progress of the excavation more and more facts about this *caitya* may come to light. According to the historians the *caitya* was built sometime in tenth century CE by Śubhaṅkara Deva II, the king of Bhaumakara dynasty.

Chaudwār

This place is situated very close to Cuttack city. A round and pillared hall has been discovered here that very much resembles a Buddhist shrine. Now, of course, it has been turned into a Viṣṇu temple.

Bāneswara Nāsi

Bāneswara Nāsi of Cuttack district is famous for the Padmeśvara temple dedicated to Padmapāṇi Avalokiteśvara. One can find also the idols of Tārā and Prajñā-pāramitā. Surprisingly, a modern Vaiṣṇava temple inside the village contains the image of Vajravārāhī, a deity of Vajrayāna branch of Buddhism.

Khairā

The village is situated in Cuttack district. One can find here the images of Padmapāṇi Avalokiteśvara, Vajrapāṇi Avalokiteśvara, Mañjuśrī, Tārā and Buddha. Of course, the beautiful image of Buddha has now been shifted to the State Museum.

Mārīcipur

This place is located in Jagatsingpur district of Orissa. The name of the village is derived from the famous Goddess of Tāntric Buddhism, viz., Marīci. She is locally known as Marīci Ṭhākurāṇī.

Garedipāncaṇa

A small village situated in Purī district is well known for the Buddhanātha temple. Though the temple is dedicated to the Hindu God Viṣṇu, the presence of eight-armed Buddhist Goddess Marīci proves the wonderful assimilation of Buddhism and Hinduism in Orissa.

Kuruma

This place is situated about 8 km from the famous Sun-temple at Koṇārka. The excavations carried out here suggest that once upon a time this place was an important Buddhist establishment. The site is famous for the beautiful image of Buddha in *bhūmisparśa-mudrā* alongwith the images of Padmapāṇi Avalokiteśvara and Revanta, collectively worshipped as Yamad dharma, inside a shed situated near the brick mound that might have been a *stūpa* once upon a time.

Vajragiri

Another important Buddhist site, Vajragiri, is situated in between Cuttack and Balasore. From the ruins of this site hoards of statues of the gods and goddesses of the Buddhist pantheon have been discovered including that of Marīci, Mañjuśrī, Tārā and Avalokiteśvara. Some of the statues of Avalokiteśvara and Mañjuśrī, recovered from this place, are now in the Orissa Museum. But the most worth-noting statue of this site is the exquisitely carved figure of Vajrapāṇi Avalokiteśvara.

Ayodhyā

Ayodhyā, situated in the district of Balasore, is famous for a temple dedicated to the Buddhist Goddess Marīci. The three-faced and eight-armed Marīci stands here in *ālīḍha* pose on a chariot drawn by seven pigs. On its top there is a slab containing the figures of *dhyānī* Buddha, Vairocana and Marīci. Besides this temple, another temple dedicated to Vajratārā is also worth noting. The image of Vajratārā is very rarely found in India.

Pārādipgarh

This place is situated very close to Pārādip, the port town of Orissa. The place is famous for a dome-shaped shrine of Avalokiteśvara. This shrine also contains the images of five *dhyānī* Buddhas. However, with the passage of time this Buddhist shrine has been turned into a Viṣṇu temple.

Tālcher

The Paścimeśvara temple situated in the vicinity of the city of Talcher contains the images of Tārā and Buddha.

Tārāpur

This site is situated in between Cuttack and Paradip. The place derives its name from "Tārā," the famous Goddess of Vajrayāna. One can also find here the images of Buddha, Prajñāpāramitā, Avalokiteśvara and Marīci.

Kendrāpaṛā

Very recently excavations carried on by the Archaeological Survey of India bring to light the existence of some important Buddhist sites in the entire region.

In fact, the district is full of such Buddhist establishments. Newer and newer Buddhist sites are coming to notice because of the recent interest of the historians. Here I give an account of some such newly discovered sites in the area.

*(i) **Musātikiri:*** This village is situated about 45 kms from Bhubaneswar. An excavation carried out here during 2004 revealed the existence of a Buddhist monastery. A 5 ft tall decapitated Buddha image was found inside the monastery, with six huge halls. This proves that a very advanced and urban Buddhist civilization flourished here.

*(ii) **Mogalapātana:*** Another Buddhist site was discovered at this place, very close to Musātikiri, sometime in April 2004. Stone images of meditating Amitābha Buddha and Avalokiteśvara were discovered here. The remnant of a big *stūpa* was also found by the villagers while digging up the site near the river Gobari. A similar monastery has been found by the villagers at Kantākiāri another village close to Mogalapātana.

Baud

This district was a great centre of Tāntric Buddhism. In colloquial Oriyā the place is called Bauddha. A colossal image of Buddha is now placed in front of the *rājā* of Baud. The people of this place worship the image as Buddha Raja. Besides one can find here the images of Ugratārā and other gods and goddesses of Tāntric Buddhism.

Besides such important places of Buddhist heritage we also come across interesting sculptures in Khadiapada and Khiching of North Orissa where a large number of images of Buddha, *pañcadhyānī* Buddhas and minor gods and goddesses of Vajrayānī order are found. Some of the fascinating statues and images recovered from these sites found their way to Calcutta Museum and Patna Museum during the British rule.

When we survey the architectural remains of Bhubaneswar, a famous Śaiva centre, we discover a very interesting dimension of the religious history of Orissa. It tells us the story of the rise and fall of different religious sects and their attempt to dominate each other. I can cite here the cases of two such temples. The first one is Kapileśvara Temple situated on the outskirts of Bhubaneswar. The present temple is dedicated to Kapileśvara or Śiva. But it can be easily guessed that once upon a time this was a Buddhist shrine. At the back of the compound wall there still exist some friezes depicting the first sermon by Buddha and other important events from Buddha's life. Also, from under a huge tree, uprooted by the recent super cyclone in Orissa, a medium-sized image of Buddha has been recovered from the temple precincts. The second such temple is Bhāskareśvara Temple situated in the old city of Bhubaneswar. The present temple is a two-storied structure with an unusually high *liṅgam*. Obviously, a Buddhist pillar has been turned into a two storey high *liṅgam*, most probably during the rule of the later dynasties patronising Śaivism.

I have given here only a select list of Buddhist sites in Orissa. But there are innumerable places where the images of the gods and goddesses of Mahāyānic as well as Vajrayānic order are found. In some places, like Kendrapara, the images are in possession of the local *zamindārs*; and in some places such images have been transformed into popular Hindu gods. However, the Orissa State Museum, situated at Bhubaneswar, has an impressive collection of Buddhist art and sculpture. A visit to this Museum can provide a glimpse of the extent of impact Buddhism had on Orissan culture.

Appendix III

Śūnya Puruṣa*

Śūnya Puruṣa is caught in the stocks!

There he is shining with compassion and forgiveness.

Eleven are the senses that surround him, lust, anger and greed ever on the guard.

Twelve sentries stand at the fortress defence; twenty-five innate tendencies — the five chieftains.[1]

Above the six circles vibrate the fifty syllables, and along the walls stream seventy-two veins.

These are the soldiers that guard the fortress ever surrounding *Śūnya Puruṣa*.

Detached, distinct, in the palace of space, *Śūnya Puruṣa* plays his games.

No one can ever touch him, but touching none he creates all.

The *śūnya* devotee sings of this Formless one chanting the thirty-two consonants and meditates on *Śūnya Puruṣa* without form.

---

* Extract from canto IX of *Śūnya Saṁhitā* by Acyutānanda Dāsa.

1. *Prakṛti* — twentyfive aspects of human nature determined by five gross elements, namely . . . earth, water, air, fire and ether (each having five tendencies). "Five chieftains" symbolises five dimensions of human mind.

Look friend, God is in your body!

From the door of the nose the swan of breath moves, travels twelve fingers'-length and takes the shape of the fortynine primal sounds.

At the door of roof its shadow can be seen.

In a form beyond words it irradiates in the world.

All see this — yet the ignorant do not see; for It is above the fourteen worlds, beyond the space of space in the great emptiness.

Now, chant the twelve essential vowels, and let the twelve sacred sounds reverberate within.

Pay no heed to this body of yours, chant of the Formless and lose yourself in delight.

Śūnya Puruṣa, is the song of *śūnya* — meditate on this *mantra* of the Formless.

This is the sacred secret you ask of.

This is how you reach concentration and then retreat.

Neither is there the need for rituals and *pūjā,* nor the need for any sacred place or position.

With folded hands focus upwards, and with upturned face meditate.

Looking up concentrate within at the confluence of the vital veins and meditate on the Indescribable.

Echo the *mantra* of the Formless in the lotus circle of your throat — repeat this essence and strive at transcendence.

Utter the thirtytwo consonants with your focus between the eyes.

Be still the way the crow stands still no movement, not even the slightest stir.

Yet that energy of curd churned in its stillness.

The way *Mandara* stays still, the way the mendicant meditates.

Without movement, silent, hold your mind pure and still, and concentrate on *Śūnya Puruṣa*.

Only then does the graceful blue shape of *śūnya*, shapeless shape, invisible grace, become visible.

Within the four-fold Godhood the Formless pervades and the lotus blooms within the pollens.

Realise this as the untouched form of the Formless.

Focus completely on your unmixed mind.

Look! *Śūnya Puruṣa* is visible!

Translated by
Priyadarshi Patnaik

Glossary

Ācārya: A spiritual teacher, also somebody having the knowledge of three holy scriptures, viz. namely Upaniṣad, *Gītā* and *Brahma-Sūtra*.

Advaita: A school of Vedānta philosophy teaching the oneness of highest reality, soul and the universe.

Arjuna: A heroic prince of the epic *Mahābhārata* who was the son of king Pāṇḍu and a friend and student of Kṛṣṇa.

Ātman: The self; the soul, indwelling spirit.

Avatāra: Incarnation of God.

Avatārī: The God incarnate.

Bhāgavata: One of the Purāṇas highlighting devotion to Viṣṇu.

Bhakti: Ordinarily understood as devotion, but has deeper significance. It may mean the passionate attachment for the God Supreme and also realising one's ownself.

Bhagavān: Ordinarily signifies God.

Bījamantra: The sacred syllables used for meditating on God.

Brahman: The Absolute Reality. Etymologically, that which grows or swells, i.e., all-compassing.

Brahmā: The name of the Creator aspect of God.

Brahmāṇḍa: the cosmos.

Caitanya: A saint from Bengal who preached the philosophy of unadulterated love, especially romantic love for God.

Cit: Consciousness.

Dharma: Literally means that which holds up the existence of anything; also essential quality; religion; code of duty; a way of life.

Dvaitavāda: The philosophy of dualism.

Gauḍīya Vaiṣṇavism: Gauḍa stands for Bengal, therefore it stands for a religious movement inspired by Śrī Caitanya devoted to the worship of Rādhā and Kṛṣṇa.

Gopī: Cowherd maids of *gopa* intensely in love with Kṛṣṇa.

Haṭha Yoga: A school of Yoga that aims chiefly at physical health and well-being.

Īśvara: The personal God.

Jīva: The individual soul.

Jīvan mukti: One who becomes liberated even while alive.

Jñāna yoga: The path of knowledge.

Kṛṣṇa: An incarnation of God and the central figure of the epic *Mahābhārata*.

Kuṇḍalinī: The dormant spiritual power of man that resides between the base of sexual organ and anus. When awakened by spiritual practice it enters the *suṣumnā* channel that is inside the backbone and starts coursing upward towards the brain.

piṇḍa: The gross body.

Paramātman: The highest Being. The soul of souls.

Sahasrāra: The thousand-petalled lotus imagined to be located in the cerebrum. It is regarded as the seat of God. When the awakened *kuṇḍalinī* power reaches the spot the spiritual aspirant becomes illumine.

Mantra: A set of holy words.

Mārga: The path.

Mokṣa: Liberation attended through spiritual enlightenment. Also called *mukti*.

Nirguṇa Brahman: The non-qualifiable highest Being.

Nivṛtti Mārga: The path of self-control.

Auṁ: The most sacred word symbolising the highest reality; also the primordial syllable.

Puruṣa: Generally implying a being of highest order. Also the word refers to individual soul as well as cosmic soul.

Śūnya: Ordinarily means void or cipher, but in Buddhist philosophy it stands for an ineffable, non-conceptualisable Reality.

Samādhi: Mental concentration of highest nature.

Viṣṇu: The preserver aspect of God.

Vaiṣṇavism: The religious order that accepts Viṣṇu or any of his incarnations as the highest Reality.

Vṛndāvana: The forest site of Kṛṣṇa's tryst with Rādhā; a pilgrimage town located on the banks of Yamunā eighty miles south of Delhi.

Santha: A spiritual leader dedicated to the spiritual uplift of the common and the ordinary.

Trikūṭa: The point located in between two eyebrows. The point is regarded as the centre of concentration in yogic *sādhanā*.

Śūdra: It refers to the four-fold classification of Hindu society, originally conceived to be determined by the potential and inherent nature of the people living in a society. Later on it turned into a classification based on birth. In this scheme of social hierarchy the brāhmaṇa is placed at the top and the śūdra on the lowest wrung of the social ladder. So the word śūdra most often came to mean the "low born." This class was denied some of the fundamental rights assigned to the other three upper castes.

Sṛṣṭi tattva: The theory of creation.

Purī: A holy place situated on the eastern part of India and situated on the Bay of Bengal.

Nilagiri: A name standing for Purī. It is believed that once upon a time the temple was situated on a blue hill.

Mūrti: The image or form of God.

Kāyā sādhanā: The culture of the body. Body, according to this method is the seat of the divine, so by perfecting the body God can be realised within the physical form of man.

Ghaṭa Yoga: The Oriyā synonym for *haṭha yoga*.

Jñānamiśra Bhakti: The path of God realisation that comes through self-realisation.

Select Bibliography

Original Oriya Texts

Bhoi, Bhīma, *Ālekha Bhajana*, Cuttack: Dharma Grantha Store, (undated).

———, *Bhajanamālā*, (3 volumes), Cuttack: Dasarathi Pustakalaya, 1963.

———, *Brahmanirupaṇa-Gītā*. Cuttack: Dharma Grantha Store, (undated).

———, *Nirveda Sādhanā*, Cuttack: Dharma Grantha Store, (undated)

———, *Stuti Chintāmaṇi*, Bhubaneswar: Utkal University, 1972.

Dāsa, Acyutānanda, *Acyutānanda Granthābalī*.

———, *Saṁhitā Khaṇḍa; Gītā Khaṇḍa* I & II; *Kavitā Khaṇḍa; Rāhāsa Khaṇḍa*, (5 volumes), ed., R. Chainy, Cuttack: Acyutananda Smruti Sansada, 1994.

———, *Cabisa Paṭaḷa*, Cuttack: Dharma Grantha Store, (undated).

Dāsa, Arakṣita, *Mahimaṇḍala-Gītā*, ed., C.R. Das, Bhubaneswar: Orissa Sahitya Akademi, 2004.

Dāsa, Balarāma, *Amarakoṣa-Gītā*, Cuttack: Dharma Grantha Store, (undated).

———, *Brahmāṇḍa-Bhūgoḷa*, Cuttack: Dharma Grantha Store, (undated).

———, *Brahma-Purāṇa*, ed., D. Pattanayak, Bhubaneswar: Directorate of Tourism and Culture, 1979.

———, *Dāṇḍī Rāmāyaṇa* (4 volumes), Cuttack: Dharma Grantha Store, (undated).

———, *Vedāntasāra Gupta-Gītā*, Cuttack: Dharma Grantha Store, (undated).

———, *Śrīmad Bhagavad-Gītā*, ed., K.C. Sahoo, Cuttack: Dharma Grantha Store, (undated).

———, *Brahma-Saṁhitā*, Cuttack: Dharma Grantha Store, (undated).

———, *Chatisa Gupta-Gītā*, Cuttack: Dharma Grantha Store, (undated).

———, *Lakṣmī Purāṇa*, ed., S.N. Dash, Cuttack: Dharma Grantha Store, 2000.

———, *Virāṭa-Gītā*, Cuttack: Dharma Grantha Store, (undated).

Dāsa, Caitanya, *Viṣṇugarbha Purāṇa*, Dharma Grantha Store, 1978.

———, *Nirguṇa Mahātmya*, Cuttack: Dharma Grantha Store, 1996.

Dāsa, Devānanda, *Vaicandra-Gītā*, Cuttack: Dharma Grantha Store, (undated).

Dāsa, Divākara, *Jagannātha Caritāmṛta*, Puri: Bada Odiya Matha (undated).

Dāsa, Jagannātha, *Artha Koili*, Published in *Koili*, Cuttack: Dasarathi Pustakalaya, 1956.

———, *Śrīmad Bhāgavata*, (10 volumes) ed. Nilamani Mishra, Bhubaneswar: Orissa Sahitya Akademi, 1994.

———, *Gupta Bhāgavata*, Cuttack: Dharma Grantha Store, (undated).

———, *Tulā Bhinā*, Cuttack: Dharma Grantha Store, (undated).

Dāsa, Sāralā, *Mahābhārata* (12 volumes), Bhubaneswar: Department of Culture, 1965.

Dāsa, Śiśu Ananta, *Hetu Udaya Bhāgavata*, ed., N. Pradhan, Cuttack: Siddha Baranga Unnayana Committee, Jagatsinghapur, (undated).

Dāsa, Yasovanta, *Premabhakti Brahma-Gītā*, ed., A.B. Mohanty, Cuttack: Prachi Sahitya Samiti, (undated).

Secondary Sources (Oriya)

Chainy, R., *Oṛiyā Santha Sāhitya Śabdakośa*, Cuttack: Arya Prakashan, 1994.

Das, C.R., *Oṛiyā Sāhityare Sānskrutika Vikāsa Dhārā*, Bhubaneswar: Orissa State Bureau of Text Book Preparation and Production, 1993.

———, *Acyutānanda O Pañcasakhā Dharma*, Santiniketan: Viswa Bharati, 1951.

———, *Oṛisāra Mahimā Dharma*, Santiniketan: Viswa Bharati, 1952.

———, *Santha (Bhakti) Sāhitya*, Bhubaneswar: Orissa Sahitya Akademi, 1982.

Dash, (Paṇḍita) Nilakantha, ed., *Śrīmad Bhagavad-Gītā*, Cuttack: New Students Store, 1980.

Dash, (Paṇḍita) S.N., *Jagannātha Mandira O Jagannātha Tattva*, Cuttack: Friends Publishers, 1985.

Kara, K.K., *Āścarya Caryacaya*, Bhubaneswar: Orissa Sahitya Akademi, 1989.

Mahatab, H.K., *Oṛisā Itihāsa*, Cuttack: Students Store, 1948.

Mansingh, M., *Oṛiyā Sāhityara Itihāsa*, Cuttack: Grantha Mandir, 1967.

Mishra, B., *Oṛisāra Matha Saṁskruti*, Puri: Graphic Points, 1998.

Mishra, K.C., *Oṛiyā Sāhityare Dharmadhārā*, Bhubaneswar: Orissa State Bureau of Text Book Preparation and Production, 1997.

———, *Oṛisi Vaiṣṇava Dharma*, Bhubaneswar: Orissa Sahitya Akademi, 1990.

Mohanty, B., *Oṛiyā Sāhityara Itihāsa*, Vol. III, Cuttack: Friends Publishers, 1977.

———, *Bhakta Kavi Jagannātha Dāsa: Eka Samīkṣā*, Bhubaneswar: Orissa State Bureau of Text Book Preparation and Production, 1994.

———, *Koṇārka*, (Special Volume on Pañcasakhā), Bhubaneswar: Orissa Sahitya Akademi, 1989.

Mohanty, D.N., *Oṛiyā Sāhityara Unmesa O Uttarana*, Part III, Cuttack: Vidyapuri, 1990.

Mohanty, S.N., *Oṛiyā Sāhityara Madhya Parva*, Cuttack: Cuttack Students Store, 1995.

Panda, B., ed., *Oṛisāra Baudha Dharma O Saṁskruti*, Cuttack: Optima Printers, 2000.

———, *Oṛisāre Tantra Saṁskruti*, Bhubaneswar: Orissa Sahitya Akademi, 1997.

Panda, R.C., *Prācī Nadira Aitihāsika Bibhava*, Bhubaneswar: Orissa Sahitya Akademi, 1991.

Patnaik, A. & Parija, G.P., *Oṛiyā Sāhityare Tantrara Prabhāva*, Bhubaneswar: Orissa Sahitya Akademi, 1982.

Pradhan, N.N., *Prācīna Oṛiyā Sāhityare Nirguṇa Dhārā*, Cuttack: Dharma Grantha Store, 1986.

———, *Oṛiyā Nirguṇa Sāhityara Bhūmikā*, Bhubaneswar: Orissa State Bureau of Text Book Preparation and Production, 1982.

Rajguru, S.N. & Das, R.N., *Oṛisāra Saṁskrutika Itihāsa*, Bhubaneswar: Orissa Sahitya Akademi, 2001.

Sahu, K.C., *Kavi Balarāma Dāsa*, Bhubaneswar: Orissa Sahitya Akademi, 1988.

Sahu, N.K., *Oṛisāre Bauddha Dharma*, Bhubaneswar: Orissa Sahitya Akademi, 1998.

Sahu, R., *Oṛisāra Santha Sāhitya*, Cuttack: Prachi Sahitya Pratisthan, 2001.

English

Avalon, Arthur, *Śāradā Tilaka Tantra*, Delhi: Motilal Banarsidass, 2001.

Baba, Viswanatha, *The Philosophy of Mahimā Dharma*, tr., S. Dash, Cuttack: Mahima Dharmalocana Samiti, 1987.

Bagchi, P.C., *Studies in Tantras*, Part I, Calcutta: University of Calcutta, 1975.

Bapat, P.V., *2500 Years of Buddhism*, New Delhi: Ministry of Information and Broadcasting, Govt. of India, 1985.

Bhandarkar, R.G., *Vaiṣṇavism, Śaivism and Minor Religious Cults*, New Delhi: Munshiram Manoharlal, 2001.

Bhattacharya, N.N., ed., *Medieval Bhakti Movement in India*, New Delhi: Munshiram Manoharlal, 1999.

Bhattacharyya, B., *An Introduction to Buddhist Esetorism*, Dehli: Motilal Banarsidass, 1989.

Bhattacharyya, B., ed., *Two Vajrayāna Works (Jñānasiddhi & Prajñopāya Vinscaya Siddhi)*, Baroda: Gaekwad Oriental Series, No. 44, 1929.

Bhattacharyya, B., ed., *Guhyasamāja Tantra*, Baroda: Gaekwad Oriental Series, No. 53, 1931.

Bhattacharyya, B., ed., *Sādhanāmālā*, 2 volumes, Baroda: Gaekwad Oriental Series, No. 26 & 41, 1925-28.

Chattopadhyaya, D. & Lama Champa, *Taranātha's History of Buddhism*, Delhi: Motilal Banarsidass, 1975.

Cowell, B. & Gough, A.E., tr., *Sarva-Darśana Saṁgraha of Mādhavācārya*, ed., K.L. Joshi, Delhi: Parimal Publications, 2001.

Das, C.R., *A Glimpse into Oriya Literature*, Bhubaneswar: Orissa Sahitya Akademi, 1982.

Das, S.C., ed., *Pag Sam Jon Zang : History of Buddhism, Its Rise, Decline and Downfall*, by Sumpa Khampo Yese, Calcutta: Calcutta University, 1908.

Dash, G.N. & Mishra, P.C., *Bibliography on Lord Jagannātha*, Puri: Sri Jagannatha Sanskrit University, 1992.

Das, Paritosh, *Sahajiya Cult of Bengal and Pañcasakhā Cult of Orissa*, Calcutta: Firma K.L.M., 1988.

Dasgupta, S.B., *An Introduction to Tāntric Buddhism*, Calcutta: University of Calcutta, 1974.

Dasgupta, S.N., *A History of Indian Philosophy* (5 volumes), Delhi: Motilal Banarsidass, 1988.

Dei, Santilata, *Vaiṣṇavism in Orissa*, Calcutta: Punthi Pustak, 1988.

Devotional Poets and Mystics (Part I and II), New Delhi: Ministry of Information and Broadcasting, Govt. of India, 1991.

Donaldson, T.E., *The Iconography of Vaiṣṇava Images in Orissa*, New Delhi: D.K. Printworld, 1999.

Eschmann, A., *et al.*, *The Cult of Jagannātha and the Regional Tradition of Orissa*, Delhi, Manohar Publications, 1986.

Ganapathy, T.N., *The Philosophy of Tamil Siddhas*, New Delhi: Indian Council of Philosophical Research, 1993.

Haberman, D.L., *Acting as a Way of Salvation: A Study of Rāganugā Bhakti Sādhanā*, Delhi: Motilal Banarsidass, 2001.

Hazra, K.L., *Buddhism in India as Described by Chinese Pilgrims, AD 399*, Delhi: Munshiram Manoharlal, 1983.

Hazra, K.L., *The Rise and Decline of Buddhism*, Delhi: Munshiram Manoharlal, 1988.

Hopkins, F.W., *Religions of India*, Boston: Ginn & Co., 1902.

Krishna, Daya, *et al.*, ed., *Bhakti: A Contemporary Discussion*, New Delhi: Indian Council of Philosophical Research, 2002.

Kulke, Hermann, *et al.*, *Jagannātha Revisited*, New Delhi: Munshiram Manoharlal, 2001.

Master, Lok. Tu., *The Prajñāparamitā, Heart Sutra*, New York: Sutra Translation Committee for U.S.A. & Canada, 1995.

Mishra, B., *Indian Culture and Cult of Jagannātha*, Calcutta: Punthi Pustak, 1986.

Mishra, K.C., *The Cult of Jagannātha*, Calcutta: Firma K.L.M., 1984.

Mishra, R.P., *Sahajayāna: A Study of Tāntric Buddhism in Orissa*, Calcutta: Punthi Pustak, 1997.

Mitra, Debala, *Bhubaneśwar*, New Delhi: Archaelogical Survey of India, 1996.

Mitra, R.L., *Antiquities of Orissa*, vol. I & II, Calcutta, 1913.

Mohanty, S., *Lord Jagannātha*, Bhubaneswar: Orissa Sahitya Akademi, 1982.

Mohapatra, R.P., *Archaeology in Orissa*, Delhi: B.R. Publishing Corporation, 1986.

Mukherjee, P., *Lalitgiri, Udayagiri and Ratnagiri*, Madras: Sangam Books, 1984.

———, *The History of Medieval Vaiṣṇavism in Orissa*, New Delhi: Asian Educational Services, 1981.

Padhi, G.N., *Śrī Jagannātha of Purī*, Puri: Sri Jagannatha Cetana Sangha, 1993.

Padhy, J., *Śrī Jagannātha at Purī*, Puri: S.G.M. Publications, 2000.

Panneerselvəm, P., "The Philosophy of Tamil Siddhas", *Journal of The Indian Council of Philosophical Research*, Special Issue, Philosophical Tradition in Indian Languages, 2002.

Panigrahi, S.C., *Bhīma Bhoi and Mahimā Darśana*, Bhubaneswar: Department of Philosophy, Utkal University, 1988.

Patnaik, Tandra, *Śabda: A Study of Bhartṛhari's Philosophy of Language*, New Delhi: D.K. Printworld, 1994.

———, "The Concept of Śūnya in Orissan Philosophy: An Overview", *Journal of The Indian Council of Philosophical Research*, Special Issue, Philosophical Tradition in Indian Languages, 2002.

Rath, B., *Glimpses of Vaiṣṇavism in Orissa*, Berhampur: Kalyani Prakashan, 1983.

Sastry, H.P., *Advayavajra Saṁgraha*, Baroda: Gaekwad Oriental Series, No. 40, 1927.

Sahu, N.K., *Buddhism in Orissa*, Bhubaneswar: Utkal University, 1958.

Sharma, C.D., *A Critical Survey of Indian Philosophy*, Delhi: Motilal Banarsidass, 1979.

Sharma, Krishna, *Bhakti and Bhakti Movement: A New Perspective*, New Delhi: Munshiram Manoharlal, 2002.

Sinha, Jadunatha, *Indian Philosophy*, 3 volumes, Delhi: Motilal Banarsidass, 1999.

Sreekumar, N., "The Voice of Dissent: From Ezuthachan to Chattampi Swamikal", *Journal of The Indian Council of Philosophical Research*, Special Issue, Philosophical Tradition in Indian Languages, 2002.

Tagare, G.V., tr., *Skanda Purāṇa*, Part V, Utkala Khaṇḍa, Delhi: Motilal Banarsidass, 1994.

Waddel, L.A., *Buddhism of Tibet* or *Lamaism*, London: Allen & Co., 1895.

Vasu, N.N., *Modern Buddhism and its Followers in Orissa*, New Delhi: Gyan Publishing House, 1986.

Yasinori, T., *Buddhist Spirituality*, Delhi: Motilal Banarsidass, 1995.

Index